Out of the Mainstream

Out of the Mainstream identifies those aspects of mental illness which can compromise parenting and affect children's development, as well as the efforts of professionals to intervene effectively. With chapters from professionals working primarily with children or adults, in different agencies and in specialist teams or in the community, the book illustrates the ways in which the needs of mentally ill parents and their children can be understood.

The book outlines different theoretical approaches which may be in use alongside each other, including:

- A systems theory approach to work with families and with agencies;
- The psychoanalytic understanding of mental illness and its impact on family relationships and organisations;
- An educational approach to supporting staff, children and parents;
- A psychiatric or bio-medical model of work.

Out of the Mainstream considers how the diverse groups of agencies, specialist teams and groups in the community can work together, even when many barriers may hinder the effective co-working between individuals and these various groups. It will be an invaluable resource for psychologists, psychiatrists, social workers, health visitors, mental health nurses, teachers and voluntary sector agency staff.

Rosemary Loshak is a social worker and a psychoanalytic psychotherapist. She was formerly Coordinator for children in families with mental illness in Tower Hamlets, London.

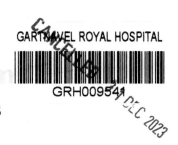

Out of the Mainstream

Helping the children of parents
with a mental illness

Edited by Rosemary Loshak

Routledge
Taylor & Francis Group

LONDON AND NEW YORK

First published 2013
by Routledge
27 Church Road, Hove, East Sussex BN3 2FA

Simultaneously published in the USA and Canada
by Routledge
711 Third Avenue, New York, NY 10017

Routledge is an imprint of the Taylor & Francis Group, an informa business

British Library Cataloguing in Publication Data
A catalogue record for this book is available from the British Library

Library of Congress Cataloging in Publication Data
Out of the mainstream : helping the children of parents with a mental
illness / edited by Rosemary Loshak.
    p. cm.
Includes bibliographical references and index.
1. Psychiatric social work. 2. Children of the mentally ill—Services for.
3. Mentally ill—Services for. 4. Parents with mental disabilities—Services for.
I. Loshak, Rosemary.
HV689.O98 2012
362.2—dc23
2012026712

ISBN: 978–0–415–68269–5 (hbk)
ISBN: 978–0–415–68270–1 (pbk)
ISBN: 978–0–203–07386–5 (ebk)

Typeset in Times New Roman
by Keystroke, Station Road, Codsall, Wolverhampton

MIX
Paper from
responsible sources
FSC
www.fsc.org FSC® C004839

Printed and bound by CPI Group (UK) Ltd, Croydon, CR0 4YY

This book is dedicated to all children, who worry about, grow up with, and sometimes help care for, a parent who suffers at times from significant mental health problems, including those who may live apart from their parent.

Contents

List of contributors   ix
Foreword   xi
Acknowledgements   xiii
List of abbreviations   xv

PART I
Themes, theories and background   1

1 Hidden children   3
  ROSEMARY LOSHAK

2 Living with a parent with mental health needs: what
  children say   14
  CASSIE BROMLEY, LIANA HADLEIGH AND AMY ROE

3 Becoming visible: the impact of parental mental health
  difficulties on children   31
  LIZETTE NOLTE

4 Working with the impossible   45
  ROSEMARY LOSHAK

5 Loss and change in the setting: the demographic,
  legislative and organisational context   62
  ROSEMARY LOSHAK

PART II
The Children and Adult Mental Health Project
(CHAMP) 2002–2012   77

6 Making a difference: the role of the coordinator   81
  ROSEMARY LOSHAK

7 Perinatal Crisis Service: psychotherapeutic work with babies
    and their families at a time of crisis   94
    SANDRA NATHANSON

8 The children's specialist in the adult mental health team   106
    ROSEMARY LOSHAK

9 How systemic work can contribute towards the development
    of collaborative work between child and adult mental health
    services   116
    PHILIP MESSENT AND NOAH SOLARIN

10 A specialist teacher in the Children and Adult Mental Health
    Project: the growth of an idea   129
    LOUISE GALLAGHER AND PEGGY GOSLING

PART III
The wider context   145

11 Providing a comprehensive service: a partnership with the
    voluntary sector   149
    CATRIONA SCOTT

12 Parental mental illness: the adult psychiatrist's perspective
    and role   163
    ELENI PALAZIDOU

13 Managing post-partum depression in the community: who
    cares for the babies?   178
    CATHY URWIN

14 Reflections: what does the future hold for the Children and
    Adult Mental Health Project?   192

    Appendix: Origins of CHAMP   197

    Index   200

Contributors

Cassie Bromley qualified as a clinical psychologist in 2008, having completed her Doctorate at the University of Hertfordshire. Since qualifying she has worked in Specialist CAMHS in Hertfordshire.

Louise Gallagher has worked in education for twenty-four years, initially as a primary teacher and since 1996 as a specialist teacher in a behaviour support team. For over three years she has worked on secondment as advisory teacher for CHAMP.

Peggy Gosling, after thirty years in education, has managed a large multi-disciplinary team, and held borough-wide responsibility for behaviour, social inclusion, multi-agency working, and related developments. Since 2008 she has pursued writing and academic interests.

Liana Hadleigh is a is a clinical psychologist and has worked in a Child and Adolescent Mental Health Team in Newham since 2010. She has a particular interest in working with looked after children and families affected by parental mental health needs.

Rosemary Loshak is a qualified social worker, now retired. She was Coordinator for children in families with mental illness and managed the CHAMP team in Tower Hamlets between 2002 and 2009. She is now a psychoanalytic psychotherapist in private practice.

Philip Messent is Head of Family Therapy, Tower Hamlets CAMHS. Philip has worked in Tower Hamlets since 1985 and has been committed throughout this time to making services accessible to more vulnerable groups. He also teaches regularly at the Institute of Family Therapy, London.

Sandra Nathanson is a child psychotherapist trained at the Tavistock Clinic, working in the East End of London since 2002. She has been working with infants and families at the Crisis Intervention Service at the Royal London Hospital since 2007.

Lizette Nolte is a clinical psychologist and systemic psychotherapist specialising in parental mental health. She is Clinical Lecturer at the University of

Hertfordshire and works in private practice. Her partner, Pieter, and sons, Jacques and Liam, are her best teachers about being family.

Eleni Palazidou is a consultant psychiatrist in East London, with a special interest in mood disorders and psychopharmacology. She is also involved in the assessment of mentally ill parents in care proceedings.

Amy Roe completed a Doctorate in Clinical Psychology at Canterbury Christ Church University in 2010. She is currently working in Greenwich for Oxleas NHS Foundation Trust, and is interested in working with families affected by mental health difficulties.

Catriona Scott qualified as a social worker in 1972. She has worked with children and families in both the statutory and voluntary sectors. Now retired, she has many years' experience of managing family support services, most recently as a Regional Manager for the charity Family Action.

Noah Solarin is a qualified social worker, and is a Children's Specialist in the Children and Adult Mental Health Team (CHAMP). Noah is doing a systemic psychotherapy training with an interest in developing a CAMHS-based family therapy service for families affected by parental mental illness.

Cathy Urwin was a child psychotherapist and an adult psychotherapist, working at the Tavistock Centre, London, and in private practice. She had a long-standing interest in working with under-fives and their parents and the impact of parenthood on identity. With Janine Sternberg, she was co-editor of *Infant Observation and Research: Emotional processes in everyday lives* (London: Routledge, 2012).

The editor and authors wish to pay tribute to the work of Cathy Urwin with children, especially in the relatively new field of parent–infant mental health. Cathy died after a short illness while this book was in publication. She has made and would have continued to make a difference in the lives and emotional well-being of so many children and will be sorely missed.

Foreword

This is a valuable and timely book for two important reasons. Collaboration between adult mental health services and those for children and adolescents has always been rather hit and miss, resulting in missed opportunities for effective joint work at a cost to parents who suffer from mental illness and their children. It is particularly timely as the tendering out of services increases the risk of fragmentation. Unless we create roles for workers whose prime responsibility is to facilitate collaboration, the danger is that this comes rather low on the agenda of any team with its own specific targets and areas of responsibility.

Both adult and child services are mainstream in their own way but only rarely are they effectively connected. Yet you do not have to be a mental health professional to recognise the need for the sort of collaboration this book exemplifies. What sort of home life is available to a child to have with an unstable parent or parents? Might the child be, in effect, doing the parenting? What happens when the parent needs hospitalisation? Can a mentally ill parent successfully meet the basic needs of children to be in a stable, reliable emotional and physical environment,[1] needs which have long been identified and understood (Kelmer Pringle 1975)?

Of course many parents who suffer from mental illness love their children dearly, hate to be parted from them and also feel guilty when they believe, often rightly, that they have let them down, and these feelings are mirrored by their children.

A mentally ill person has a fragmented mind. The psychotic processes involved lead to splitting of the 'good' and 'bad' (as a way of trying to preserve the 'good'), because the belief is that to hold all together in mind would not only be catastrophic but also unbearably painful. These parts are then projected into others: some who are identified as 'good' and others as 'bad'. In the case of those who are depressed and suicidal, the 'bad' is located in themselves such that they often feel undeserving of help and deserving of death. Consequently they have difficulty in using 'good' care. Either way these dynamics easily lead to breakdown in relationships. If the professionals in the system of care are not wise to these processes then the danger is that communication between them breaks down as they too become unconsciously contaminated by the fear that to hold the whole system in mind would be too much to bear and that any attempt to do so would be futile. In this case the system of care mirrors the fragmented and distorted mind of the suffering person, and the opportunity to provide a containing network of care which could facilitate integration and understanding in the minds of the service users, adults and children, is missed. The challenge therefore is to help and support both parties.

This book takes on that challenge. Starting with the 'hidden children' who for the most part are voiceless, dependent and afraid, it explores the impact of mental illness on family life (Part I), then takes the reader through the stages of creating an integrated service (Part II), which (in Part III) is extended to include the wider network of care. In doing so this book leads the way for others in the field to follow.

An integrated system of care in which the different service providers focus on creating and maintaining effective, non-blaming communication between themselves and with their clients is one that is capable of containing the disturbance, reducing risk, and enabling mutual understanding and emotional development in all the participants.

Angela Foster
Co-Editor of *Managing Mental Health in the Community:*
Chaos and Containment
(Routledge, 1998)

Note

1 The need for love and security, for new experiences, for praise and recognition and for responsibility. The assumption here is that the parent is capable of introducing new experiences and responsibilities as appropriate to the child's development. The impact of inappropriate parenting is also explored.

Reference

Kelmer Pringle, M. (1975) *The Needs of Children.* London: Unwin Hyman. Reprinted by Routledge.

Acknowledgements

First and foremost the editor and authors wish to thank the parents and children who consented to material appearing in this book, and the senior management and staff of both the mental health trust and the local authority adults' and children's services where the project took place. Both agencies have formally given approval for this work to be published, for which we are grateful. Without their enthusiasm and readiness to consider new ways of working, the Child and Adult Mental Health Project would not have been possible.

We have had much support and assistance from Dr Elizabeth Walters, Dr Navina Evans and staff members of the borough's CAMHS teams, from Darren Summers (Primary Care Trust), from Helen Jenner, Liz Vickerie and Liz Southcombe (Education Department), from staff of the Crisis Intervention Service (Royal London Hospital), and from Dr Begum Maitra, Dr Jennifer Walters, Karen Daniel and the Hackney CAMHS Parental Mental Health Team.

We have learnt a great deal from others in the field including the Parkside Parental Mental Health Team at St Charles Hospital (Brent, Kensington, Chelsea and Westminster), the National Children's Bureau, the King's Fund, and Judy Hildebrand at the Institute of Family Therapy.

The Children's Workforce Development Council provided essential 'start-up' funding for the initial pilot post of children's specialist.

The editor is grateful to Angela Foster, for agreeing to write a Foreword for this book, for her knowledge and understanding of the complexity of the work, and for her interest and encouragement throughout.

Many individuals have made important contributions to either or both project and book, including Mick Morgan; Karen Badgery; Rose de Paeztron; Patrick Lonergan, Raffaella Katsanis and Shukri Hussain (Family Action); Oliver Kianchehr, Rehana Uddin and Fateha Hussain (CHAMP); Dr Snehal Shah and Coenie Nolte; and we thank Dr Pieter W. Nel for his support and encouragement.

The editor owes much gratitude to Philip Messent who generously supported the project from the outset, to Ian Williamson who willingly undertook its management, to Peggy Gosling who has helped with the bibliography, to Lizette Nolte who has been generous with her ideas, to all the contributors for their time and trouble in writing chapters, and to Harvey Taylor who has given vital advice and encouragement throughout.

The extract from Philip Pullman's book *The Subtle Knife* is reprinted with permission as follows:

The Subtle Knife
Text and inside illustrations © Philip Pullman 1997
Reproduced with permission of Scholastic Ltd
All rights reserved.

Brief excerpt ('I used to feel there was something like a dark grey cloud – could even speak') from *Under My Skin: Volume One of My Autobiography, to 1949*, by Doris Lessing. Copyright © 1994 by Doris Lessing. Reprinted by permission of Harper Collins Publishers.

We are grateful to the following for permission to reprint from their published works:

Gwyn Daniel and Jasmine Chin, for permission to reprint from:
(2010) 'Engaging with agency cultures in parental mental illness training'. *Context 108*, pp. 47–50.

Karen Daniel, for permission to reprint from:
Daniel, K. (2010) 'The dance of attempting to break down barriers: working with children and families where a parent is experiencing mental health difficulties'. *Context 108* , pp. 56–58.

Institute of Psychoanalysis, for permission to reprint from:
Williams, P. (ed.) (1999) *Psychosis (madness).*

Palgrave Macmillan for permission to quote from:
Howe, D. (1995) *Attachment Theory for Social Workers.*

Routledge for permission to reprint from:
Bower, M. (ed.) (2005) *Psychoanalytic Theory for Social Work Practice.*
Foster, A. and Zagier Roberts, V. (eds) (1998) *Managing Mental Health in the Community: Chaos and Containment.*
Hinshelwood, R. (2004) *Suffering Insanity; Psychoanalytic essays on psychosis.*

Tavistock Centre for Couple Relationships and Paul Pengelly for permission to reprint from:
Woodhouse, D. and Pengelly, P. (1991) *Anxiety and the Dynamics of Collaboration.*

Taylor & Francis for permission to reprint from:
Loshak, R. (2007) 'There is a war on! Someone is going to get killed'. *Psychoanalytic Psychotherapy* 21(1): 20–39.

Abbreviations

CAF	Common Assessment Framework (www.education.gov.uk)
CAMHS	Child and Adolescent Mental Health Services
C4EO	Centre for Excellence in Outcomes in Children's and Young People's Services (www.c4eo.org.uk)
CMHT	Community Mental Health Team (adult)
CPA	Care Programme Approach (www.dh.gov.uk/home/publications)
CWDC	Children's Workforce Development Council (ended March 2012)
DCSF	Department for Children, Schools and Families (formerly part of DfES, now included in DfE)
DfES	Department for Education and Skills (obsolete)
DfE	Department for Education (www.education.gov.uk)
DH	Department of Health (formerly DoH) (www.dh.gov.uk)
ECM	Every Child Matters (archived: see DfE website)
NCB	National Children's Bureau (www.ncb.org.uk)
NICE	National Institute for Health and Clinical Excellence (www.nice.org.uk)
NSF	National Service Framework (www.dh.gov.uk/home/publications)
PMHCWN	Parental Mental Health and Child Welfare Network (www.pmhcwn.org.uk)
SCIE	Social Care Institute for Excellence (www.scie.org.uk)
TAC	Team Around the Child (www.education.gov.uk)

Part I

Themes, theories and background

This book describes the development of a parental mental health project over a period of ten years. The years during which this happened were a time of rapid change within health and social care sectors, but also an exciting time of growth presenting a real opportunity to make a difference in some children's lives. The 'Children and Adult Mental Health Project' seized the moment and attempted to build a network in one inner city borough with a focus on the children of parents with mental illness, making full use of existing resources.

While the project itself has given rise to the book and is central to it, there are two major themes which underlie it. These are outlined in Chapter 1 and are further developed in the following chapters in Part I. The first theme is that these are a group of highly vulnerable children who nevertheless largely remain hidden from view, whose emotional and ordinary developmental needs may remain entirely hidden from professionals involved with their parents, from teachers and others working with them. The three authors of Chapter 2 pick up on this theme by talking to children and reporting what they have to say about their experiences, so that we hear their voices directly.

Writing from the viewpoint of a systemic family therapist, Lizette Nolte, in Chapter 3, supports children's views of their experiences with research evidence about the impact of parental mental illness on both the not so ordinary task of parenting, and directly on children. Lizette ends with a plea for more talking to and with children about their parent's illness. This need not be confined to the clinic setting of Child and Adolescent Mental Health (CAMHS) but may be approached by a number of other professionals, particularly those in adult mental health. It is this change in working practice that the project has sought to bring about.

The second major theme is that of the relevant agencies working together. This has been recognised as a difficulty in most child abuse inquiries of preceding years, a difficulty which is arguably increased when one of the agencies involved is concerned with mental health, an area which many find difficult to understand. The problem is identified in Chapter 1 and illustrated with a case example which had a direct bearing on the start of the project.

In Chapter 4 this difficulty is considered from a psychoanalytically informed approach to the understanding of mental illness, and its impact on the minds and functioning of the adults and the organisations which try to work with it. Anxiety dominates the work of any mental health organisation and this chapter attempts to show how defences, both individual and organisational, are put in place to cope with this, often to the detriment of working together.

The various chapters present different theoretical viewpoints, which will recur throughout the book. This perhaps illustrates a frequently encountered problem in working together: that of managing differences, not only of theory but of professional background, and training.

In the late 1990s, the years leading up to the start of this project, there were major structural reorganisations within health and social services which came about as a response to the 1990 NHS and Community Care legislation, which provided for adult mental health care in the community. These changes affected both adult mental health and child mental health services, resulting in a loss of long-standing and valued team and supervisory relationships. For the editor, this experience of loss served as a catalyst for change, for moving into this new area of work with parental mental health. Loss and change may be thought of as a 'leitmotif' carrying through the whole book. Chapter 5 considers its impact directly, describing the context in which the project took place. The context is one of time, and place, of an unremitting experience of loss and change experienced alike by families and those working with them. In devoting space to what is in part a historical overview we are also establishing the importance of our relationship with the past for the present, and showing the impact of disrupted relationships.

1 Hidden children

Rosemary Loshak

This book is concerned with a group of children who, though vulnerable, remain hidden from their teachers, friends and neighbours, and professional networks. Philip Pullman, in his trilogy 'His Dark Materials', helps us to understand one of the reasons for this:

> Will had first realised that his mother was different from other people and that he had to look after her when he was seven years. . . . So he kept his mother's trouble secret . . . . And he learned how to conceal himself too, how not to attract attention from the neighbours, even when his mother was in such a state of fear and madness that she could barely speak. What Will feared more than anything, was that the authorities would find out about her and take her away and put him in a home among strangers.
>
> (Pullman 1997: 8–11)

Anne Sexton was an American poet who committed suicide in 1974. She had two daughters and had been hospitalised in a psychiatric unit during the early years of her eldest daughter's life. In a powerful poem she indicates the meaning her first child held for her, as a way of finding herself (Sexton 1981).

In a radio interview in 2010 her daughters describe their experience of feeling that there was 'not a lot of room for us' and 'battered by the illness because we did not understand what was going on. People withdrew from the illness.' Her youngest daughter spoke of there being 'always a fear of violence that would erupt and they would start a fight, – it wasn't a safe house'. They describe feeling angry, guilty, anxious and trying not to think about what was happening (BBC Radio 4 2010).

Children are affected by and cope with parental mental illness in many different ways. Some will remain hidden from view and become young carers, with little independent life of their own, unable to separate from a dependent and needy but loved parent, and socially isolated from their peers as the stigma of mental illness casts a shadow over them also. Some may face real risk of physical injury, or, in rare cases, death, particularly the very young who are most at risk. Not all will suffer actual harm but they will be vulnerable to their emotional, social and physical development being compromised.

This book describes a project extending over ten years which attempts to bring the plight of children of mentally ill parents to the forefront of the minds of the professionals involved with them or their parents. The aim is to intervene early to prevent the crisis which is the realisation of their worst fears, fears of separation, family breakdown and of someone being hurt. In 2002 a coordinator was appointed in the local authority to work across the interface between child and adult services. She was supported by a steering group which at a very early stage had identified the need for experienced children's social workers to be located in the adult community mental health teams. Such posts were finally created and filled four years later and it is their work that is set out in this book as one possible model of providing services for families affected by mental illness.

A training video made by the Royal College of Psychiatrists allows children and young people whose parents suffer from a mental illness, which has at some point required their admission to hospital, to tell their stories, and lets us glimpse the daily reality of their lives. What is striking about many of these children's accounts is the absence of other adults who will take responsibility, whether family members or professionals. The young people feel they are left to manage alone, sometimes when there is no food in the house, sometimes with a parent attempting suicide, or family violence (Cooklin 2006).

That these children do so often remain hidden is related to the nature of mental illness and to society's response to it. A frequent feature of psychotic illness is the denial of the need for help or of difficulties. An Australian study reported that of 124 parents with a psychotic illness, 49 per cent did not want help with their children but preferred to cope on their own, and 30 per cent feared their child being taken away (McLean *et al.* 2004). The fear of losing one's child is not without reality. In the 1950s, admissions to asylums were often linked with a shameful pregnancy, whether an illegitimate birth or as a result of rape. In a study of admissions to an Essex asylum, Gittins found that women were 'certified' for bearing such children while psychiatrists still admitted teenage mothers of illegitimate babies into the 1950s (Gittins 1998).

The children were often removed from the mother and placed for adoption. The stigma remains, and a vestige of the old attitudes towards the mentally ill having children remains evident in our collective difficulty in recognising the need.

With a variety of more recent developments in service provision these children have slowly been finding their own voice, and it is with this process and these children that this book is primarily concerned. While support for parents and recognition that parenting is a valued social role is an essential aspect of the work described, the focus is on the child in the context of his or her family and wider social network.

Working together to help children and families

This is a second but central theme of this book. The initial appointment was intended not to provide direct services to families, but to address the problems of working together which were recognised by senior management in both health and social care at the time, as obstacles to providing an effective and supportive service to families. There was an expectation that procedures would be established and policy put in place to overcome obstacles and provide effective training programmes for staff.

A personal anecdote is relevant to the problems encountered: prior to taking up this newly created post this author had been, for many years, a social worker in a multidisciplinary child and adolescent mental health service working psycho-dynamically with parents and children, separately and together as families, and often as co-worker with a colleague of another discipline, usually psychiatrists, psychologists or child psychotherapists. This role provided opportunities for links with adult mental health services, through the hospital social work team which historically covered both adult and child mental health, through a caseload which included several parents who were themselves users of adult mental health services, and through some direct work with adult outpatient psychiatry. It formed the groundwork, the secure base for this venture into community adult mental health in a new role.

The following vignette from her work in that setting illustrates difficulties that can arise among colleagues when working with families where a parent has a mental illness.

> I was leading a work discussion group for child protection advisers, who were experienced health visitors. They formed a team within the borough who provided consultation and support to their colleagues about child protection matters. Our discussions were about complex situations which often aroused strong feelings. We shared our anxiety about the matters of life or death where infants and small children were involved. One such discussion concerned a pre-school child and her single mother who was described as acting bizarrely and appearing depressed. The group member expressed a strongly held view that the child was seriously at risk, and urgent action required, possibly to take the child into care.
>
> Taken aback by what seemed a premature rush into action, I was also surprised by my own equally strong reaction, that such a step was drastic and unnecessary, a view that I conveyed. At our next meeting I was asked to support my unusual view with evidence, as the group were agreed that the mental illness of a parent represented a danger to such a young child.

This brief vignette indicates how polarised positions of potential conflict can quickly develop to distort professional thinking and the quality of communication when anxieties are high, and few facts are known. It signals the second theme of this book which is an attempt to understand the impact of severe mental illness on the professionals working closely with it, on their organisations, and on their efforts to work collaboratively.

In the above example neither participant had firsthand knowledge of this mother and child. Responses were determined rather by individuals' strongly held beliefs and attitudes regarding mental illness, by their different assumptions about the role of the other's profession, as well as by what may be termed their 'personal baggage' (the sum of our own childhood experiences which have been our motivation for entering the caring professions, but which can also operate to blind us to current realities) (Hallett and Stevenson 1980). They were, however, already engaged in a working relationship with me and the group had provided a setting in which self-reflection was possible. Where this possibility does not exist such conflictual interactions may come to typify professional networks attempting to work together, whether among individual workers or between whole agencies.

This incident prompted more discussion and led this author to research the topic of parental mental illness, both in relation to the available evidence, which was limited at that time (Quinton and Rutter 1984), and to her own self-knowledge. It came to serve as a trigger to the developments which led ultimately to the project described in this book. However, such developments do not occur in isolation; they require a 'climate change' in society, shared interest from a group of colleagues and an organisational context in which they become possible. These gradually came about in the 1990s as awareness of the numbers of children living with a parent who had a 'severe and enduring' mental illness slowly increased (Gopfert *et al.* 1995; Mayes *et al.* 1998).

In April 2010 a cloud of ash spewed across Northern Europe from an Icelandic volcano, grounding all flights for several days and bringing a state of paralysis to the travel industry and rage and frustration to travellers. After the event we learnt that the Civil Aviation Authority had been trying for at least two years prior to this event to bring together representatives of the airline industry and engineers and environmental scientists to agree a safe level of ash in the atmosphere in which planes could fly. The parties were reluctant to meet, apparently fearful of the possible financial and legal consequences of making an incorrect decision, exposing them to too much risk of bad publicity and damages claims in the event of a disaster. There were too many vested interests, and the industry was highly risk averse.

The situation is analogous perhaps to that which can exist among statutory health and social care agencies carrying heavy responsibilities for people and situations which are inherently full of uncertainty and anxiety. The following example is the organisational response to the death of a child in 1998 in the borough. Clinicians and managers within the borough had already recognised the likely distress experienced by many children of parents with mental illness. There had been a very well-received conference on the subject in 1997 and a joint working group convened to set up 'cross-over' training workshops. However, the latter had had a limited response from staff. The death of a child made the matter urgent and the inquiry gave the impetus to appoint a coordinator, recognising that the effort needed to ensure more effective working together could not be managed within existing staff resources.

A 'Part 8 Review'

A 'Part 8 Review' is an inter-agency response to the death of a child as a result of non-accidental injury or neglect. In 1988 the Department of Health published the first 'Working Together' document (to which Part 8 refers) which provided guidelines and requirements for relevant agencies to communicate and cooperate in the protection of children (DHSS 1988).

Reder *et al.*'s 1993 study of child abuse inquiries was completed prior to the publication of this document and had identified a number of problems in inter-agency communication and working which may have been contributory factors leading to a child's death (Reder *et al.* 1993). These included, as did a Department of Health report of 1991, a confusion of roles, the absence of a pivotal worker at the time the child died, mirroring the dynamics of the case in the professional network, and the need for a secure setting for staff in child protection work (DoH 1991). The concept of a secure setting included such factors as continuity of management, regular and good supervision, clear procedures, clear agency boundaries and stable organisational structures (Reder *et al.* 1993). Many of these problems will still be seen to be present in the case outlined below. Neither of these early studies made reference to parental mental illness, a highly significant factor in this case.

In the late 1990s in the borough an infant died as a result of neglect. The non-English-speaking parents had failed to understand the potential seriousness of the child's illness and had been unable to access adequate and timely medical help. The case led to a local Part 8 Review to understand the events which led up to this tragedy. There were more than twenty agencies or services involved with this child's family at the time, forming a system in which failed communication was a significant feature.

The family included a father thought to have a serious mental illness who was awaiting assessment and appropriate treatment, but not engaging with services whose workers found it difficult to make contact. Such contact as occurred was often through the mother, a recent immigrant to the UK who had a very limited command of basic English. She was struggling to cope with her husband's difficult moods or behaviours and with the sole care of three pre-school children. Both parents were isolated within their own community by the father's illness and in the wider society by their culture and language differences. They were viewed by professionals as uncooperative and 'difficult'.

Difficulties of working together

Factors identified in the external agency's report share common features of other such reports, including a failure to recognise the importance of formal communication within and between agencies, a 'dearth of inter-agency planning', an absence of a theoretical underpinning and a lack of recognition in adult mental health services of 'patients as parents' or of adult services' role in child protection (TH ACPC 2001). The responses from each of the three agencies involved, namely the local authority, the mental health service and an acute hospital trust, dealt with gaps in training, failed lines of communication and a lack of understanding of the role of adult mental health staff in child protection. The report contributed directly both to the creation by the local authority of the post of 'Interface development coordinator' to which this author was subsequently appointed (this job title was later amended to the more descriptive 'Coordinator for children in families with mental illness'), and to the appointment of an Assistant Director for Safeguarding Children in the new mental health trust.

In initial meetings in the coordinator role with team staff and senior managers in both health and the local authority, the author encountered a more detailed awareness of the difficulties which inter-agency work can bring. Managers were both aware and concerned that multi-agency involvement can, when services are overstretched, result in no one taking responsibility for decision making and holistic assessment of need becoming less likely, as there is an assumption that the other agency is responsible. Reder *et al.* noted that 'the knowledge that someone is doing something reduces anxiety for other members of the network and the case becomes less of a priority for them' (Reder *et al.* 1993: 67).

The lack of a holistic and interactional view of a family's difficulties, and the failure to take a historical family perspective of individuals' lives, of losses, of strengths and difficulties rather than a 'snapshot' of incidents treated in isolation from each other has been a feature of many inquiries, including that following the death of Victoria Climbié.[1]

Mental health staff, in common with other professions, complained that they referred children to what was then Social Services, only to be told that 'there were no concerns'. They recognised that different priorities might be operating but rarely had they been able to establish the working relationships with childcare colleagues that would permit discussion about criteria for referral, consultation about how to manage a situation, or advice about what further information might be needed. Agencies and their teams appeared to operate from the 'silo' mentality and from a defensive structure so often noted in the literature (Reder *et al.* 1993; Woodhouse and Pengelly 1991). Assisting in managing this interface and overcoming these barriers, sometimes by providing direct help to staff in making appropriate and informed referrals, has been a central role for the coordinator and later for the children's specialists in the mental health teams.

There was no established mechanism by which the single agency responses to the report could be brought together, and managers had also been concerned that there was no coordinating person in the management of the case. This is a recognition of the reality that no one agency has authority over other agencies. In 1989 the inquiry into the death of a child in Islington had commented:

> A fundamental issue which has not been resolved is whether the role of other agencies is to supply the Social Services department with the relevant information in their possession to enable the department to carry out its statutory function of protecting children or whether they are all generally cooperating fully and equally in the child's interests, regardless of the legitimate need of their own agencies.
>
> (DoH 1991: 42)

A duty to cooperate is now clearly stated in the 2004 Children Act, in the latest edition of *Working Together*, and with the introduction of 'integrated teams' with multi-agency representatives operating at the point of referral to Children's Social Care, the idea that children are everybody's responsibility is becoming more embedded (DfES and DoH 2006).

Although the report had been critical of adult mental health services' failure to see their 'patients as parents' this was not unusual at the time. In 1991 the Department of Health had noted that psychiatrists seldom figured in reviews of child deaths. More or less concurrent with the local Part 8 Review was the publication of a further study of child abuse inquiries, this time of 'Part 8 Reviews', by Reder and Duncan (1999), in which they identified parental mental illness or substance abuse as a significant factor in child deaths with 43 per cent of parents having an active mental illness or current history of substance abuse at the time of the child's death. At the time, although at least 25 per cent of mentally ill adults were parents of children under 16, very few authorities across the country had recognised the implication of this for services, or had put anything in place to ensure joint working. The newly created mental health trust at that time had a named consultant child psychiatrist but no named nurse for child protection. This was very soon rectified by the creation of the post at assistant director level for safeguarding children, and in time by the development of a small team of 'named nurses', who developed a training programme for mental health trust staff about child protection.

Wider organisational factors such as instability, changes in structure, a lack of clearly defined procedures, a lack of regular supervision, and high staff turnover have all been identified as contributory factors when a child dies (Reder and Duncan 1999). Locally, managers and staff commented on the effects of high staff turnover or the absence of permanent staff in communication and liaison between teams. High staff turnover may operate at all levels of a department, not only in front-line services; between 2002 and 2009 six successive third-tier managers were responsible for the coordinator role and for the whole of children's front-line fieldwork.[2] The direct and indirect effect on service users is an experience of constant disruption which mirrors the disruption in their own lives and the fragmentation of their own coping capacities.

Where services involved with a family are characterised by such fragmentation and lack of coordination the effect on vulnerable parents may be to increase anxiety, arouse fears of intrusion and loss of control, and ultimately to undermine precarious parenting skills.

It was noted that staff from the mental health team and from the childcare team visited on the same day, each without the knowledge of the other. Although these are matters of coordination and communication they also demonstrate the need for knowledge and theory. 'Cross-over training' alone will not be adequate to help staff think about the consequences of separating children from their parents, the need to assess attachment, to know how to approach a parent who may be psychotic or to work with personality disorder. These are complex tasks likely to flood an inexperienced worker with anxiety; all require theoretical knowledge of a high order. While this kind of knowledge and thinking has been embodied in the overall approach to post-qualifying staff education in the local authority, embedding it in practice inevitably takes considerable time and requires stable teams and consistently good supervision.

The difficulties that characterised the adults in the family – lack of cooperation with others, being 'difficult', withdrawing from contact, fear and anxiety, isolation – could be said to have been mirrored in the professional network surrounding them (Britton 2005). The professional 'family' might also be considered to have been under 'siege' with individual staff seeking to tighten the boundaries around their work to protect themselves, as were their agencies, like overburdened parents, not hearing their anxieties, instead being preoccupied with their own.

Concurrently with the responses to the death of the child in 1998, but independently of that event, a group of professionals in different settings had become increasingly aware of the widening gap between adult mental health and child mental health, where previously there had been long-standing working relationships across settings and disciplines. Initially this author, as a CAMHS social worker, together with a mental health team manager and a children's team manager, met to share concerns about children, already known to their teams, of mentally ill parents, and the difficulty of accessing services for them. The group aroused interest and was soon joined by an adult psychiatrist, a child protection lead officer and a voluntary sector manager. Later, representatives from education and nursing became part of the group, which in time became the steering group for CHAMP (the Children and Adult Mental Health Project).

The work of the CHAMP team has complemented developments in the mental health trust to ensure that mental health staff members are also supported in the complex task of working collaboratively, to think holistically about service users and their families and in their efforts to put in place preventive services. These may over time not only provide early interventions for children but also thereby reduce the risk of family breakdown and repeated admission to hospital. By facilitating communication and mutual understanding at the interface, the project aims also to reduce the sense of isolation among mental health staff, manage anxiety and facilitate collaborative work.

Organisation of the book

This book is intended to help practitioners of all disciplines in mental health and children's services, including education, to develop a clearer understanding of each other's role, to recognise in themselves and others the impact of the work on themselves, on their agencies and on their working relationships, and to work more collaboratively for the benefit of children. However, it is not exclusively for practitioners: as Woodhouse and Pengelly make clear, we all work in an organisational context, in which management and commissioning have a vital, and often much vilified role (Woodhouse and Pengelly 1991). The nature and responsibilities of our organisations are determined in turn by the society of which we are also a part. We believe therefore that the book is also relevant and important to managers and policy makers who determine change and the structures in which we work. We are all part of an interrelated and interconnected system.

Theoretical approaches to these problems have been diverse; some have applied systemic concepts (Daniel and Chin 2010; Munro 2010; Reder and Duncan 1999; Reder *et al.* 1993) while others have applied psychoanalytic thinking to the working of organisations (Britton 2001; Cooper and Lousada 2005; Foster and Zagier Roberts 1998; Hinshelwood 1998). Social work is necessarily concerned with loss and change, while Yelloly has shown how Freudian humanism was the foundation of social work's non-judgemental and self-determining values (Yelloly 1980). Current childcare social work is much informed by attachment theory and concepts of resilience. In adult mental health services a medical/biological model dominates, while behavioural therapies have developed considerably in the focus on recovery. These will all emerge in the context of this book as the different authors contribute from their own perspectives. The psychoanalytic knowledge of human development has provided a framework for thinking about and under-standing mental illness as well as its impact on the individuals and organisations working with it, and this will be described and demonstrated.

Protecting children, service users and staff

Contributing authors have made extensive use of casework material throughout, and this has demanded that close attention is paid to the need to protect service users and children by ensuring that they remain anonymous. In most cases this has been achieved by presenting illustrative vignettes in which details are omitted or changed, and which may not relate directly to one service user but rather describe situations that many may experience. Where more detailed case histories are given to demonstrate the nature of the work, and of changes that take place, any identifying information has been changed and permission has been given for publication. We are grateful to those service users and their children who have been generous in this way.

However, the book is also concerned with staff mostly from one local authority and its partner mental health trust, which will be readily identifiable to their employees. Where possible we have also sought their consent to inclusion of material which may relate to them. Because we have considered history and context relevant and of importance, it is also inevitable that some readers may identify the area of the project. We are grateful to both agencies for giving their approval to the publication of the book and for the support and advice they have given throughout. It is important that the book is not written in a spirit of criticism, blame or fault-finding, but rather aims to understand processes, often unconscious, which can interfere with the collaborative task, and cause many of us at times to 'turn a blind eye' to the plight and circumstances of some children. Without the interest, enthusiasm and cooperation of very many staff in both agencies, this book, and indeed the project, would not have been possible.

Notes

1 Victoria Climbié died in 2000 as a result of injuries inflicted by her carers over a long period of time. The failures of local agencies who knew Victoria were heavily criticised in the inquiry report produced by Lord Laming which led to legislative changes incorporated in the Children Act 2004.
2 Management responsibility was held jointly by the adult mental health social care manager and the children's fieldwork manager.

References

BBC Radio 4 (2010) *Consorting with Angels*, London: BBC Radio 4, 17 January. ©BBC 2010.

Britton, R. (2005) 'Re-enactment as an unwitting professional response to family dynamics', in Bower, M. (ed.) *Psychoanalytic Theory for Social Work Practice*, Abingdon: Routledge.

The Children Act (2004) *Every Child Matters*, Norwich: TSO.

Cooklin, A. (2006) *Being Seen and Heard: The Needs of Children of Parents with Mental Illness*, London: Royal College of Psychiatrists (DVD).

Cooper, A. and Lousada, J. (2005) *Borderline Welfare: Feeling and Fear of Feeling in Modern Welfare*, London: Karnac. Available from: http://www.karnacbooks.com/isbn/9781855759053.

Daniel, G. and Chin, J. (2010) 'Engaging with agency cultures in parental mental illness training', *Context*, 108, April, pp. 47–50, Association for Family Therapy. AFT Publishing.

Department for Education and Skills and Department of Health (DfES and DoH) (2006) *Working Together to Safeguard Children*, London: HMSO.

Department of Health (1991) *Child Abuse: A Study of Inquiry Reports 1980–1989*, London: HMSO.

Department of Health and Social Security and the Welsh Office (1988) *Working Together: A Guide to Arrangements for Inter-agency Cooperation for the Protection of Children from Abuse*, London: HMSO.

Foster, A. and Zagier Roberts, V. (eds) (1998) *Managing Mental Health in the Community: Chaos and Containment*, London and New York: Routledge.

Gittins, D. (1998) *Madness in its Place: Narratives of Severall's Hospital 1913–1997*, London and New York: Routledge.

Gopfert, M., Webster J. and Seeman, M.V. (eds) (1995) *Parental Psychiatric Disorder: Distressed Parents and their Families*, Cambridge: Cambridge University Press.

Hallett, C. and Stevenson, O. (1980) *Child Abuse*, London: Allen and Unwin.

Hinshelwood, R. (1998) 'Creatures of each other', in Foster, A. and Zagier Roberts, V. (eds) *Managing Mental Health in the Community: Chaos and Containment*, London and New York: Routledge.

Mayes, K., Diggins, M. and Falkov, A. (eds) (1998) *Crossing Bridges: Training Resources for Working with Mentally Ill Patients and their Children – Reader for Managers, Practitioners and Trainers* (DoH), London and Brighton: Pavilion Publishing.

McLean, D., Hearle, J. and McGrath, J. (2004) 'Are services for families with a mentally ill parent adequate?', in Gopfert, M., Webster, J. and Seeman, M.V. (eds) *Parental Psychiatric Disorder: Distressed Parents and their Families*, Cambridge: Cambridge University Press.

Munro, E. (2010) *The Munro Review of Child Protection: Part One: A Systems Analysis*, London: Department of Education.

Pullman, P. (1997) *The Subtle Knife*, London: Scholastic Children's Books.

Quinton, D. and Rutter, M. (1984) 'Parental psychiatric disorder: effects on children', *Psychological Medicine* 14: 853–880.

Reder, P. and Duncan S. (1999) *Lost Innocents: A Follow-up Study of Fatal Child Abuse,* London: Routledge.

Reder, P., Duncan, S. and Gray, M. (1993) *Beyond Blame: Child Abuse Tragedies Revisited,* London and New York: Routledge.

Sexton, A. (1981) 'The Double Image', in *The Complete Poems of Anne Sexton*, Boston, MA: Houghton Mifflin.

Tower Hamlets Area Child Protection Committee (July 2001) *A Review into Events Leading up to the Death of NH.*

Woodhouse, D. and Pengelly, P. (1991) *Anxiety and the Dynamics of Collaboration,* Aberdeen: Aberdeen University Press.

Yelloly, M.A. (1980) *Social Work Theory and Psychoanalysis,* New York and London: Van Nostrand Reinhold.

2 Living with a parent with mental health needs

What children say

Cassie Bromley, Liana Hadleigh and Amy Roe

Introduction

The experiences of young people whose parents have mental health difficulties have rarely been investigated (Gladstone *et al*., 2006; Leverton, 2003; Mordoch & Hall, 2002). Previous research has often focused on the associated risks for children, rather than on how some of these children continue to do well (Leverton, 2003; Mordoch & Hall, 2002). These dominant narratives of risk can become problematic when they constrain us from noticing experiences that may be useful in assisting us in understanding what helps these young people to do well (Madsen, 2007). While valuable, the results of such studies fail to capture the richness and complexities of young people's experiences of living with parents with mental health difficulties in a meaningful way. Qualitative research methods allow for a more in-depth exploration of young people's day-to-day lived experience, and give us an opportunity to learn first-hand about their lives (Leverton, 2003; Mordoch & Hall, 2002). Therefore there is a need to widen the scope of research to include a focus on competence and resilience (Seligman, 2005).

Attachment theory (Bowlby, 1973) has been used to help understand factors which may influence resilience. It proposes that a child's experience of interactions with attachment figures becomes an internal working model, which produces expectations about the self and others, and governs affect, the ability to cope with stress and to seek and engage in support. It is suggested that the development of an internal working model may be mediated by how experiences are processed, or made sense of by the individual, and incorporated into their autobiographical narratives (Fonagy *et al*., 1996). Therefore understanding how children make sense of their experiences is important in understanding resilience.

Systemic approaches emphasise the importance of considering the different roles and relationships within the family system. Perceptions of what children can manage at different ages are dependent upon social, economic and cultural contexts. It is therefore important to understand from children how they construct their relationship to parental mental health difficulties, the strategies they use to manage stressful experiences, and how the position they adopt can change at different times, at different developmental stages, and within different contexts.

Encouragingly, some international research has begun to address this (Fudge & Mason, 2004; Garley *et al*., 1997; Handley *et al*., 2001; Maybery *et al*., 2005;

Meadus & Johnson, 2000; Polkki *et al.*, 2004; Riebschleger, 2004). In the UK a handful of studies, drawing predominantly on young carer samples, have been published (Aldridge & Becker, 2003; Armstrong, 2002; Stallard *et al.*, 2004; Webster, 1992). Common themes arising from these studies include young people's lack of understanding about their parents' difficulties, anxiety about their parents' and their own mental health, and experiences of economic disadvantage and isolation.

In summary, there has been limited research into the richness and complexity of these young people's experiences. Further research would help to develop an understanding of the attachment and transactional effects within such families that lead to increased resilience. It would inform clinical practice and improve support for families.

In this chapter an overview of the findings of three qualitative studies, recently carried out across three inner city boroughs, is presented. The overall aim of these studies was to build on the previous research into parental mental health. More specifically, to focus on exploring young people's experiences of living with a parent or carer with mental health difficulties and in a way that pays careful attention to their richness and complexity. Two of the studies interviewed adolescents (Bromley, 2008; Roe, 2010), while the third focused on younger children (Hadleigh, 2011). The children's parents had a range of mental health difficulties from depression to psychosis and the children were recruited through a variety of services including Young Carers, a parental mental health project, CMHTs and CAMHS.

The studies used Interpretative Phenomenological Analysis (IPA) (Smith *et al.*, 2009) of interviews with young people about their experiences of living with parental mental health difficulties. IPA explores individual experiences, rather than making generalisations about the larger population. IPA's stance in relation to the researcher's role is important because IPA involves a double hermeneutic; this means the researcher attempts to make sense of the participant making sense of his or her world. The analysis aimed to highlight generic themes, in addition to individual stories, thereby examining both divergence and convergence.

As with qualitative methodology in general, the aim of the research was not to come up with a complete, final or 'true' account of experiences of all children living with parental mental health difficulties. Rather, this account should be viewed as partial and incomplete, and the reader is invited to consider the verbatim extracts and the interpretations made in context (Smith & Osborn, 2008).

It is necessary to acknowledge that the findings presented provide an in-depth insight into the salient themes of the young people's experiences in three specific IPA studies, and the findings' transferability must be considered within this particular context. Young people who chose not to participate or who did not have contact with the services used for recruitment might have qualitatively different experiences of parental mental health problems to those participating. Hence the recruitment strategy needs consideration when contemplating the findings' transferability.

Uncertainty in understanding parental mental health difficulties

Young people talked about how they became aware and tried to make sense of their parents' difficulties. They spoke about how they felt this had developed with age and experience, with few saying that they had received an explanation, instead being left to make sense of what was going on themselves. Young people also experienced uncertainty about what the implications for the future might be.

Developing awareness

All of the young people were aware of their parents' mental health difficulties, and seemed to become aware mainly through observations, such as changes in their parents' emotions, behaviour or conversation.

Joel: By looking at and analysing and seeing how things are.

However, for some it wasn't a process of developing awareness; their experience was that they had always known things this way.

Amrita: No one really told me, it was like I sort of like knew.

Others described a complex process whereby what they had seen as normal became increasingly problematic through the intervention of others.

Joel: It wasn't something I really became aware of . . . it just sort of happened and came like bang, like it wasn't like a process, and if it was a process I was too young to see the signs anyway. One day she was at home, the next day we got put into care . . . I didn't know why, 'cos I didn't think there was nothing wrong with her.

It was suggested by Bromley (2008) that the extent to which they acknowledged their parents' difficulties may be embedded in their construction of 'normality' within the family. For some, the tension between acknowledging differences and describing 'normality' seemed born out of a desire not to be stigmatised or seen as different.

Understanding of mental health

The young people often sought information to aid their understanding of their parents' mental health difficulties. Some drew on discourses of illness to explain mental health difficulties. These were either learnt through school or through awareness of professional contact with their parent, making a health narrative explicit through the giving of medication or due to the discussion of 'health'.
      Farhana tried to ask her father.

Farhana: Like why did it happen . . . and how do you feel and why do you feel like smoking and why do you do stuff like this, and he just ignores.

She experienced difficulty with being able to discuss this with her father. Equally, Joel discovered that it was difficult to discuss with others because of the strong feelings it might provoke.

Joel: 'Cos like if your mum's ill someone would be scared to talk to you about it, because if they say that you're [understanding is] wrong they think that you might get angry or something . . . so there's no one to talk to.

They therefore experienced frustration at not being able to discuss their thoughts, or get answers to their questions.

While some children tended to hold a simple single explanation for their parents' difficulties, some tried to develop a more complex understanding, incorporating ideas of genetics and systemic factors, looking beyond the familiar.

Katie: I don't really think it's coincidental that her Mum had it, my Mum had it, and now I have it. It's obviously something genetic, or something going round in our family. So therefore I think if she didn't have it, then I wouldn't have it.

Similarly, younger children's understanding of their parents' mental health needs was not fixed to one explanation; instead they were able to hold differing definitions. For them, mental health, physical health or religious explanations did not have to be mutually exclusive. Sidz, one of the younger children, used an interpersonal, behavioural and religious context to define her father's mental health needs.

Sidz: I'm not really sure because normally at home he's fine but just sometimes he speaks a lot like sometimes when I say something then he says it again just to make sure and that's why my mum and I get angry because, you know, we say it again and again but we know how he is so we try our best.

Sidz: Like, erm . . . you know the rubbish thing had fallen and then he starts getting the hoover out and like for one hour he starts hoovering and hoovering. So he's actually really into neat things that's why.

Sidz: Because you know I go to Mosque and they always say these things to keep them away, you know these, I don't think if you know but jinns.

The various definitions of mental health given by young people indicate that this is not fixed and may represent the fluidity of this concept for them. However, some appeared to find it difficult to integrate these ideas, and therefore a satisfactory understanding remained elusive.

Katie: Well a lot of people have explained it to me, told me, you know, what it's about and how it works. But I . . . still don't really understand it.

A striking element in the young people's experiences was the uncertainty that seemed to envelop their parents' difficulties. Some clearly experienced strong emotions when faced with uncertainty, feeling scared, not knowing what was happening. Katie's reaction demonstrates how being aware of something without understanding can lead to feeling unsafe.

Katie: I was kind of worried 'cos I didn't really know what was going on, I didn't understand why she was so upset or why she was so distressed. So I was kind of scared.

To manage these uncomfortable feelings respondents attempted to make meaning and develop explanations for their parents' behaviour. Young people who hadn't had the opportunity to discuss it tried to make sense of it themselves. They often sought to make sense of their parents' difficulties by looking to the familiar, connecting their parents' difficulties to external factors or life events, tending to understand it as having developed following stressful experiences. Both younger and older children highlighted relationship difficulties as the cause of their parents' mental health difficulties.

Joel: She wasn't like that mental ill. What she was, was angry because of stuff that my Dad did, and they can sometimes mistake the way that someone reacts with anger and they mistake it for mental illness and given pill, pill, pill, pill and then and that's what I think actually makes them ill.

Nandita: Outside people looks at my mum and then she gets a bit worried, that's it.

It seemed that in their search for meaning respondents drew on the resources at their disposal, but also explanations that made sense to them in terms of what they had witnessed. While these understandings may be grounding, enabling them to maintain a continuous link with their parent as in principle reachable, others also experienced it as worrying, since it left them to wonder whether they were to blame.

Ellie: It's confusing like. Is it me or my Dad, or is it the whole family, who is it, is it one of us or is it parts of us . . . I felt I just wanted to like go away from my family, just wanted to be on my own.

Living with uncertainty: change, recovery and the future

Young people were also aware that their parents' mental health needs changed across time. Some remembered life before the difficulties started. Older children talked of difficulty coping with the fluctuation or unpredictability of their parents' behaviour and of preparing themselves for the future.

Nalini: Obviously you have that thing in your head that you just have to brace yourself for the next time she breaks down . . . you've just got to get ready.

They tried to make things seem more predictable, which was interpreted by the researcher as trying to gain some control over what they were experiencing.

Ellie: I'd just wait until she acts weird again and then, like I told you so she'd act weird again.

However, these concerns were accompanied by hope for their parents' recovery and noticing signs of progress. They were aware that there may be times when their parent experiences difficulties again, but the young people were keen to think about what they could do to prevent this and support their parents' recovery, as is discussed in the following section.

The complexity of the parent–child relationship

Young people's relationships with their parents were complex. Caring was a reciprocal process between them. Young people's desire to care for their parents and to be cared for by them was underpinned by the strong bonds between them. Young people appeared to use the relationship with their parent to help themselves cope, focusing on the positive parts of the relationship to manage the impact of the more difficult parts.

Caring for parents

Young people expressed a wish to care for their parents and adopted protective, caring and responsible roles towards their families. The desire to look after their family and ease their parents' difficulties illustrated the strong bonds and reciprocity between them.

Emir: She's my mum and she born me and then I need to take care of her.

Lucy: You sort of get on with your mum and your dad more from the experiences, if that makes sense, 'cos you get a bigger bond, stronger bond.

For young people whose parents had been in hospital there was a strong wish to re-establish the connection with them. Separation was experienced as painful and so they actively sought to reconnect or rebuild their relationships with them.

Lucy: Because from them being in hospital you don't see them, then you just want to get closer to them.

The desire to care was demonstrated in a variety of ways by younger children and adolescents alike. Some did household chores, some reassured their siblings, some their parents, and some tried to minimise their parents' stress by behaving well. Nandita's mother asked for her support to go to places, finding her presence reassuring.

Nandita: She says that oh can you be with me can you come somewhere with me, that's it.

Messi described providing practical help to manage the physical consequences of his father's mental health needs.

Messi: Erm . . . he sometimes he does wee on the bed and then it's hard work changing it.

It was apparent that some assumed responsibility for their parents' well-being, considering their needs and helping them when upset, offering themselves as people their parents could depend on for support and love.

Alara: Sometimes I'm like worried to leave her alone, at home when I'm going to school . . . even like when I went to school I used to always think about her.

Farhana: He always says I'll have it [medication], just go and sleep and stuff, I'm like no you have it now and you go to sleep . . . like the parent.

Ben: Sometimes I come in and sleep with her.

Interviewer: OK, does that help mum then sometimes?

Ben: Yeah cos she knows I'm next to her.

Young people talked of their wish to foster their parents' recovery and felt they had an important role to play. Some spoke of how helping their parents made them feel good and how they wanted to make their parent smile, laugh and have a nice time. It was also apparent that their emotions seemed to mirror their parents', such that they felt upset by their parents' distress and concerned about what it might mean, as well as happy when their parents were no longer experiencing difficulties.

Lucy: If you motivate them, be nice to them, go places with them, listen to them and sort of visit them, and just randomly help them, they do get better.

However, they also recognised the limits of what they could do and experienced frustration at their powerlessness to help.

Nalini: I wish I could do more, I'm doing my bit but I wish I could do a little bit more. The thing is I don't know what that is to make things easier.

At times, the sacrifices made as a consequence of placing their parents' needs before their own were experienced as frustrating. They recognised that other young people did not do the things they did, and sometimes the commitment to helping their parents got in the way of what they wanted.

Hayley: It's not always good though, 'cos we have to collect our little brother [from school] . . . It's annoying. . . . When you've got something planned . . . you've gotta cancel it.

Ben: Sometimes when I'm just tired and I'm just tired and sleepy and just wanna go to sleep at night. But when my mum says can you just get me a glass of water I just say OK and I get one.

Thus the desire to care was juxtaposed with some young people feeling frustrated and restricted by their parents' difficulties, demonstrating the complexity of the connection between young people and their parents, and the difficulty balancing their parents' needs with their own needs.

Experience of parenting

Also salient was the young people's experience of feeling cared for and looked after by their parents, demonstrating that caring was reciprocal between them. It appeared that, in spite of mental health difficulties, parents showed resilience by continuing to meet their children's needs. The warmth and affection for their parents was clear when young people talked about what they valued about their relationships. Among their descriptions was the sense that their parents were doing their best to try to maintain a familiar routine. For the young people, parents showing interest in their development and providing boundaries symbolised caring.

Chris: She acts like our Mum and stuff, like we have to ask for stuff, we have to . . . say when she tells us? To come back home like, she isn't just like one of those parents that say 'Oh yeah you can do whatever you want'.

For some young people they noticed this improved over time, valuing the time spent together.

Amrita: Um, it's got better because she spends more time and stuff with me, always cooking with her and activities and stuff.

Some young people appeared to have adapted their expectations, such that normal events were valued and seen as special.

Interviewer: OK, anything else that she does that's special?

Ben: Er, that she makes dinner for me and my dad.

For Almas, the effort her father made was enough to make her happy.

Almas: Erm [pause] he does like hardly talk to me but then he tries to talk to me and I get more happy when he tries to talk to me.

Some young people spoke of how they supported their parents to take a parenting role by seeking help from them. Ashley showed awareness of the importance of continuing to seek help from both parents, to demonstrate that they were viewed equally as parents.

Ashley: Sometimes he helps me at maths, 'cos I'm no good at maths. . . . Yeah because like if you, erm, went to, erm, mum first how would dad feel and, er thingy, we said that sometimes we go to dad and then we go to mum.

Sidz helped her father take a parental lead in a task, by encouraging him to demonstrate his nice handwriting to her.

Sidz: Erm, sometimes you know when, 'cos my handwriting isn't that good and I've seen on CDs that he writes really nice handwriting so I tell him to write first on a paper and then I write after him.

It was apparent that, even though young people felt parented and cared for, some had simultaneous experiences of their parents being unavailable, producing feelings of isolation and loneliness.

Alara: She used to be miserable all the time, and she didn't want no one to come and see her . . . she wanted to stay alone from everyone and she was always sleeping and taking sleeping pills and sleeping, and I got really upset 'cos I felt alone.

Amrita: Uh it's kind of hard for me to talk to her, she doesn't really like say much . . . sometimes I feel a bit angry, that I can't ask something or she doesn't answer me properly.

For younger children who were dependent on parents to accompany them to places, their parents' unavailability had an impact on their social interactions too, further increasing their sense of isolation.

Almas: Well erm [pause] I'm not sure, like people go out, we don't.

Some of the young people seemed to develop an understanding about the fluctuations in the connection and disconnection with parents that allowed them to cope with the periods of unavailability.

Ellie: I just didn't want to see her because she's always acting weird, like, I didn't see her as a Mum to me anymore I just saw her as somebody that's just there. . . . I think I talk to her more, now yeah. . . . Me being around her more and seeing the kind of person that she is. I've just got to see how she is, that's it, I've got to understand her more.

Nalini: Because she's not well that's why she's acting like that. Whereas if she was to be OK then I would be like, hold on you're my Mum you should be there for me.

Hence it appeared that some young people seemed to manage the fluctuation in parental availability by perceiving the good times as fragile and more valuable, which further strengthened the bond with their parents.

Adaptations, strength and resilience

Young people described varying ways they and their family changed in order to manage their parents' mental health needs. Some developed their own creative ways of supporting their parents and managing the emotional impact of parental mental health needs. Young people also talked about their relationships being a source of support. They identified personal qualities which they felt helped them to cope, qualities which seemed important for their sense of self-worth. They described resilience to difficult experiences, but also wondered how their experiences had affected them.

Using resources and adaptive coping

Consistent support from family, friends and services was valued by the young people, as it allowed them to feel accepted and not alone. It also provided some relief from feeling responsible for their parents.

Young people and their families developed strategies to manage parental mental health difficulties, including providing direct assistance with medication and financial support.

Almas: So my dad felt really bad and then erm, my erm, my grandma wanted my dad so he's gonna go to Turkey but my uncle gave him the money. But my sister's going with him because to help him with his medicines. Yeah so that's why my uncle paid for him, for my dad to go to Turkey.

Developing ways of promoting parents' independence while ensuring their safety was illustrated by Almas and her sister.

Almas: Well yeah my sister does, erm like, sometimes when he goes to buy cigarettes by himself but sometimes he loses his way so he just sits down somewhere or he goes to a shop where he waits there and my sister will know where he is and so my sister will go and pick him up.

To cope with the emotional impact of parental mental health needs, some young people used taught strategies to manage difficult emotions.

Messi: If sometimes you get angry you just get a paper, scribble on it with red until you're finished and rip it off, scrunch it into a big ball, rip into pieces and then throw them at the wall as hard as you can.

Others developed their own strategies. These adaptive strategies revealed the resilience of these young people.

Chris: Like you're feeling like you're forgiving yourself for blaming yourself . . . it's releasing all the grief. So you don't feel that way anymore . . . because you've realised that you can lift up the sadness so you can get on with stuff. That's like the easiest way to do . . . it's not really a technique.

Distraction was used by many to cope with difficult feelings in relation to parental mental health difficulties, the need to escape apparent in their words.

Emir: Sometimes, sometimes I try and take it out my head and do something else.

Ben: Er I just er, forget about it and sometimes play with my toys and watch TV.

Other activities young people engaged in to distract themselves were playing, listening to music and sleeping. The benefits of distraction seemed linked to their wish to contain difficult thoughts and avoid getting into a negative cycle of escalating difficult feelings.

Talking about parental mental health difficulties was an area that young people had mixed feelings about.

Ashley: Talk about, erm, their problems. And then if they want, erm if they want, erm, like a meeting around here and then and then with nobody else so it could stay private.

Some, like Hayley, directly expressed their reluctance to talk with friends and parents.

Hayley: Sometimes you don't always wanna talk. Like I know people say you should like let it out, but sometimes that's not always what you wanna do.

Finding it hard to talk seemed related to concern for how others might react and a wish to avoid thinking about what was difficult or uncertain.

The benefits of talking within the family about parental difficulties were also evident. Katie's experience of talking with her mum about anxiety shows that talking openly could be helpful.

Katie: I kind of felt like 'Right well I should just go for it. If she doesn't want to speak about it then, that's it, she's your Mum, she's one person, you know, you really shouldn't feel embarrassed to talk to' so I, you know, I just went for it. And she did answer me. And then after that I kind of felt comfortable about it.

Help with relating to their parents was valued by the young people. They appeared to view their family relationships as an important resource that required nurturing.

Sidz: To get them into activities maybe so then it'll keep them, to maybe more, speak more to their dad and feel more confident to speak out to their dad. That's how I feel sometimes I actually don't want to talk to my dad about school I just talk to my mum 'cos she's mostly around me, so yeah.

Young people found it helpful to know that they were not alone in their experiences. Lucy talked of how she valued being with others whose parents also had difficulties.

Lucy: The fact that you do have people there who've got similar difficulties to how I am, and you haven't got to really worry about it.

Young people found participating in activities away from home, and having the opportunity to have fun and talk, helped them to cope.

Interviewer: What's good about playing then?

Ben: Er, that you have fun.

Ben: That you, that you play and you don't and you're not being like stuck inside and you play outside and it's good.

Nalini was aware how different her life was at school compared with life at home.

Nalini: They try to make me happy, cheer me up, you know, things like that. But then it's like I'm living a double role basically. At school I'm so happy with my friends but when I come home it's like oh my God, serious Nalini.

Ellie described how with everything going on at home school felt like a place to rest.

Ellie: Well most times in school I just stare into space, 'cos like in school I feel I want some rest now, it's too much.

Friends influenced the resources young people could draw upon. Some experienced friends as understanding.

Farhana: I talk to people who have difficulties at home as well.

Others were unsure how much they understood what the young person was going through or how much they could help.

Nalini: Even though I've got really close friends that I talk to most of the time it seems that they don't understand what I'm going through.

Some young people identified when external resources did not go far enough; this seemed linked to a lack of continuity.

Hayley: She's had a few counsellors and stuff, and they haven't really helped because she's getting one after another, and right now she doesn't have one. So I don't think they're helping.

Young people's views of what would help them were likely to be influenced by the impact they felt their parents' mental health needs had on their own life. Therefore, whether the impact was felt to be predominantly relational or individual appeared important to the type of help they would have chosen to engage in.

Experiencing oneself as having positive qualities and skills

Young people described themselves as having a range of different qualities: 'patience', being 'calm', 'understanding', 'easy to get along with', 'supportive', and having 'maturity'. They recognised their need for strength and hope to cope with what they were experiencing.

Nalini: You've just got to have faith, hope for the best and never give up.

A sense of independence was also mentioned by young people.

Ellie: Like if I didn't have a Mum I'd still cope . . . I do my work on my own, and I know how to cook some stuff, and clean and stuff. Just the stuff that it takes to really live.

A positive view of self-sufficiency was particularly compelling in the experiences of those accessing Young Carers. Viewing their independence and ability to look after themselves as advantageous, the young people normalised taking responsibility for themselves.

Hayley: Well you don't actually realise that you've learnt it, it's just like the only time that you realise is when you hear someone saying like, 'I don't know how to wash my own clothes', or . . . I've got some friends that their Mum cleans their room, does their clothes, makes them breakfast and whatever. . . . When they live out they're not gonna have those skills for themselves.

Coping was not straightforward and some young people felt they did not cope. Change was not always easy and this may have influenced usual ways of coping, including emotional expression.

Joel: What do you mean by how did I cope? I don't know.

Ellie: I cried a lot and nothing changed so I just had to wait.

Young people talked about feeling that they had become hardened in coping with difficult experiences.

Lucy: You can grow sort of like thicker skin to how you act around people sort of things, and you don't really take it if they say anything nasty about you.

Ellie: Like, maybe if someone was to die right now I wouldn't care, I like have no heart, no feelings, of being sad anymore. Like I wasn't emotional like how my brothers were and wanted me to be.

Young people had no option but to adapt to their parents' mental health needs, and this affected many areas of their lives. They gained strength and positive qualities through this process but it was a difficult road for which help from services was not always available. As a result their resilience was often developed from the resources they utilised around them.

Conclusion: implications for practice

Increasing young people's visibility was a key aim of this chapter as their experiences are invaluable when shaping services. They have provided much to think about in terms of how services support families experiencing parental mental health needs. Based on their voices, here are our ideas about what services need to consider.

The nature of help-giving

The findings suggest that developing a trusting relationship with young people is necessary before they feel able to talk about their parents' difficulties. Young people valued non-pathologising and safe relationships to talk through their feelings about their parents' difficulties. For some, talking about their difficulties may not be the best way to engage them, as avoiding thinking about negative experiences associated with a parent's mental health needs may be a way of coping. Given the complex nature of relationships between parents with mental health difficulties and their children as well as the concerns and fears identified both for young people and parents, it may be helpful to start from a positive stance whenever possible. Talking about positive things within or outside their home life may feel more helpful and easier. One might use the frame of reciprocity as a starting point for a conversation about parental mental health needs. This may facilitate them to talk about things that they struggle with as well as their strengths in coping with adversity. This could then direct work towards strengthening their existing skills and resources while also working to address the difficulties they identify.

It is important to acknowledge that young people often take on additional caring responsibilities, and it is essential that these are identified and understood from the young person's perspective. Often caring can foster a sense of pride and achievement. The implication, therefore, is not that all caring responsibilities are harmful even for young children; however, it is important that caring is balanced with positive activities that are free of responsibilities.

The young people's experiences show that a lack of awareness of parental mental health or confusion about these difficulties can induce complex feelings in some young people. Given the suggestion that understanding of parental mental health can enhance resilience (Oppenheim, 2006), the findings support the need for these young people to be offered help to make sense of their parents' difficulties. Parents can play a crucial role in children's sense making, and professionals should ensure that they are part of this process whenever possible, and actively seek to help parents support their children in this complex task. The young people's experiences highlight the importance of families being encouraged to develop their own shared understanding of the parents' mental health difficulties. This might focus on external factors and life events, and suggests that professional explanations (e.g. using diagnostic criteria) may not always be necessary or helpful. Encouraging families to have ongoing conversations about the implications of mental health needs for their lives may foster young people's communication about their parents' difficulties and help them overcome any uncertainty.

Experiencing positive relationships was helpful to young people and they were aware when there was a lack of this experience for both them and their parent. This emphasises the importance of having a focus on the relationships of families with parental mental health needs within therapeutic work that combines family interventions alongside individual interventions. Collaboration between adult and child services would help ensure that parental mental health is considered as a family issue.

The context of help-giving

Encouraging consistent sources of support for young people through family, friends and the community is advantageous. Voluntary services can also play a vital role in meeting the needs of these young people with the potential to offer consistent long-term support to families. Young people were interested in meeting others in similar situations, highlighting the importance of services such as Young Carers and Kidstime workshops (Cooklin, 2006).

The need for more education and public awareness about mental health needs seems fundamental. The young people's experiences highlight the importance of learning about mental health needs in order to develop their understanding as well as reduce the stigmatising attitudes young people experience and hold about mental health. Schools, religious institutions, libraries, the media and other forums used by children, should make mental health a bigger priority for young people, and mental health services play a vital role in providing knowledge and information for this.

Acknowledgements

We would like to thank all the individuals who helped recruit young people for the studies. Without their help this chapter would not have been possible. We would also like to express our gratitude to all the young people who participated and generously shared their experiences, in addition to their parents, who gave permission for them to be interviewed.

References

Aldridge, J. & Becker, S. (2003). *Children Caring for Parents with Mental Illness: Perspectives of Young Carers, Parents and Professionals.* Bristol: The Policy Press.

Armstrong, C. (2002). Behind closed doors – living with a parent's mental illness. *Young Minds Magazine, 61,* 28–30.

Bowlby, J. (1973). *Attachment and Loss, Vol. 2. Separation, Anger and Anxiety.* London: Hogarth Press.

Bromley, C. (2008). An Interpretive Phenomenological Analysis of Young People's Experiences of Living with a Parent with Mental Health Problems. Unpublished DClinPsy. Thesis. University of Hertfordshire.

Cooklin, A. (2006). Children of parents with mental illness. In L. Combrinck-Graham (ed.) *Children in Family Contexts: Perspectives on Treatment* (2nd edn) (pp. 265–291). New York: Guilford Press.

Fonagy, P.E., Leigh, T., Steele, M., Steele, H., Kennedy, R., Mattoon, G. *et al.* (1996). The relation of attachment status, psychiatric classification and response to psychotherapy. *Journal of Consulting and Clinical Psychology, 64,* 22–31.

Fudge, E. & Mason, P. (2004). Consulting with young people about service guidelines relating to parental mental illness. *Australian e-Journal for the Advancement of Mental Health, 3,* 1–9.

Garley, D., Gallop, R., Johnston, N. & Pipitone, J. (1997). Children of the mentally ill: A qualitative focus group approach. *Journal of Psychiatric and Mental Health Nursing, 4,* 97–103.

Gladstone, B.M., Boydell, K.M. & McKeever, P. (2006). Recasting research into children's experiences of parental mental illness: Beyond risk and resilience. *Social Science and Medicine, 62,* 2540–2550.

Hadleigh, L. (2011). Living with a Parent with Mental Health Needs: What Children Say. Unpublished DClinPsy. Thesis. University of East London.

Handley, C., Farrell, G.A., Josephs, A., Hanke, A. & Hazelton, M. (2001). The Tasmanian children's project: The needs of children with a parent/carer with a mental illness. *Australian and New Zealand Journal of Mental Health Nursing, 10,* 221–228.

Leverton, T.J. (2003). Parental psychiatric illness: The implications for children. *Current Opinion in Psychiatry, 16*(4), 395–402.

Madsen, W.C. (2007). *Collaborative Therapy with Multi-Stressed Families: From Old Problems to New Futures* (2nd edn). New York: Guilford Publications.

Maybery, D., Ling, L., Szakacs, E. & Reupert, A. (2005). Children of a parent with a mental illness: Perspectives on need. *Australian e-Journal for the Advancement of Mental Health, 4*(2), 1–11.

Meadus, R.J. & Johnson, B. (2000). The experience of being an adolescent child of a parent who has a mood disorder. *Journal of Psychiatric and Mental Health Nursing, 7,* 383–390.

Mordoch, E. & Hall, W.A. (2002). Children living with a parent who has a mental illness: A critical analysis of the literature and research implications. *Archives of Psychiatric Nursing, 16*(5), 208–216.

Oppenheim, D. (2006). Child, parent, and parent–child emotion narratives: Implications for developmental psychopathology. *Development and Psychopathology, 18,* 771–790.

Polkki, P., Ervast, S.-A. & Huupponen, M. (2004). Coping and resilience of children of a mentally ill parent. *Social Work in Health Care, 39,* 152–163.

Riebschleger, J. (2004). Good days and bad days: The experiences of children of a parent with a psychiatric disability. *Psychiatric Rehabilitation Journal, 28*(1), 25–31.

Roe, A. (2010). Young People's Experiences of Living with a Parent with Psychosis. Unpublished DClinPsy. Thesis. Canterbury Christ Church University.

Seligman, M.E.P. (2005). Positive psychology, positive prevention and positive therapy. In C.R. Snyder & S.J. Lopez (eds) *Handbook of Positive Psychology* (pp. 3–9). New York: Oxford University Press.

Smith, J.A. & Osborn, M. (2008). Interpretative phenomenological analysis. In J.A. Smith (ed.) *Qualitative Psychology: A Practical Guide to Research Methods* (2nd edn) (pp. 53–80). London: Sage.

Smith, J.A., Flowers, P. & Larkin, M. (2009). *Interpretative Phenomenological Analysis Theory, Method and Research.* London: Sage.

Stallard, P., Norman, P., Huline-Dickens, S., Salter, E. & Cribb, J. (2004). The effects of parental mental illness upon children: A descriptive study of the views of parents and children. *Clinical Child Psychology and Psychiatry, 9*(1), 39–52.

Webster, J. (1992). Split in two: Experiences of the children of schizophrenic mothers. *British Journal of Social Work, 22,* 309–329.

3 Becoming visible

The impact of parental mental health difficulties on children

Lizette Nolte

In this chapter I will be discussing the impact that mental health difficulties in a parent might have on a child. In recent years literature on the potential effects of parental mental health difficulties on children has proliferated as our awareness of this group of children has increased. Thus, these children and their lived experiences within the context of parental mental distress are gradually becoming more 'visible' rather than 'hidden', as described by Lancaster (1999). However, there remains a lack of awareness, knowledge and skill in understanding and responding to the needs of this group of children.

Approaching this topic from a primarily systemic and narrative perspective, I am immediately confronted with the issue of language and context. It presents the dilemma of how we talk about human distress, and brings an immediate awareness of the power of the medical discourse to conceptualise distress and emotional struggle. Constructs like mental illness or mental health problems immediately invite ideas of illness and treatment, and an internal focus. In this chapter I have moved away from using the word 'illness' to describe the mental distress, discomfort and disturbance that human beings experience at times in response to life stresses and trauma. However, I am aware that this does not fully address the tension there often exists between how distress is conceptualised within a medical context and how families talk together and prefer to talk to practitioners about their struggles.

As we start this exploration together it is important to note that I will not here be talking about a linear causality. One cannot say that any particular mental health problem in a parent will lead to any specific outcome in a child (Duncan & Reder, 2000). Rather, mental health problems in a parent exist within the context of the life of the parent, the family, community and society. It is therefore not any particular diagnosis of a parent that 'causes' harm to children, but rather the particular psycho-social context (Rutter & Quinton, 1984) of the parent and child that will determine the impact the difficulties of the parent will have on the child. Furthermore, the fact that a parent experiences mental health difficulties does not automatically imply a negative impact on the parent–child relationship, nor does it suggest inevitable problems in a parent's ability to parent their child (Falcov, 1998). On their own, mental health problems in a parent present little risk of significant harm to children (Cleaver *et al.*, 1999). Many factors mediate the impact any difficult family event will have on a child. Therefore, we will be exploring what might have a potentially negative impact on a child, but also looking at what is protective of children.

Finally, we should not imply that the parent–child influence is unidirectional (Lippett & Nolte, 2007). Becoming a parent and the challenges and rewards of parenting have a significant impact on a parent and on their well-being, and both the potentially positive and negative implications of these factors need to be considered as part of our thinking.

I will now go on to discuss the potential impact of mental health difficulties on parenting.

The impact of mental health difficulties on being a parent and on parenting

> If we value our children, we must cherish their parents.
>
> (John Bowlby, quoted in Bowlby, 2007)

Becoming a parent is often a deeply meaningful experience and most parents want the best for their children. However, for parents who suffer from mental health problems parenting can be a more complex experience (Kelly, 1999). For some, family life and the responsibilities and challenges of parenthood may even be experienced as having a negative effect on their well-being and recovery (Lippett & Nolte, 2007). We know that many parents with mental health difficulties are able to parent their children well (Falcov, 1998). However, mental health problems pose a number of specific challenges for parents and can potentially impact upon parenting.

Good parenting requires that parents provide a safe physical and secure emotional environment for their children. Parents need to be able to understand the needs of their children and respond to these needs in a self-reflective way. There is also a need for parents to provide their children with guidance and modelling for how to be in the world and for what is required of one within the community, culture and society in which one lives (Gopfert *et al.*, 2004). For parents with mental health problems these areas may be challenging due to managing the specific manifestations and consequences of their emotional distress in addition to the normal challenges and stresses of parenting (Nicholson *et al.*, 1998). Furthermore, not only are people dealing with the effects of their mental health problems, but often also the effect of psychotropic medication.

In addition to this potential day-to-day struggle with the tasks of parenting, becoming a parent within the context of mental health problems often brings to mind for a person their own experiences of being parented and their relationship to parenting. It may be that they experience ambivalence about being a parent, lack a role model for parenting or link the arrival or presence of the child with the difficulties they are experiencing. This could get in the way of a strong and positive relationship between the parent and the child (Cleaver *et al.*, 1999).

Some particular concerns also often play on the minds of parents with mental health problems. They often live with a fear that their children will be removed from their care (Lippett & Nolte, 2007), and this has potentially significant implications for them and for their parenting. Furthermore, they frequently have a concern about the mental health of their children (Nicholson *et al.*, 1998) and they may want to deny that there are any effects on their children, or alternatively scrutinise their children for signs of mental health difficulties.

Finally, many of the contextual stressors that often accompany mental health problems can potentially make parenting a more complicated and challenging task (Goodman *et al.*, 1995). The relevance of the wider social, economic and political context to parenting and mental well-being is well established, and poverty, lack of education or employment, unsuitable housing, social isolation and other stressful life events have been shown to put much additional pressure on parents (Gopfert *et al.*, 2004). Parents with mental health problems are also frequently acutely aware of and have to deal with the stigma attached to mental health difficulties in society, in the media and in their communities. Potential social marginalisation and isolation means that the support we all need and use as parents may not be available to someone with mental health problems.

In summary

It is therefore clear that mental health difficulties may take parents away from many of their preferred and desired ways for relating, distancing them from their hopes and dreams for themselves and their lives and relationships, their parenting and the lives of their children.

I will now go on to more directly explore the specific impact mental health problems in a parent may have on a child. In this section I will be using examples from my own practice working with families where a parent is experiencing mental health difficulties. I have changed all names and identifying information in these examples so as to protect confidentiality. These examples come from my work within a specialist Parental Mental Health Team, situated within CAMHS, which received referrals from adult mental health services.

The impact of parental mental health difficulties on children

Many factors mediate the impact of parental mental health problems on children. These include the nature, severity, pervasiveness and duration of the mental distress. Also important is the age and developmental stage of the child and the support and sensitivity of other adults, both within the family and community and among the professional network, to the child's dilemmas. All these factors will contribute to the impact the parent's difficulties will have on the child.

Specific areas of impact will now be considered.

Attachment

Attachment theory (Bowlby, 1969) helps us understand how early experiences are held as narratives or 'internal working models' that shape our experiences, actions and sense of self as we go through our lives (Vetere & Dallos, 2007). Early attachment relationships are characterised by attachment behaviours by the infant (e.g. moving closer to the care giver) when there is a perceived threat or stressor (e.g. presence of a stranger, unfamiliar circumstances, etc.) and exploration from the 'secure base' of the care giver when the level of perceived threat is low. Therefore, a crucial developmental need through childhood and into adulthood is the requirement in children for their parent to provide a safe, secure and reliable 'base' from which they can explore and to which they can return. As the child develops, the parent needs to gradually support a sense of autonomy and self-confidence while maintaining connection (Bowlby, 2007; Hill, 2004).

Accessibility and responsiveness are thought to be building blocks of relationship security. Parents with mental health problems may struggle to tolerate closeness with their children and psychotropic medication may also reduce responsiveness. The ability to tolerate frustration could be undermined when parental distress is severe, or parents may be preoccupied and therefore struggle to focus on their children (Hall, 2004). Parents with mental health difficulties may also be unable to respond with warmth to their child, or they may be particularly critical or rejecting of a child.

It is therefore clear that secure attachment relationships between a parent and child can be disrupted when parents are not able to be consistently and positively available to a child, where the parents are not able to focus on and respond to the needs of the child and where a parent might struggle with closeness to and distance from the child. Different children are affected differently by difficulties in their attachment relationships, with some children reacting with intense emotion to situations while others will try to keep the emotional intensity in relationships to a minimum.

> One 3-year-old girl who came to the attention of our service was observed to withdraw into a corner to soothe herself whenever she felt upset or scared and only engage with the adults around her again once she felt better. She was also observed to stand some way away from her mother making small meowing sounds when she needed something from her, instead of the very clear and insistent way most toddlers have to gain the attention of a parent.

Insecure attachment relationships not only affect the relationship between the parent and child, but can have an impact on the child's experience in the world and their ability to form, maintain and negotiate interpersonal relationships.

A child's meaning making in relation to the parent's difficulties significantly influences the impact these difficulties might have on the attachment relationship between the parent and child. A child may perceive a parent's difficulties as something separate from the parent (e.g. as an 'illness') and therefore not really part of the relationship. In such circumstances a crisis of parental distress could be seen as not changing the overarching experience the child has of the parent. However, if the parent's behaviour is experienced as part of the identity of the parent, it could pose a significant challenge to the continuity of a child's experience of the parent and their relationship (Hill, 2004).

The importance of meaning making in relation to parental distress will now be explored in more detail.

Meaning making and coherent narratives

There is much evidence that the capacity to give a clear and coherent account of one's experiences and relational life is a significant factor in resilience; that is, one is protected by the ability to tell a credible and consistent story about one's experiences, while also having some tolerance for uncertainty and contradiction (see e.g. Cooklin, 2004; Focht & Beardslee, 1996; Fredman & Fuggle, 2000).

Parental distress and disturbance can expose children to many potentially traumatic, fear-inducing and confusing experiences. We know from research that when we experience such potentially traumatic events, often our meaning making around these events becomes confused and our stories of these experiences become incoherent and fragmented (Byng-Hall, 2002).

The ability to develop more detailed, coherent and reflective narratives, which will be protective for children, is linked to a number of factors. Where family circumstances and relationships are emotionally safe and open, it will positively impact upon coherent meaning making. However, families differ in how clearly, openly and reflexively they are able to talk about their painful experiences and, for families where there are parental mental health problems, there are a number of obstacles in the way. The awareness of stigma can greatly inhibit open dialogue. In addition, parents and other adults may hope to protect the child by not talking to them about what is going on. They may worry that talking may upset, frighten or confuse children or that it will make children feel different or embarrassed about their parent. In particular, parents often worry that information about parental distress may damage their children. They may argue that children do not need information and that they probably do not notice what is going on. They also worry that such a conversation may be too difficult and that they would not know what to say.

However, not talking to children about their parents' mental health problems is likely to cause a child to feel upset, afraid and confused.

> Tyrone (6) and Raymond (7), two brothers whose mother had become unwell the week before and had been sectioned and removed from the home in the middle of the night by a police car to be taken to hospital, explained that they thought their mum was in prison, because the police had come to take her away, but that they did not know what she had done wrong. They felt ashamed as the neighbour had come out and seen the police car. They were worried because they thought the prison must be a very scary place and they were sad because they did not know when they might see their mother again.

In the absence of an explanation, children will come to their own conclusions about the meaning of the parent's behaviour and this could be damaging to the relationship between parent and child and may leave the child particularly fearful of the future.

> Wayne (12) was living with a foster parent and knew that his mum could not look after him because she was ill. However, when she repeatedly did not turn up for contact visits with him, he thought that she did not care about him, because as he told me, when you are ill you can still remember things or pick up the telephone and let someone know you are not able to make an appointment.

Furthermore, not having a context for the parent's actions may be more likely to make the child feel embarrassed or ashamed of a parent and may make them feel that what is happening must be kept a secret, thus contributing further to the stigma surrounding mental health issues.

Despite the clear need to give children accurate and age-appropriate information, the dilemma of how to help children make sense of what is going on can be highly confusing and distressing for parents (Focht & Beardslee, 1996). Parents need to make decisions about whether to talk to their children or not. If they do decide to talk to them, they need to decide at what age, what information to share and how to deal with any awkward questions or negative reactions from their children. Many parents wish for guidance in this regard.

Safety and health

Children need love and security to thrive. However, at times children's physical and emotional safety and well-being can be compromised by the impact of a parent's mental health difficulties.

Physical neglect can pose a danger for children living with a parent who has mental health problems. This could be due to many of the issues that can accompany mental health difficulties, including distorted experiences of reality, difficulties with concentration and focus, ambivalence about parenting, lack of support, etc. This could mean that children are not provided with meals, are not clean, do not have a clean uniform in the mornings for school, do not have their regular immunisations, etc.

> I worked with a family where both parents experienced mental health difficulties. They had a daughter, Dilek, who was 5 years old. Her mother told me how Dilek had once taken a raw frozen breaded chicken fillet from the freezer, put it in the toaster and toasted it and then tried to eat it. Clearly she was hungry and her parents were not able to provide her with a nourishing meal. Dilek was also teased at school for 'smelling bad' as she was left to her own devices when having a bath and brushing her teeth.

Emotional difficulties experienced by a parent might also impact upon a child, for example, where a parent has difficulty with showing love and warmth towards a child, with tolerating activity or noise from the child, or holds unrealistic expectations of the child. In such circumstances the child's emotional and physical health might be threatened.

> I met with Britney, and her 4-year-old daughter Melody, where Britney was struggling to tolerate the normal activity levels of a young child. In response to this she withdrew into her bedroom, watching television for up to eight hours at a time, not allowing Melody into the bedroom and scolding Melody for attempts to get her attention, threatening that she would 'give her away' if she did not stop. Melody was not emotionally or physically safe in this situation.

Emotional unavailability of a parent can also lead to children being out of control, too self-reliant and pseudo-mature or exposed to danger.

If a parent struggles with discipline and with setting appropriate limits for a child (e.g. due to lack of awareness, lack of energy and focus or lack of confidence), the child may not be safe.

> Tara, aged 7, went missing one night and was finally found at 9 p.m. with a group of young people much older than her – Tara's mother had been dozing on the sofa and had not seen her leaving the house earlier in the day. When Tara was returned to her home her mother said that she was out of control and that she did not listen to her. It was clear that Tara's mother did not feel able to set boundaries for her.

Sometimes within the context of parental mental health problems, parents may not be able to set limits within or outside of the home and this may also compromise a child's safety. Children may end up living in chaotic and unpredictable environments and may witness and be frightened by bizarre or threatening behaviour of a parent.

> Jenny, a mother of twin boys, became very upset when she told me about how, some years before in response to voices she was hearing, she had made the boys stand outside in the bitter cold, guarding the house, which she felt was being threatened at the time. She worried about whether they still remembered this event and whether they had been frightened by it.

In the most severe and fortunately very rare cases, parents may harm their child (e.g. physically or sexually abuse them) as part of their experience of or responses to mental health concerns. In the most extreme circumstances we know that children have died at the hands of a parent who was experiencing mental health problems. A specific context for this is where a parent is having psychotic experiences and a child is included in the distorted beliefs of their parent.

An example might be where a parent believes that their child is possessed by an evil spirit and, in an attempt to be rid of the spirit, the parent kills the child.

However, it is important to remember that of the children who die from abuse or neglect each year, the large majority of these do not have a parent with mental health problems (Hall, 2004). A further context where there should be concern about the safety of a child is where the parent is suicidal and there is the possibility that the parent may also be having homicidal thoughts.

For professionals working with families where a parent experiences mental health issues the safety of the children should be a highest priority.

Development (physical, cognitive, emotional)

Many factors relating to parental experience of mental distress can impact upon the emotional, intellectual and physical development of children. Due to a parent who may be emotionally unavailable, a lack of stimulation and interaction with a parent, a chaotic and unsupportive environment or a lack of socialising, children may fall behind in their development (Hall, 2004). This is of course crucial in the earlier years of life, and in my work with parents I often met young children under the age of 3, who had severe delays in talking, walking, toilet training, eating patterns, interacting and imaginative play. This of course has significant implications for children's lives and learning.

Older children are also affected in their development. They need to master skills as they enter the world of formal education and develop self-confidence. If the parent is unable to facilitate this, they may struggle with school attendance and performance, and with understanding appropriate behaviour in different situations (Cleaver *et al.*, 1999).

> For example, in a family where there was a severely depressed mother, she was concerned about the fact that she was not able to focus on helping her two sons, aged 6 and 8, with their homework. Their teachers were also becoming concerned that they were falling behind and not achieving their full potential.

Children may also express their concerns, fears and distress about the situation at home by developing difficulties in school (e.g. struggling to concentrate, being fearful, lacking in confidence, finding it difficult to form relationships or exhibiting behavioural problems).

> Patrick (aged 10) who came from a home where his mother was very unwell and exhibiting bizarre and frightening behaviour got into trouble at school for expressing frustration by breaking things in class. He was taken into care when his mother was hospitalised, but it took a long time for him to find his feet again in school and he worried that the reputation he had of being 'trouble' would follow him through the rest of his time in school.

When during their teenage years children gradually become more independent and spend more time away from home, young people who have a parent with mental health difficulties often find that they are expected to be at home to help with caring for their parent or as emotional support for the parent, or they find that they are too concerned about their parent to fully enjoy activities away from home. Thus their developing sense of independence is interrupted. These are also the years when young people gain a sense of their own identity. This may be difficult when a young person does not feel that they have had a good parental role model.

> Riana (15) was angry with her mother who suffered with depression because she did not want to come from a 'crazy family' – she wanted to be 'normal' and fit in. She struggled in school to make friends and started to cut her arms to express her distress.

In addition, during this time difficulties at school may continue as described above, influencing the opportunities and life chances the young person may have.

Mental health and well-being

It is known that children who have a parent with mental health problems have an increased risk of experiencing mental health difficulties themselves. In their seminal paper, Rutter and Quinton (1984) found that one-third of children will not go on to develop any difficulties, one-third will develop transient problems and one-third will have persistent difficulties. The mental health and well-being of a child of a parent with mental health difficulties might be affected by the specific symptoms or characteristics of the parent's difficulties (e.g. bizarre beliefs or self-harm); by the psychological or social effects of the difficulties (e.g. lack of energy and ability to carry out responsibilities); by associated changes to relationships and family life (e.g. separations due to periods in hospital; changes in roles; relationship difficulties); or by associated lifestyle and socio-economic factors (e.g. financial difficulties, housing problems).

Children are most directly affected when they witness a parent's bizarre or unusual behaviour or hear about their strange beliefs, or when they are included in the parent's concerns and expected to contribute to the parent's management of these concerns.

> Susan had a diagnosis of OCD and feared contracting HIV or other illnesses. She had a ritual of checking the children's clothing, expecting them to strip down just inside the front door, perform a cleaning ritual and then put on clean clothes that she had prepared for them. This happened every time they returned to the house, even if they had only been out in the garden.

Strange behaviours or beliefs of the parent could lead to the child being embroiled in the behaviour of the parent or taking on the parent's beliefs.

Children of parents with mental health problems often experience guilt and feelings of responsibility for the difficulties the parent is experiencing. The conflict between the love for their parent and their anger and resentment with their parent can be overwhelming. Their vigilance and underlying insecurity when a parent is vulnerable, out of control or suicidal can leave them perpetually fearful (Landau *et al.*, 1972). Children may be afraid that their own feelings or experiences are early signs of mental health issues. However, it has also been found that in contrast some children within this group have been seen as highly competent and even 'invulnerable'. What is clear is the 'hard emotional work' (Shah & Goodbody, 2011) that these children often need to do in order to manage the challenges throughout their lives presented to them by their parent's difficulties.

Socialising/relationships

Relationships and socialisation can often be affected when a parent has mental health issues. Many aspects of parental distress may contribute to this (e.g. parents' actions may be inconsistent or disorganised, or parents may struggle with interpersonal boundaries and have difficulties with intimacy, etc.). Due to these factors, children of parents with mental health problems may struggle with communication, have difficulty in relating to peers or have few friends. When a parent is uninvolved with their child, preoccupied or unable to provide structure and containment, children may be undisciplined and show aggressive behaviour (Landau *et al.*, 1972). They may be bullied or bully other children. As children grow older there may be conflicts over discipline, control and autonomy; and the normal conflict between parent and child may be either exacerbated or absent (Lancaster, 1999).

> Suzie (15) and her mother, Anna, described how they would often argue about 'normal' things like what time Suzie needed to be at home or how much television she could watch, but Anna sometimes felt afraid by how angry Suzie would get and on one occasion Suzie had slapped her mother and pushed her against the wall.

Children naturally often feel an intense sense of loyalty towards their parents. This might lead to them feeling very protective towards a parent with mental health problems and taking responsibility for their parent's well-being.

> Antoni, aged 5, told me that he had to always check on his mother as she sleeps on the sofa because he had to make sure that she was still breathing – he would hold his hand under her nose to feel the warm air, but sometimes he could not feel it and would panic and wake her up. Then he would be told off.

Children may also worry about showing happiness or enjoying themselves when their parent is going through a difficult time. They may feel that they need to cheer up their parent or make them laugh, or rouse them, for example, into anger.

Children and young people may also experience a sense of shame owing to the behaviour of their parent. They may feel embarrassed at times due to the stigma associated with mental health problems.

> Taleisha (14) described how she and her mother would be on the bus on their way somewhere. Suddenly her mother would shout at someone and accuse them of staring at her and this would lead to an argument. Taleisha feared such situations as it made her feel embarrassed, and she worried that friends from school might see her and her mother in such a situation.

Children may also worry about their parent's interaction with their school – they may wonder whether their parent will act appropriately when collecting them from school or when talking with teachers, or be seen as 'strange' by other parents. They may also feel unable to invite friends over to their home and therefore become more socially isolated.

> I was touched by a conversation with a family where the father, Mr Polat, was unwell and unable to work. Mrs Polat, mother of Elif (12) and Nur (14), became tearful when she was telling me that it was Elif's birthday the next week, but that they could not afford a cake or present and could not invite friends over, because they did not have a nice flat with appropriate furniture, and she was not sure how Mr Polat would act around strangers.

Children of parents with mental health problems often live in fear of the family breaking down or that they might go into care. They also often have to cope with periods of separation and disruption when a parent needs to be in hospital.

At times, children can take on parental roles to fill the vacuum of care in the family – this might be extremely useful and indispensable for the family (Byng-Hall, 2002). However, parent–child relationships can also become reversed at times when the child or young person takes responsibility for either the emotional or physical care of the parent. This can involve ensuring that the parent takes their medication, watching them to prevent self-harm, taking care of household tasks, looking after siblings, making their own decisions, etc. It can also involve providing emotional support to the parent during difficult times.

> Denelle, a 12-year-old girl, described to me how she would be woken in the middle of the night by her mother in a state of distress. Her mother needed her to sit with her, rub her back and talk with her for hours until she felt calm again and could drift off to sleep. This left Denelle drained and exhausted the next day, unable to concentrate in school and worried about whether her mother was OK at home alone.

Despite outward appearances of high competence, the child with parental responsibilities can sometimes feel inadequate, guilty or self-blaming. They may feel sad or low in mood at times and may experience unrelenting worry. This again speaks to the hard emotional work they have to do.

What protects children?

Given the above, we can see that children living with a parent with mental health problems may be seen as vulnerable to the effects on them and their lives on many different levels. However, we know that not everyone is affected in the same way when faced with these adverse experiences. We will now go on to explore the factors that are protective of children.

Resilience may be seen as the process of or capacity for adapting successfully despite challenging or threatening circumstances. It cannot be seen as a special individual trait, but rather it is something that can be fostered in children, for example, through the development of skills, the fostering of confidence, the building of supportive relationships, and the promotion of positive experiences and achievement. Practically this could include developing a good hospital plan with a family that includes alternative care arrangements and ensuring regular visits during periods of hospitalisation, minimising disruption and maintaining daily routines (e.g. by involving reliable other adults), and developing or enhancing particular skills for coping.

Parents can play an important part in fostering resilience. Parents who are able to identify the areas and times when their parenting skills are most vulnerable can enable the psychological interventions and practical support in the home around these times, and this will strengthen positive coping strategies and foster competence and resilience in the parent, thus protecting children.

Talking to children about their parents' mental health difficulties

It has already been mentioned that helping children to develop a clear understanding of their parents' difficulties is protective for them. Professionals can play an important role in this (e.g. by providing the child with opportunities for conversations about parental mental distress and for asking questions).

Professionals can work alongside parents to develop this awareness. Helping the child see the mental health problem as separate from the parent and from the parent–child relationship is highly significant in protecting children (White & Epston, 1990), as is the child having a sense of being loved by the parent even when things are difficult.

Factors that should be considered when providing families with guidance in relation to talking to their children about parental mental health problems include that information should be age appropriate and focus on what is observable for the child (i.e. be 'experience near' (White & Epston, 1990)) and considering when best to talk to children (e.g. when things are not at crisis point and they are calm enough to take in the information (Duncan & Reder, 2000)). It is helpful to start by asking children what they already know and what they have noticed. Often practical information might be the most useful (what has happened, where is the parent, when can they see them, what will happen next, who are the professional people around, etc.). Furthermore, children need to be told that the parent's difficulties are not their fault, that it is not their responsibility to make it better, and their questions about 'catching the illness' should be answered (Cooklin, 2004). Some authors have provided guidelines about how to facilitate such conversations (see e.g. Cooklin, 2004; Daniel & Wren, 2005; Focht & Beardslee, 1996; Walters, 2010).

Conclusion

In conclusion, it is clear that the impact parental mental health difficulties will have on a child will be mediated by myriad factors. It is therefore important to think about the interplay between the particular challenges and resilience factors for the child, the parent, the parent–child relationship, and the relational, social and environmental contexts. The balance between all of these factors will determine the outcome for the child and the impact the parent's difficulties could be said to have on the child. Therefore it is important that we do not assume. We should remain curious about children's understanding and experience of their circumstances, of what care-giving tasks mean, their experience of being with their parents at difficult times, and what they think would help. Therefore, the most important thing is to be aware of the children within the context of parental mental distress and to maintain open conversation with these children.

I hope I have been able to convey the complexity, layeredness and subtleties embedded in any answer to the question of how a parent's mental health difficulties impact upon their child. There are no easy answers, but that should not stop us asking the questions, 'seeing' these children and actively working for better outcomes for them.

References

Bowlby, J. (1969) *Attachment and Loss: Attachment.* New York: Basic Books.

Bowlby, R. (2007) 'Passionate about attachment'. *Context,* April: 3–4.

Byng-Hall, J. (2002) 'Relieving parentified children's burdens in families with insecure attachment patterns'. *Family Process,* 41(3): 375–378.

Cleaver, H., Unell, I. & Aldgate, J. (1999) *Children's Needs – Parenting Capacity: The Impact of Parental Mental Illness, Problem Alcohol and Drug Use, and Domestic Violence on Children's Development.* London: TSO.

Cooklin, A. (2004) 'Talking with children and their understanding of mental illness'. In Gopfert, M., Webster, J. & Seeman, M.V. (eds) *Parental Psychiatric Disorder* (2nd edn, pp. 294–305). Cambridge: Cambridge University Press.

Daniel, G. & Wren, B. (2005) 'Narrative therapy with children in families where a parent has a mental health problem'. In Vetere, A. & Dowling, E. (eds) *Narrative Therapies with Children and their Families – A Practitioner's Guide to Concepts and Approaches* (pp. 121–139). London: Routledge.

Duncan, S. & Reder, P. (2000) 'Children's experience of major psychiatric disorder in their parent – an overview'. In Reder, P., McClure, M. and Jolley, A. (eds) *Family Matters – Interface Between Child and Adult Mental Health* (pp. 83–95). London: Routledge.

Falcov, A. (ed.) (1998) *Crossing Bridges: Training Resources for Working with Mentally Ill Parents and their Children*. London: Department of Health/Pavilion Publishing.

Focht, L. & Beardslee, W.R. (1996) 'Speech after long silence: the use of narrative therapy in a preventative intervention for children of parents with affective disorder'. *Family Process*, 35: 407–422.

Fredman, G. & Fuggle, P. (2000) 'Parents with mental health problems: involving the children'. In Reder, P., McClure, M. and Jolley, A. (eds) *Family Matters – Interface between Child and Adult Mental Health* (pp. 213–226). London: Routledge.

Goodman, L.A., Dutton, M.A. & Haris, M. (1995) 'Episodically homeless women with serious mental illness – prevalence of physical and sexual assault'. *American Journal of Orthopsychiatry,* 65(4): 468–478.

Gopfert, M., Webster, J. & Nelki, J. (2004) 'The construction of parenting and its context'. In Gopfert, M., Webster, J. & Seeman, M.V. (eds) *Parental Psychiatric Disorder* (2nd edn, pp. 62–84). Cambridge: Cambridge University Press.

Hall, A. (2004) 'Parental psychiatric disorder and the developing child'. In Gopfert, M., Webster, J. & Seeman, M.V. (eds) *Parental Psychiatric Disorder* (2nd edn, pp. 22–49). Cambridge: Cambridge University Press.

Hill, J. (2004) 'Parental psychiatric disorder and the attachment relationship'. In Gopfert, M., Webster, J. & Seeman, M.V. (eds) *Parental Psychiatric Disorder* (2nd edn, pp. 50–61). Cambridge: Cambridge University Press.

Kelly, M. (1999) 'Approaching the last resort: a parent's view'. In Cowling, V. (ed.) *Children of Parents with Mental Illness* (pp. 60–75). Melbourne: ACER.

Lancaster, S. (1999) 'Being there: how parental mental illness can affect children'. In Cowling, V. (ed.) *Children of Parents with Mental Illness* (pp. 14–33). Melbourne: ACER.

Landau, R., Harth, P., Othnay, N. & Scharfhertz, C. (1972) 'The influence of psychotic parents on their children's development'. *American Journal of Psychiatry*, 129: 70–75.

Lippett, R. & Nolte, L. (2007) 'Talking to parents about talking to their children about parental mental distress'. *Clinical Psychology Forum*, 173: 37–40.

Nicholson, J., Sweeney, E.M. & Geller, J.L. (1998) 'Mothers with mental illness 1: The competing demands of parenting and living with mental illness'. *Psychiatric Services*, 49: 635–642.

Rutter, M. & Quinton, D. (1984) 'Parental psychiatric disorder: effects on children'. *Psychological Medicine*, 14: 853–880.

Shah, S. & Goodbody, L. (2011) Personal communication, 10 December 2010.

Vetere, A. & Dallos, R. (2007) 'Attachment narratives and systemic therapy'. *Context*, April: 5–9.

Walters, J. (2010) *Working with Fathers – From Knowledge to Therapeutic Practice*. Basingstoke: Palgrave Macmillan.

White, M. & Epston, D. (1990) *Narrative Means to Therapeutic Ends*. New York: W.W. Norton.

4   Working with the impossible

Rosemary Loshak

Yet work with psychosis is not normal work. It is not to be confused with any general kind of work. It is work with the incomprehensible.

(Hinshelwood 2004: 162)

The need for theory

Writing about psychosis, Hinshelwood states, is 'about the dark side of experience' (Hinshelwood 2004: 2). Stevenson recognises something similar in introducing the need for theory in social work practice:

there is a pressing need to examine issues of communication and cooperation at deeper levels and to use theories which illuminate the darker places of our attempts to work with others and, of course with the families, on whom our concern is focussed. We neglect such theory at our peril.

(Stevenson 2005: xiv)

Inquiry reports or serious case reviews following the death of a child from abuse consistently indicate that a contributing factor was the absence of a theoretical underpinning in the work of the professionals involved (Reder and Duncan 1999; Laming 2003). The absence of a theory of human development, of individual relationships, and of pathology, may contribute in a variety of ways: an individual's history of trauma or of violence may not be taken into account, 'snapshots' of the here and now may fail to identify a pattern in responses to events, and assessments may lack a dynamic aspect, failing to be aware of the meaning of particular relationships for an individual.

Most significantly, the complex feelings evoked in staff by their clients may not be understood by staff themselves, by organisations and by policy makers, and may give rise to increased anxiety and to the danger of inappropriate action. Howe notes:

the need for the social worker to understand what is going on if he or she is to remain patient and available and not give up on the case, and not be provoked into acting rigidly and bureaucratically because of feelings of fear and anxiety, uncertainty and intolerance.

(Howe 1995: 222)

It is this fear and anxiety that gives rise to defences aimed at the survival of the individual, which can become rigid and institutionalised to protect the whole organisation. It is the understanding of these processes that is the subject of this chapter.

Inquiries themselves have too often increased levels of anxiety and led to increasing pressure for organisational control. Stevenson noted the resulting improvements in control structures, while commenting that:

Paradoxically, these (usually) sincere attempts to change things for the better have to an extent increased the tension and fear because there has been so little attempt to provide opportunities for understanding the impact of the work and its agency context.

(Stevenson 2005: xv)

In her review of the child protection system Eileen Munro makes a similar point about the effect on practice of the reforms (Munro 2010).

Munro makes a further observation that:

There is also strong evidence that workers, in seeking to engage with a family, can get pulled into relationships with one or more members that distort their overall perception of the family. A classic example is being so focussed on helping the mother that the child's needs are overlooked.

(Munro 2010: 17; 1.26)

In more complex situations dysfunctional individual or family patterns of relating may, when not fully understood, be mirrored among the workers and teams involved; this is described and explored by Britton:

contact with some families may result in professional workers or their institutions becoming involved unknowingly in a drama which reflects a situation in the relationships of the family or within the minds of some of its individual members, and that this is not recognised but explored in action. ... In some cases the pattern of response of education departments, schools, social services or doctors takes on uncannily the shape of the family; quarrels are pursued between workers who seem as incompatible in their views as are the parents; high-handed intervention by senior colleagues echoes the domination of a family by the intrusions of an opinionated grandparent. In another case a succession of workers uncharacteristically failed to communicate with each other or to acknowledge other workers' existence, thus echoing the family pattern of a child who had been at different times abandoned by both his parents, long since separated, who related to him independently without acknowledging the other's existence.

(Britton 2005: 165–168)

Where there is a multidisciplinary team with long-established relationships these difficulties may be recognised and worked through. A history of shared experience and of respect for each discipline's contribution and role enables team members to recognise such patterns and to notice uncharacteristic responses among themselves or their colleagues. Such a team can create opportunities for reflecting on complex relationships and providing a thoughtful collective response to the service user:

> The service needs to be able to tolerate and 'digest' the disturbance as well as manage it. In other words we need to be able to contain the disturbance therapeutically. This is no simple task, and the services often defend against the impact of the disturbance by becoming omnipotent in their thinking and consequently ineffective in their practice. Facing this reality requires the team and the workers to know and work within their limitations. Limitations can be reduced and the capacity for containment and management increased if the work and the experience of it is shared among a group of people, i.e. the whole team.
>
> (Navarro 1998: 147)

Some degree of containment of this sort can take place in specialist teams, in which all members of the team focus on a particular client group. Most social care organisations have specialist 'panels' or 'boards' which include representatives of other agencies, whose members meet on a regular basis with a clearly defined and limited task; examples are safeguarding children boards, school improvement panels with a focus on children at risk of exclusion, fostering panels, and adult protection panels. Such panels typically bring together some of the most experienced staff within an organisation and provide a context in which thinking and shared expertise develop over time.

Where, however, the task is not so circumscribed, where a number of agencies are involved whose representatives meet irregularly and infrequently, and at a point of crisis, such a considered response is much harder to achieve. The effect on the organisation is to focus on the present, a 'snapshot' approach which discounts history and hinders the building of relationships. Ultimately it increases isolation among staff and leads to fragmented and omnipotent decision making.

Managing difference

The realities of multidisciplinary and community-based work demand that a variety of theoretical approaches from different disciplines with widely differing traditions coexist in a context of learning and curiosity. This richness within the community is reflected among the authors in this book, who bring systems theory, a medical model, psychodynamic approaches, sociological and education theory as well as psychoanalytic concepts to bear on the task of working with mental illness, and working together.

No one theory can provide clarity in all situations. Some professionals, particularly social workers who need knowledge of the development of the individual personality, its dynamics and internal world, as well as of external realities which may impinge, will require different theories to structure diverse information.

When different professions come together as in the multidisciplinary team, or when working across agency settings, theoretical differences are inevitable and can contribute to creative team work, bringing other perspectives to a problem, stimulating thinking and finding new solutions.

The growth and development that can follow are as important for staff satisfaction as for service users; for many,

> it is necessary gradually to develop and acquire clinically relevant frameworks of understanding. Acquiring these frameworks is a lifelong personal process and one is always looking for additional insights to deepen the framework of reference. No single framework is comprehensive enough to cover all situations; each has its limitations. We are continually challenged to find new and meaningful understandings and to integrate them.
>
> (Lucas 2009: 9)

The authors of this book who are from different disciplines and theoretical backgrounds share a concern with the individual in relationship, to his internal world, to his family, or to wider social contexts, such as school and community, and with his or her development. There are shared values which include recognition of the importance of the meaning of individual experience, and a need to work with the healthy part of the personality or system, implying a belief in the possibility of growth and development. Finally there is a shared view that relationships with colleagues are central to the task, and that working together effectively ensures the best service for patients and their families. In this chapter the contribution of psychoanalytic theory to an understanding of mental illness, including psychosis, and its application to the task of working together, will be described as one way of thinking about the difficulties encountered.

Psychoanalysis as a way of understanding mental illness

> A thing which has not been understood inevitably reappears; like an unlaid ghost it cannot rest until the mystery has been solved and the spell broken.
>
> (Freud 1909: 122)

Psychoanalysis can be a form of treatment, but also a way of understanding mental processes. This view is endorsed in the NICE *Schizophrenia Clinical Guidelines* which recommend that:

Healthcare professionals may consider using psychoanalytic and psycho-dynamic principles to help them understand the experience of people with schizophrenia and their interpersonal relationships.

(NICE 2009: 8.8.7.1)

Psychoanalysis can help us recognise how the past can come alive in the present; internalised early relationships of infancy and childhood are remembered, repeated and when brought to consciousness, worked through in adult life. When they remain unconscious they are not subject to the changes wrought by time, and with all their original strength they continue to affect us, our self-esteem, our relationships and our enjoyment in life.

The work of Freud, Klein, Bion, and of more recent writers such as Richard Lucas and Paul Williams increases our understanding of loss, trauma, anxiety and psychosis. Williams and Lucas, among others, have argued powerfully for a psychoanalytic presence in modern mental health service provision, to bring attention to the unconscious meaning of the illness 'in the context of the person's life history, personality development, internal object world, and current relationships with staff' (Williams 2010: 1). It is only through the experience of a shared meaning that individual suffering can be placed in its context, and understood so that further development can happen.

The depressive position

The context for the joint working project described in this book is one in which an unremitting experience of loss and trauma has threatened at times to overwhelm not only sections of the population but also those working with them in the public services. With the borough's long history of receiving immigrants, and with memories of war affecting both the new and the indigenous populations, loss and trauma may be passed down through generations. This is vividly described by Doris Lessing, who writes:

I used to feel there was something like a dark grey cloud, like poison gas, over my early childhood . . . the old darkness of dread and anguish . . . my father's emotion, a very potent draught, no homeopathic dose, but the full dose of adult pain. I wonder how many of the children brought up in families crippled by the war had the same poison running in their veins from before they could even speak.

(Lessing 1995: 10)

Loss of a significant other, or of an aspect of oneself, such as one's job or one's health, will precipitate a reaction which can readily be understood by others; grief, anger, tears and sadness, a searching for the lost person. The process of recovery requires that the mourner bit by bit relinquishes the presence of the other, gradually becoming able to face the reality of change, and to pick up the threads of their life.

In *Mourning and Melancholia* Freud differentiated this ordinary response to loss from a state of melancholy or depression in which the sufferer is unable to mourn, but remains in a state of perpetual grief and torment, unable to let go (Freud 1917). Freud attributed this state to an unconscious hostility which gives rise to guilt. The person who is absent is blamed and hated for having deserted the sufferer, who then hates him- or herself for harbouring such thoughts, and judges him- or herself as unlovable. As Freud describes it, 'the shadow of the object falls upon the ego' (Freud 1917). The mourner is left with a conflict of ambivalence, a mixture of love and hate which has dominated the lost relationship.

Melanie Klein conceptualised a mind with a capacity to tolerate such conflicting feelings without becoming overwhelmed by guilt for wrongdoing, as functioning in what she termed the depressive position. In this state of mind one is able to recognise good and bad in one's relationships, and in oneself, without forming harsh judgements. The capacity to forgive and thus to reinstate in memory lost figures and to repair damaged internal relationships is an important aspect of human development and growth of the personality.

The paranoid-schizoid position

Klein also identified more primitive anxieties which may dominate and lead one to make use of much earlier defences of splitting the world into good and bad, loved and hated figures. In this state, which she termed the paranoid-schizoid position, the self is also split, with unwanted aspects of the personality being pushed out of conscious awareness. Britton describes the consequences when whole families behave in such a way:

> The members of a family whose relationships are experienced in the main in the paranoid-schizoid position (Klein 1965) as opposed to the depressive position, are likely to feel persecuted rather than guilty; ill rather than worried; enmity rather than conflict; desperation rather than sadness. They are liable to feel triumphant or if not to feel squashed and to see others as either allies or opponents. Their tendency to take flight . . . is linked to their belief that psychic experience can be split off and left behind: by the same token there is a sense of being hunted and a fear of being cornered.
>
> (Britton 2005: 169)

While these positions reflect developmental stages as the infant begins to be able to take in the world as it is, with good and bad in one and the same person, they are also positions between which we may oscillate throughout our lives. We may all be subject to paranoid functioning at times of emotional strain, and if we do not have secure internal relationships which bring a sense of trust in the world despite difficulties, we will be vulnerable to an accumulation of bad external events and to the possibility of illness.

These two positions are associated with very different kinds of anxiety; while the depressive position is characterised by guilt, by anxieties about damage and the capacity to repair, the paranoid-schizoid position is associated with more primitive infantile anxieties. Klein has demonstrated how the infant, utterly dependent upon maternal care, and whose sense of self is determined by his or her bodily needs, may experience acute anxiety about a disruption of care, with fears of being abandoned to die of starvation, or of annihilation.

An unconscious body memory of such anxieties may be reactivated later as the growing child or adult faces external threats to his or her existence. If such an external event threatens to overwhelm the individual it is experienced as catastrophic; it becomes a trauma, an impingement upon our ordinary state of being, which is experienced physically as an attack on the body and emotionally as a threat to the sense of self. In a severe traumatic state the individual's sense of self will be overwhelmed by a flood of unwanted stimulation, and fragmented, so that ordinary functioning is disturbed.

Psychotic processes

When someone is suffering from a severe psychotic illness, anxieties of the paranoid-schizoid position dominate. Freud first described the processes of projection of intolerable pain and fragmentation of the mind and its contents in his study of the writings of the German judge Schreber (Freud 1911). After a period of depression following failures in his career, Schreber suffered a breakdown in which he believed he was being persecuted, notably by his psychiatrist, Dr Flechsig. As his disturbance increased, his delusions became fragmented and increasingly bizarre. Freud sought to understand these fragments, relating them to Schreber's homosexual erotic feelings towards his doctor and the conflict these feelings produced for a man of his stature and reputation. It is relevant that Schreber's father was renowned for promoting strict disciplinarian methods of child rearing, involving harsh punishment regimes, which the child Schreber probably also endured. The residues of infantile conflict of feelings of love and hate for such a father must have been brought close to consciousness as a result of his depression and in his encounter with his doctor, a possible father figure. These would create an intolerable burden of unacceptable and inexpressible feelings bringing the 'soul destruction' of which Schreber himself complained.

Where such thoughts and feelings cannot be processed, the sufferer's responses may appear bizarre or frightening. Dr Leslie Sohn, psychiatrist and psychoanalyst, relates an early encounter as a medical student with a young woman who is psychotic; she has just been delivered of a dead baby; he spends several hours with her, as she speaks in a delusional way about a (fantasised) dead husband, *not* a dead baby. Some days later he meets her again in a psychiatric ward and

> Being curious and a friendly sort of chap, I went up to her and said 'Hello, how are you?'. She replied that she had no idea who I was, nor did she know how I knew her. And she walked away. Mrs G could not have suffered a more catastrophic loss; she'd expected a healthy, live baby and as far as

I know she never violently attacked anyone except her own mind and its memories and contents. The narcissistic blow to me was enormous.

(Sohn 1999: 23)

Mrs G is demonstrating the severely damaged capacity to bear external reality which is the characteristic feature of psychosis, which affects the individual's relationships and places a considerable burden on carers. Other features are a confusion and disorder of thought, a loss of a sense of self, a state of self-absorption, belief in one's own imaginings, delusions and hallucinations, a loss of the use of words as symbols, and their use instead as concrete ideas. Sohn is describing not only the process of destruction of all her mental functions, memory, thinking and perception, but also that of evacuating unwanted, intolerable stimuli, and the effect of this defence upon the other, that is, the hurt, which is so powerfully projected into him.

Unwanted aspects of the self's personality may be projected into another who, if sensitive to such processes, may identify with these aspects and feel and react as if they are their own. The other may then respond as if taking on the role unconsciously demanded of them by their client, patient or partner. The other has been made to conform to the roles belonging to the sufferer's internal world of infantile relationships, rather than being able to function as his or her real self. It is such 'role responsiveness' that can result in the mirroring processes among workers described earlier and named by Britton as 'complementary acting-out' (Britton 2005: 167).

Williams describes the power and force of such projections, likening them to 'psychosomatic missiles that are expelled or fired into the other' (Williams 2010: 15). Describing intensive work with a psychoanalytic patient suffering from 'crippling psychotic anxieties', he conveys the effect upon himself as 'Feeling inept, moved, that I was being bullied (or else being a bully), held to ransom, or that the analysis was destined to fail' (Williams 2010: 32). It is such projections that induce a real fear of mental illness among workers.

These defences form part of a mental structure that has been further elaborated by Bion. He suggests that the mind has 'turned against itself', and attempts to destroy its own functioning, that is, the processes that are essential to thought, attention, perception, cognition, memory and judgement, in the interests of being rid of an unbearable truth. It is this that leads to the fragmented and chaotic thought processes that Schreber's story describes.

Meaninglessness and despair

Attempts to rid the mind of unbearable contents, by projective identification, splitting and by attacking thought processes themselves, ultimately result in a state where there is no meaning, a kind of psychic death. Hinshelwood describes very powerfully this state and its effect on those close to the sufferer, whether family or in a professional role:

Typically that distress is not formed or articulated in words; meaning itself gives way to an experience of meaninglessness. And this is contagious. It has a direct effect on others and, in fact, percolates through the whole system. Psychotic patients are very effective at this non-verbal impact. Being a communication of meaninglessness its communicative function is lost. It becomes merely an emotional impact, an unidentifiable experience.

(Hinshelwood 1998: 19)

In his account of his experiences as a tank commander in the First World War the 20-year-old Wilfred Bion described the despair which is the effect of prolonged exposure to shelling and battle:

It did not take long for interest in life to die out. Soon I found myself almost hopeless. I used to lie on my back and stare at the low roof. Sometimes I stared for hours at a small piece of mud that hung from the roof by a grass and quivered to the explosion of the shells. . . . I found myself looking forward to getting killed, as then at least one would be rid of this intolerable misery.

(Bion 1997: 94)

Bion here puts into words the desperation of the psychotic whose mind is under attack as if by shelling. 'Almost hopeless', Bion was also observer of his own state of mind. An important development in his understanding of psychotic functioning was his elaboration of the concept of a split between a psychotic part and a non-psychotic, or sane part of the personality which is aware, somewhere, of reality. Freud had observed this split in his patients:

One learns from patients after their recovery that at the time in some corner of their mind (as they put it) there was a normal person hidden, who like a detached spectator, watched the hubbub of illness go past him.

(Freud 1940: 202)

It is this part of the patient, sometimes in their parental role, with which one may be able to work.

However, Lucas, former consultant general psychiatrist at St Ann's Hospital, Haringey, and psychoanalyst, made clear the dangers when mental health staff members are unable to recognise which part of the personality they are faced with. He wrote:

Professionals often remain unaware of the commonest presenting symptom of psychosis and its diagnostic implication. If one consults a standard psychiatric textbook, one will find that the commonest symptom is not, as one might expect, persecutory delusions or auditory hallucinations, but lack of insight. This lack of insight presents as denial of any problems with associated

rationalisations. In other words if we are not aware that denial and rational-
isation are the commonest presenting features of psychosis we are in danger
of succumbing to the rationalisations and missing the underlying psychosis.

(Lucas 2009: 7)

Separateness of being

For the parent psychotically preoccupied with their own internal world, the child
may be experienced as an extension of him- or herself, rather than as a separate
being with their own mind and personality. Any suggestion of difference or
separateness in the external world is experienced as humiliating, causing shame
and paranoia. The sufferer expects others to see the world as he does, and may be
provoked to conflict or desperate action when confronted with reality. It is such
'one-person' thought processes that may lead a parent to kill their child as well as
themselves.

This fear of separateness is experienced in relation to the 'otherness' in all
relationships, not just between parent and child. Britton speaks of 'a primary
mutual hostility of human beings' which is present to some extent in all of us
(Britton 2005). In psychosis this dominates through a relentless pull towards a
world in which separateness is denied, and relationships, difference and thinking
are experienced as threatening. Sameness, lack of change and inertia provide the
only route to safety.

This is a state more readily associated with the long-stay wards of the old
asylums. It may, however, characterise family life for some children today.

Working with severe mental illness: the impact on staff

Families struggling with major loss form much of the caseload of any childcare,
mental health or primary care worker in the borough, and engender a state
of hopelessness and despair which can be overwhelming. In a workshop for
childcare social workers about parental mental illness, group members wanted
answers, not to the problems presented by severe mental illness such as schizophrenia, but rather to the unremitting diet of depression in their workload, which
was not diagnosed or treated. In these circumstances staff members, whose job
satisfaction is contingent on being able to help, and to prevent harm to children,
are likely to become identified with the helplessness, anger and guilt of their
clients, and to find relief from these feelings through frequent sickness, or changes
of job.

For both mental health and childcare staff high levels of anxiety are raised
in their work. One mental health worker, invited to think about the children of her
clients, replied, 'Don't make me more anxious than I am already, I have enough'.
Paralysing anxiety is felt at all levels of the organisation, and is largely un-
contained, and undigested. A senior manager, presented with information about
disturbed mothers of young babies, commented, 'I know more than I did and it
makes me more anxious'.

Highly skilled professionals in both adult and child mental health settings have expressed intense anxiety and pain when asked to talk to a child, particularly a teenager, about their parent's mental illness. Feelings of failure, identification with the young person's fears of inheriting the illness, and the associated stigma can cause a paralysis of thought. Staff members need to retain a high level of sensitivity, self-awareness and reflective capacity to be able to tolerate their own fears as well as those of their clients.

For childcare teams the dominant anxiety concerns severe or fatal injury to a child, which is rare. However, in adult mental health services, violence, murder and suicide are frequent occurrences in an inner city area with high indices of deprivation, overcrowding and joblessness. For adult mental health staff the fears are that their clients may carry out some act of violence against themselves or another, including, as Hinshelwood states, against their mental health worker:

> It is the fear of something going quickly out of control. This may be experienced as either madness or violence, a mind going out of control. It makes us afraid of our patients and we give it a meaning – that they may become violent and injure us.
>
> (Hinshelwood 1998: 20)

Faced with such anxieties, including fear of the patient, all staff may become vulnerable to insomnia, flashbacks, anxiety, depression, loss of memory and of confidence. Hinshelwood describes the process of demoralisation which can result:

> If many staff are subject to feeling despair, then the first danger to the team is that it will become collectively demoralised. People cannot give each other the support, encouragement and praise that is needed when they themselves feel they are not doing a good job.
>
> (Hinshelwood 1998: 21)

High levels of absence, sickness and staff turnover are the result. In the absence of containing structures and in the interest of self-preservation a variety of defences will be employed; these include avoidance of stress-inducing situations, withdrawal and isolation from colleagues, blaming others or other agencies, and a manic belief in one's omnipotence and ability to deal with everything.

Families whose lives are characterised by inertia, resistance to change and meaninglessness are difficult for professionals to bear so that thinking about them feels impossible. Appointments or home visits are easily cancelled. No change takes place, despite comprehensive 'care packages'. Those professionals who try to engage more deeply with the family are either repelled or invited to become part of the family system, seen as 'friends' rather than having authority invested in their role. They can be drawn into colluding with family dynamics by 'turning a blind eye' to the real difficulties and to what no one can bear to acknowledge, often the level of violence in the family and the severe neglect or abuse of children (and sometimes also of the ill adult) – physical, emotional, and possibly sexual.

The organisation develops its own defences; knowledge of the family becomes fragmented and scattered among different agencies who can find no forum for coming together or for effective communication; agencies take up different positions, as professionals identify with different family members and remain divided, blaming each other for failings; strenuous efforts to provide 'support' resemble the hyperactive behaviour of a child trying to get a reaction from an unresponsive, despairing parent. Professionals may find themselves trying to inject liveliness and to bring about change in a meaningless and emotionally dead family life.

Organisations and systems working together

Isobel Menzies-Lyth (1959) noted the high levels of sickness, anxiety and stress experienced by nurses in a general hospital, and related this to the defences mobilised by the nature of their work: this is described by Hoyle in her discussion of resistance to change:

> The primary task for the hospital was to accept and care for ill people who cannot be cared for in their own homes. The work of the nurses therefore, arouses strong and mixed feelings of pity, compassion, and love; guilt and anxiety, hatred and resentment because of the aroused feelings; envy of the care given to the patient.
>
> (Hoyle 2004: 89)

The difficulty in bearing such feelings led to defensive responses which included denial of emotional pain, distancing from the patient, and preoccupation with routine tasks. However, these also *increased* anxiety, denying the nurses a meaningful relationship with the patient and reducing their job satisfaction (Menzies-Lyth 1959). Similar processes have been identified among childcare social workers in particular, as Munro notes:

> The ones who lose out most are the very children the system is designed to protect. The reforms have driven compliance with regulation and rules over time, with social workers increasingly operating within an over-standardised framework that makes it difficult for them to prioritise time with children, to get to know them, and understand their feelings, wishes and worries. It is then in turn, difficult to provide the flexible and sensitive responses that match the wide variety of needs and circumstances that are presented.
>
> (Munro 2010: 7)

In the late 1980s Woodhouse and Pengelly, working in what was then the Tavistock Institute of Marital Studies, conducted a research workshop to study the particular anxieties and dynamics inherent in the task of collaboration. Combining a systems approach with an understanding of unconscious dynamic factors, their underlying assumption was 'a conception of the person as a *dynamic and open system* embedded in larger, interacting ones with physical, emotional and social/cultural dimensions' (Woodhouse and Pengelly 1991: 9).

They noted that with increased levels of anxiety, both individual and organisational defences are likely to become more rigid. They can become embedded within the organisational structure and reduce the capacity for openness, cooperation and change.

Instead, the primitive nature of the anxieties generated from the work with very ill people with a damaged capacity for relationships will result in the very early defences described by Klein and Bion. These take the form of suspicion and blaming of other agencies, splitting organisations into good and bad, evacuating feelings of inadequacy and helplessness and projecting them into the other agency, which is identified as useless, ineffectual or even irresponsible. The paranoid and split mental functioning of clients and patients is mirrored in workers' responses to otherness and difference; their inertia and fragmented thinking directly affects communication between staff in different agencies. Organisations become preoccupied with defensive strategies to maintain their boundaries.

Where more than two agencies are involved, the presence of a third may increase anxiety about difference arousing feelings of rivalry, exclusion and possessiveness. One way to be rid of such difficult feelings is to resort to blame and criticism. The capacity to come together to think about ways to deal with the realities of the task at hand is thus jeopardised by the 'unconscious impact of anxiety, the defences aimed at dealing with it and the conflict of feeling it generated which undermined the ability to think and to work collaboratively' (Woodhouse and Pengelly 1991: 224).

In considering the children of parents with mental illness, we are necessarily concerned with many interacting systems in which creative collaboration is a basic requirement. These will include relationships within and between the following:

- the family system with the child at its centre, and the ill adult within the family
- the ill adult and the mental health system
- the child's daily world of school, peer groups, etc.
- the childcare system of child health and Children's Social Care
- the parallel professional systems as they come together; of services for children, including education, and of services for adults including social care and health, both physical and mental
- the local community of voluntary organisations, churches, neighbours, etc.

Such complex work benefits from a containing structure which can provide continuity over time in the context of secure relationships, and in which a capacity for reflecting and thinking is retained in the face of massive anxiety and projective processes. Such a capacity is rarely available in today's public sector organisations, modelled, as they currently are, on business practices.

Cooper and Dartington have shown how this complexity is further increased by changes in the traditional hierarchies in which authority rested. Today there is a need for professionals to negotiate their own authority, not only within one complex organisation, but in any work group in which several agencies may be participating (Cooper and Dartington 2004).

What works?

An effective system is characterised by sensitivity and openness to a range of emotional responses; it needs to be flexible rather than rigid in its boundaries with other systems; and those working within it need to feel sufficiently safe to explore, to ask questions and to be curious about their patients or clients, whether adults or children, their lives and relationships.

The human organisation

In inter-agency work the role and primary task of each of the participants has to be kept in mind, maintaining a clear boundary between self and other, and recognising rather than obscuring differences so that they can be openly discussed. However, Halton suggests that it is not only the role that is important but one must also keep in mind the fundamental human quality of the organisation and its work (Halton 2004). Halton's approach is consistent with the depressive position in which concerns about damage and a wish to repair are predominant, over the wish to take flight into action or 'quick fixes'. The reflective and creative attitude

> keeps in mind the needs and feelings of the individual performing the role and recognises that everyone has other people to deal with apart from the immediate transactions with oneself.
>
> (Halton 2004: 110)

When interactions become dominated by paranoid-schizoid functioning the

> suspicion, mistrust and hidden rivalries interfere with the healthy exchange of differences.
>
> (Halton 2004: 111)

A reflective space

The need for a space in which there is room for reflection may be concrete – there are times when one needs a degree of physical distance from one's patients or clients in order to be able to think about them (Garelick 2011); or it can be found in supervision, or in case discussion groups.

Woodhouse and Pengelly offered such a space in their series of workshops, studying collaborative work among the professions. They noted that short-term interventions can be effective in the work as well as mutually satisfying for those involved:

> [Most successful collaborations] consisted of short-term or one-off concerted action focussed on a single specific issue, where the social worker and other

practitioner were agreed about their strategy, and their agencies were not in conflict. They were therefore unlikely to be split by the influence of the client's anxieties and defences. . . . Each of these short term interventions was instigated by the social worker, seemed well-timed and proved a turning point in the work. The social workers were not assailed by the anxiety of doing more harm than good; the concerted action did not have the quality of a defensive collusion or ganging up against the client, but rather functioned to contain anxiety and enable unpalatable truth to be faced.

(Woodhouse and Pengelly 1991: 183)

It is such interventions that characterise the efforts of the coordinator post and the CHAMP team described throughout this book.

A systemic approach in meetings

Daniel and Chin (2010), in the context of more recent training workshops provided for multi-professional groups across adult and children's services, emphasised the value of introducing a systemic approach which focuses on mutual learning and discovering the other as a resource rather than blaming the other for failing. They suggest that such an approach can improve staff confidence and increase flexibility in working across agency boundaries.

The statutory framework of child protection or adult mental health Care Programme Approach meetings demand that a single agency take responsibility for their organisation and management. Non-statutory 'joint working meetings' led by an experienced clinician without a management or statutory remit in the family (e.g. school-led Team Around the Child meetings) can be helpful in creating a climate of openness and willingness to cooperate rather than one characterised by anxiety, inhibition and defensiveness. Family dynamics may be better understood and workers can gain confidence in their own expertise and professional autonomy.

A physical presence

In describing the role of a CAMHS psychologist providing regular sessions in an adult community mental health team, Chin writes:

Developing a connection has undoubtedly been the most useful aspect in working across services, and I find that being a physical presence in each team helps to provide an opportunity for different explanations about services and their service users to develop. It demystifies and promotes understanding of the other's culture, allowing teams to learn the language that is used to talk about people and problems and to develop a respect for the differing thresholds for worry and risk.

(Daniel and Chin 2010: 50)

Chin emphasises the need for a non-judgemental approach, a willingness to listen, and the ability to ask sometimes 'obvious' questions. The coordinator and the children's specialists in adult mental health demonstrate a model with many similarities, but utilising mostly social work staff. Social workers can bring a different experience to such a role, with their knowledge of the community, their understanding of the child in the context of his or her family, and of the social networks of which child and family are a part.

The capacity to relate

For all professions, it is our capacity for relatedness which differentiates us from those clients where this is so impaired by mental illness. Several authors (Howe 1995; Armstrong 2004; Cooper and Dartington 2004) suggest it is also the building block which will lead to new models of containment in this 'networked' world. Karen Daniel states:

> In the last four years while working with the adult mental health teams, I have learnt from others who have skills and ideas different from my own. There is nothing like working together on a case to enhance mutual understanding and respect.

(Daniel 2010: 58)

References

Armstrong, D. (2004). Section Three: Working relations in a new organisational order. Introduction. In Huffington, C., Armstrong, D., Halton, W., Hoyle, L. and Pooley, J. (eds) *Working Below the Surface; The Emotional Life of Contemporary Organisations.* London: Karnac.

Bion, W.R. (1997). *War Memoirs 1917–1919.* London: Karnac. http://www.karnacbooks. com/isbn/9781855751538, reprinted with kind permission of Karnac Books.

Britton, R. (2005). Re-enactment as an unwitting professional response to family dynamics. In Bower, M. (ed.) *Psychoanalytic Theory for Social Work Practice.* Abingdon: Routledge.

Cooper, A. and Dartington, T. (2004). The vanishing organisation; Organisational containment in a networked world. In Huffington, C., Armstrong, D., Halton, W., Hoyle, L. and Pooley, J. (eds) *Working Below the Surface; The Emotional Life of Contemporary Organisations.* London: Karnac. http://www.karnacbooks.com/isbn/9781855752948, reprinted with kind permission of Karnac Books.

Daniel, K. (2010). The dance of attempting to break down barriers: Working with children and families where a parent is experiencing mental health difficulties. *Context 108*, pp. 56–58. Association for Family Therapy. AFT Publishing.

Daniel, G. and Chin, J. (2010). Engaging with agency cultures in parental mental illness training. *Context 108*, pp. 47–50. Association for Family Therapy. AFT Publishing.

Freud, S. (1909). Analysis of a phobia in a five year old boy. In Freud, S., *Standard Edition 10*: 122. London: Hogarth Press.

—— (1911[1958]). Psychoanalytic notes on an autobiographical account of a case of paranoia. In Freud, S., *Standard Edition 12*: 1–82. London: Hogarth Press.

—— (1917a). *Mourning and Melancholia. Standard Edition 1.* London: Hogarth Press.

—— (1940). *An Outline of Psychoanalysis. Standard Edition 23.* London: Hogarth Press.

Garelick, A. (2011). Finding a space to think and a way to talk. *Psychoanalytic Psychotherapy*, Vol. 25, No. 1, March. Abingdon: Routledge.

Halton, W. (2004). 'By what authority? Psychoanalytic reflections on creativity and change in relation to organisational life'. In Huffington, C., Armstrong, D., Halton, W., Hoyle, L. and Pooley, J. (eds) *Working Below the Surface: The Emotional Life of Contemporary Organisations.* London: Karnac. http://www.karnacbooks.com/isbn/9781855752948, reprinted with kind permission of Karnac Books.

Hinshelwood, R. (1998). Creatures of each other. In Foster, A. and Zagier Roberts, V. (eds) *Managing Mental Health in the Community: Chaos and Containment.* London and New York: Routledge.

—— (2004). *Suffering Insanity; Psychoanalytic Essays on Psychosis.* Hove and New York: Brunner Routledge.

Howe, D. (1995). *Attachment Theory for Social Workers.* Basingstoke and London: Macmillan.

Hoyle, L. (2004). From sycophant to saboteur – response to change. In Huffington, C., Armstrong, D., Halton, W., Hoyle, L. and Pooley, J. (eds) *Working Below the Surface; The Emotional Life of Contemporary Organisations.* London: Karnac. http://www.karnacbooks.com/isbn/9781855752948, reprinted with kind permission of Karnac Books.

Klein, M. (1946[1975]). Notes on some schizoid mechanisms. In *Envy and Gratitude and Other Works 1946–1963.* London: Hogarth.

Laming, Lord (2003). *The Victoria Climbié Inquiry.* London: The Stationery Office.

Lessing, D. (1995). *Under My Skin.* London: Harper Collins.

Lucas, R. (2009). *The Psychotic Wavelength.* Hove and New York: Routledge.

Menzies, I. (1960). A case study in the functioning of social systems as a defence against anxiety: a report on a study of the nursing service of a general hospital. *Human Relations* 13: 95–121. Reprinted in Menzies Lyth, I. *Containing Anxiety in Institutions: Selected Essays Volume 1.* London: Free Association Books.

Munro, E. (2010). *The Munro Review of Child Protection: Part One – A Systems Analysis.* London: Department of Education.

National Institute for Health and Clinical Excellence (NICE) (2009). *Schizophrenia Clinical Guidelines CG 82.*

Navarro, T. (1998). Beyond keyworking. In Foster, A. and Roberts, V.Z. (eds.) *Managing Mental Health in the Community: Chaos and Containment.* London and New York: Routledge.

Reder, P. and Duncan, S. (1999). *Lost Innocents: A Follow-up Study of Fatal Child Abuse.* London: Routledge.

Sohn, L. (1999). Psychosis and violence. In Williams, P. (ed.) *Psychosis (Madness).* London: Institute of Psychoanalysis.

Stevenson, O. In Marion Bower, E. (2005). *Psychoanalytic Theory for Social Work Practice.* Abingdon and New York: Routledge.

Williams, P. (2010). *Invasive Objects; Minds Under Siege.* New York: Routledge.

Woodhouse, D. and Pengelly, P. (1991). *Anxiety and the Dynamics of Collaboration.* Aberdeen: Aberdeen University Press.

5 Loss and change in the setting
The demographic, legislative and organisational context

Rosemary Loshak

Despite the impact of information technology, and of the market culture which has dominated management styles for so long, our public sector health and child welfare services remain concerned with humanity, with people, with their relationships, the patterns and fabric of their lives, and with the meanings they attach to experiences. Just as in work with a child or family one seeks to know and understand something of the context in which they may be struggling, so it is relevant also, in thinking about the difficulties individual professionals and their agencies have in working together, to understand and to hold in mind something of the history of relationships, and of the socio-economic and political climate in which they operate.

This chapter attempts to give a picture of the inner city borough which is the setting for the work, its history, its people and their struggles. This will be set against a historical and legislative framework for current policies in mental health and children's services, and an outline of the local organisation of services as it existed at the time the project took place. Inevitably, further changes are in the offing. It will be seen that the underlying theme is one of constant loss and change, for the people of the borough and also for the professional community within it. This places heavy demands on staff members, who are asked to cope not just with the complexity of their clients' lives, but also with a need for constant adaptation to change and for new learning. Whether this also represents an opportunity for growth and development is dependent on their and their organisation's space for containment and for reflection.

Because of the unique history of the borough, and the pride with which this shared history is held, any attempt to describe it is likely to render the borough easily recognised. The purpose of this chapter is to demonstrate the influences of particular local characteristics upon the organisations providing services. While many of the socio-economic features and the inter-agency difficulties will be shared by other authorities, there is no 'one size fits all', and the organisation of services must be informed and determined by local need. It is written in a spirit, not of criticism or of despair, but rather in an attempt to show what is valuable and yet vulnerable to destructive processes.

The social context: the borough history and its people

Originally a collection of villages, three ancient parishes were formed into a borough in 1965, clearly bounded on one side and its identity determined by the river, which historically was the source of employment in its docks, and a point of entry for refugees and immigrants over several centuries. It lies adjacent to the commercial and financial heart of the city, yet is in sharp contrast to it. Its history is a labour history of the working man and of an underclass, in which events such as the Match Girls' Strike of 1888, and the marches of the 1930s against Oswald Mosley's fascism stand out. It has been a history of radicalism and reform, which has never failed to attract researchers and sociologists. Thus it was the home of the first university settlement which sought to bring about radical change through educating the future political elite of the country in the life and conditions of the working classes and the poor. This was to be achieved by bringing Oxford graduates to live and work as volunteers with the aim of improving the lives of the poor through providing education and opportunities for recreation and enjoyment.

The population suffered heavy losses in the Second World War, and in the postwar period were subject to new housing policies, 'overspill' and the creation of new towns in rural areas. Michael Young, sociologist and researcher, in an influential study, examined the impact of postwar housing policies upon urban family life, which was traditionally bound by strong kinship ties across generations, but which became threatened when these ties were disrupted (Young 1957). Young described a social structure in which there is a 'network of local attachment'. The foundation of this was as follows:

> the ancient family consisted not only of parents and children, but also of uncles and aunts, nephews and nieces, cousins and grandparents. Kindred were bound together throughout their lives in a complex system of mutual rights and duties.
>
> (Young 1957: 41)

Families lived together in close proximity. The relationship between mother and daughter was vital and of practical importance, as mothers, who knew the rent collectors, were well placed to help their daughters in getting homes (Young 1957).

However, as council ownership of housing increased, this old system gave way to new priorities as the council allocated tenancies on the basis of need, with the result that families were no longer in close proximity and a mother had 'none of the special influence with local authorities that she had with private rent collectors' (Young 1957: 41–42).

Yet mother–daughter relationships have remained strong, while housing policies have continued to be a source of tension which needs to be understood in the context of this background.

Immigration

David Widgery, a local GP and writer, knew well the 'multiracial and non-conformist character' of the borough, which had been shaped by generations of immigrants, seamen, refugees and exiles (Widgery 1991). Such diversity has been characteristic of the borough over the centuries due to the presence of its docks and port. In the seventeenth century the Huguenots fled religious persecution in Europe, setting up a silk-weaving industry in their homes, their craft still reflected in local street names – Tenter Street, Weavers Fields. They were followed by the Irish, by European and Russian Jews, by Chinese and Vietnamese, by Somalis, and by those from the New Commonwealth countries of Pakistan and Bangladesh. Today the indigenous white population is in a minority with the 55 per cent majority originating from more than twenty different countries, including African, Asian, Caribbean and European nations.

Today it is the Bangladeshis who constitute 30 per cent of the population and who have settled as a result of changes in immigration policy in the 1980s. This community had historic links with the area through the lascars – seamen employees of the East India Company which traded in jute with Bengal, they first settled close to the docks which were their source of work. In the 1980s, large numbers of women and children joined their men who had until then managed a single life here while supporting their families at home. It is often overlooked that many of these families were fleeing the impact of the war of independence from West Pakistan less than ten years earlier (1976), when East Pakistan became the new state of Bangladesh. This was a period of widespread killings, rape and pillage by the Pakistan army and many members of the first generation still carry the emotional scars from that time.

Of the women and children arriving to join husbands, the majority had no English, and were impoverished migrants from a war-torn, rural peasant economy, many with low levels of literacy in Bengali. Like numbers of migrants before them, many had experienced overwhelming losses, of family, of community and of the daily pattern of life, only to find themselves in vermin-infested and over-crowded conditions provided by slum landlords. One young married woman living in a Victorian slum tenement block longed for the quiet beauty and companionship of her village and missed most the ability to bathe daily in the open air. Here, she and her family occupied one second-floor room, damp with mould on the walls, a shared outdoor toilet in the yard below, and a cooker occupying one corner of the room which provided living, sleeping and eating space for five.

The loss and the disappointed expectations, often complicated by grief and mourning for the death of relatives back home or by chronic ill health, brought depression, victimhood and sometimes a helpless dependence for both men and women. This too often led to professionals feeling deskilled and impotent in their struggle to understand or bring lasting change.

It had been a time of racial violence in the borough. For the indigenous white population the very neediness and poverty of the new arrivals perhaps stirred memories of their own circumstances of a generation earlier, and of their long-buried feelings of loss and helplessness in the blitz. The white population, in direct competition for council housing and jobs, openly and unashamedly expressed their racist rage on buses and in the streets, where immigrant women were spat at. Teenage gang fights culminated in the death of a Bangladeshi youth, who is now commemorated in a local park named after him.

Yet today the borough is a place of vibrancy and constant change. It is a young borough with over 60 per cent of children under 16 years of Bangladeshi origin. The rapidly growing population results from both a high birth rate and more newcomers from many countries coming to start a new life. Nearly thirty years on from the first influx of families, the Bangladeshi population is in the third generation and its troubled history is slowly fading from the collective memory. No longer identified as the 'Bangladeshi community' within the borough, they are, like other immigrant groups before them, an integral part of its institutional and daily life – leaders of the council, a substantial part of the public service workforce, creating a vibrant arts culture and successful in business, part of the British Asian community of the nation. In 2010, one of two Muslim women Members of Parliament in the country was elected in the borough; born in Bangladesh, educated at a local comprehensive, an Oxford graduate and Associate Director of the Young Foundation, she writes:

> My story is a typical East End story. I grew up in [the borough] having moved to the UK from Bangladesh when I was seven years old. My family's migration is part of a long tradition of people who came here to build a better future for themselves and those around them.
>
> (www.Rushanaraali.org 2010)

Poverty and deprivation

However, in the early 1980s the council owned approximately 80 per cent of the housing, and there were high levels of unemployment. The borough scored highly on the Jarman Underprivileged Area Score, a measure indicative of a higher demand for primary health care, and including overcrowding, numbers of children under 5, single-parent households and recent immigration. More recent measures have included the local environment and have taken account of physical and mental health, and children's educational attainment. Despite dramatic improvements in housing and increased new building, results from the 2001 Census showed persistent overcrowding with nearly 30 per cent of households affected, and a high proportion (38 per cent) of benefit claimants, so that the borough still ranks third in the Indices of Deprivation across the whole country (Office of National Statistics 2007). Very substantial improvements have occurred in educational attainment, and these are described fully in a later chapter.

Health: physical and mental

With high levels of deprivation inevitably there are also massive health inequalities, not only between the borough and the rest of the country, but also internal to the borough. Life expectancy varies across the borough by ten years. While it is the case that the Bangladeshi and the Afro-Carribean populations have significantly higher rates of heart disease and diabetes, poorer health and reduced life expectancy are found in those parts of the borough with the most overcrowding and the worst housing and environmental conditions. Local housing policies of the 1980s restricted rehousing across neighbourhoods, effectively creating white enclaves and minority ghettos, a situation which later housing policies have done much to improve.

The 2001 Census asked a new question concerning long-term illness and disability. This resulted in information indicating substantial differences in 'disability-free life expectancy' relating to social class and area type, such that

> those in disadvantaged circumstances not only experience shorter expectations of life but also shorter proportions of life expectancy free from a limiting long term illness or disability.
>
> (White and Edgar 2010)

In the borough, over one-third of *all* households have an adult with a long-term limiting illness and more than 10 per cent of all households have dependent children with no adult in employment (ONS 2004).

The primary care trust estimated that locally rates of emergency admissions for psychotic illnesses are three times higher than the national average (Yacub 2007). Suicide rates are high, though slowly decreasing, and there is a high incidence of depression, much of which remains undiagnosed and untreated.

Nationally it is estimated that two million children live with at least one parent who has a mental illness, and most of these adults will not be in work (SCIE 2008). However, there is a significant gap here in government statistics which is reflected at the local level and is a major obstacle to providing services for this group of highly vulnerable children.

The organisation of health and social care, adult and child services

> We live in an age of small government, in which responsibility for welfare now rests with a range of public, independent, and private organisations whose structural ties to wider society, state and democratic and political processes, are weak by comparison with the network of strong 'intermediate institutions' based in the workplace – trade unions, local government, community and professional organisations – that mediated relations between the state and civil society until they were swept away by the Thatcher revolution (Hutton 1996).
>
> (Cooper and Lousada 2005: 65)

The structure and organisation of local health and social services are a reflection of society's current priorities and relationship to the needs of its dependent members. Such priorities and relationships are a reaction to changing demography and needs, to developments in knowledge, to public or media reaction to events and, increasingly, to the demands of the market economy. New legislation arises as a result of such changes and may follow national inquiries when blame for an avoidable death is placed on failing services. It is then followed by national policy drivers in an attempt to ensure implementation, and accompanied by inspection and monitoring to ensure compliance.

Our public services, in health or social care, for adult or child, have developed separately through their history, and at the time of the project were becoming increasingly separate as we saw the growth of large corporate organisations with their own identities in the form of mental health trusts within the NHS, and children's trusts in the local authority.

In an attempt to show the distinct histories, functions and priorities of these organisations, and in order also to convey the pace of change over the past twenty years spanning the turn of the century, we shall describe their development along separate paths, in response to changes in the way society conceives of its responsibilities towards the mentally ill and towards children in need.

Mental health services

In the latter part of the nineteenth century the mentally ill were isolated in asylums, large, self-contained institutions for the containment of madness, and of those deemed unfit or unable as a result of 'mental deficiency' to take their place in society. They existed at first in parallel with the Poor Law system and in many cases occupied buildings which had previously been workhouses. In 1914 there were over 350,000 beds in asylums across the country but by 1954 this number had already halved, with emerging concern about the effect on the individual of long-term institutional care, fostering dependence. The advent of drugs which could control the symptoms of psychosis, notably chlorpromazine in the early 1950s, increased the pace of change as more patients could be managed on medication in their own homes. The Mental Health Act of 1959 removed the practice of 'committal' for an unlimited period and detailed the circumstances under which patients could be formally admitted and detained in hospital against their will. It placed greater emphasis on outpatient and community-based provision of services. Enoch Powell's (the then Minister of Health) speech of 1960 condemned asylums as 'doomed institutions' and laid a foundation for some inpatient services to be located in district general hospitals. By 1997 to 1998 only 45,878 beds remained, and most of the old institutions had closed (Bartlett and Sandland 2007). These same authors are unequivocal in their view that this shift in policy in the care of the mentally ill was determined by cost rather than by therapeutic aims, and that it predated the introduction of the new medications (Bartlett and Sandland 2007). Powell's paper also separated the two aspects of care, the personal and social care from the medical, which had previously been regarded as intertwined. This change was implemented in due course with the NHS and Community Care Act of 1990.

A worrying number of homicides by severely mentally ill patients no longer detained in a safe environment (for example, the murder in 1992 of Jonathan Zito by Christopher Clunis, known to have been suffering from paranoid schizophrenia) contributed to awareness of the failings of the system of mental health care in the community (Coid 1994). The NHS and Community Care Act of 1990 had designated local authorities responsible for the non-medical care of patients who needed long-term provision. It coordinated a complex web of services, legislation and guidance, and attempted to make community mental health teams (CMHTs) the gateway to secondary health services. The Care Programme Approach (1990) identified CMHT staff, nurses or social workers as 'care coordinators' responsible for putting together a package of services for community-based care. Referral for admission or services was to be through the CMHT. The vignette below suggests something of what has been lost in this new arrangement, and provides a different perspective of the old asylum.

> 'M' was referred by her GP to the consultant psychotherapist. The GP knew his patient well and felt she would benefit from some 'talking therapy' to help her with fears and obsessive thoughts which stemmed from childhood traumas. She was seen by a psychotherapist in the old Victorian building which was then still the psychiatric hospital. Although two family members had been inpatients there in the past, she was reassured rather than discomfited by this. It seems she felt the institution, rather than stigmatising her, contained her own anxieties about breakdown. M's fear of becoming 'mad' was very powerful, but she was able to make good use of the psycho-therapy and showed improvement in her ability to work and in her family relationships.

Had 'M' been referred to the CMHT, as policy guidance of the time suggested, she might have been offered a social intervention such as a befriending group, as she would not have met the criteria of 'severe and enduring mental illness'. Her underlying state of terror and feelings of persecution and guilt would not have been heard, leaving breakdown more likely.

The need for a safe place where severe disturbance can be contained is clearly felt by Children's Services staff and other professionals outside mental health services who may fail to appreciate the 'gatekeeping' and managerial function of the CMHT, instead expecting that a clearly unwell parent will be removed urgently to hospital care, so that children may remain safely in their own home.

In the ten years following the Part 8 Review described in Chapter 1 of this volume, there have been continuous developments in adult mental health services, including a revised Code of Practice for the 1983 Mental Health Act, a new Mental Capacity Act (2007) which introduced Community Treatment Orders, and several national policy initiatives, including the National Service Framework (1999).

Locally, mental health service provision has seen massive changes since 1984. In 2000 a new mental health trust was created covering four neighbouring local authorities whose primary care trusts were responsible for the commissioning of mental health services. In the borough in which CHAMP was established, developments included a new inpatient mental health unit of ninety-six beds, four CMHTs (staffed by psychologists and occupational therapists as well as consultant psychiatrists, mental health nurses and social workers), an assertive outreach team, a community rehabilitation team, a personality disorder service, and a home treatment team. Forensic services are provided across the whole trust, as is specialist inpatient provision for mothers and babies. Outpatient services include psychology, psychotherapy, short-term crisis work and a perinatal mental health service. Child and adolescent outpatient services are provided locally with a trust-wide inpatient unit in a neighbouring borough.

By 2009 the rapid developments over the relatively short life of the enlarged trust had put in place a modern, comprehensive mental health service, with good governance, extensive user involvement and strong academic links, to the benefit of patients and staff.

A difficult area for the mental health trust has been the recruitment of staff from the ethnic minorities in the local population, leading to barriers of language and cultural understanding. Bangladeshi residents are over-represented among service users in relation to the population, yet there continue to be few staff who share the same language or cultural background. Those staff who find themselves as the sole representative of another culture within a team may experience considerable isolation. It is not unusual in adult mental health services to encounter families where violence against women and children continues to be seen as a norm, or where young women have been sent to the UK by their relatives to marry and therefore care for a man who has a serious mental illness. Such young women, without support from parents and friends, without spoken English, are highly vulnerable to becoming unwell themselves under the strain of caring for their husbands and children (see Chapter 1). For a team, such experiences arouse strong feelings, and a lone ethnic minority worker may find him- or herself expected to account for such practices, leading to inevitable tensions within the team.

In parallel with changes in the organisation within the NHS, there have been changes in the local authority affecting the provision of mental health social work and social care services. These were placed historically in an adult department, originally under a director of social services, but since 2008 under its own director responsible directly to the chief executive of the council. Relations between the trust and the local authority for the provision of social work services have been subject to change and uncertainty, contributing to confusion about the role and lines of accountability.

Children's services

As in the care of the mentally ill, developments in the state's relationship with children in need have come about only slowly with changes in society. Under the nineteenth-century Poor Laws communities had responsibilities towards orphaned or abandoned children whose parents were unwilling or unable to provide for them, but it was not until the 1948 Children Act of the postwar Labour government that these duties were formally transferred to all local authorities, who were required to assist children in need of help, as well as take over their care when necessary. This legislation led to the creation of the specialist children's departments and formed the basis for child care practice for the next forty years.

One of the tensions was the sanctity of family life and the still central role of the father in society. In 'The Suspicions of Mr Whicher', based on a true story from 1860, a 3-year-old child is brutally murdered, and in the subsequent investigation the father of the family is able to argue for the privacy of his family life, and effectively prevent the police from entering his home, collecting evidence or interviewing family members, the only possible suspects (Summerscale 2009). The new and somewhat despised profession of detective is further reviled by the public, whose strong Victorian family values ensure that sympathies increasingly come to lie with the family and its right to privacy. Elements of this story will be familiar to social workers in child protection today!

It was not until the 1970s that changes in legislation (Guardianship Act 1973, Divorce Reform Act 1969, and the Matrimonial Causes Act 1973) meant that the primacy of the father's position in relation to children was altered. The mother was for the first time given the same rights in relation to her children as the father, and society could be said to approach a system where a father's rights no longer had primacy (Bedingfield 1998).

The debate continued between parental rights and any rights a child might have, until with the 1989 Children Act Parliament finally passed a child-centred law in which 'the welfare of the child is paramount in almost every decision a court makes regarding the care and upbringing of that child' (Bedingfield 1998: 9).

It is crucial to note that this 'welfare principle' applies in the case of a child subject to legal proceedings, as 'to some it comes as a surprise to realise that Section 1 (1) CA89 applies only to the courts, not to local authorities or other agencies' (Davis 2009: 34).

Less experienced childcare social workers may be heard to assert in inter-professional meetings 'the child's needs are paramount', rather than to make clear their own duties toward a child. They thus act as if health professionals have no priorities of their own and without recognising that they are not empowered to dictate other professionals' or agencies' actions. This stance may lead well-informed psychiatrists, under a duty of care to a patient who may be dangerous or suicidal, to limit their cooperation in providing reports or information only to cases which are before the court. Such exchanges, based on flawed understandings of the law, can lead to frustration, distrust and impasse between childcare staff and psychiatrists.

The 1989 Act was a response to the 1988 report by Baroness Butler-Sloss of the Cleveland Inquiry, in which she drew attention to the complexity of the childcare system, and to a child's right to be heard and to be a party to proceedings (Butler-Sloss 1988). She insisted that a child is not an object, but has views and feelings of his or her own, which must be listened to and taken into account. The Act also altered the basis for the local authority's relation to the parents of children in its care and made working in partnership with parents a requirement under law.

As in mental health services there have continued to be high-profile inquiries into the deaths of children, which have brought further changes, most notably the Victoria Climbié Inquiry which led to the 2004 Children Act (Laming 2003). This introduced a statutory requirement for services to share information and to cooperate, making specific reference to adult mental health services. The most recent edition of *Working Together* provides guidance about parental mental health and child welfare (DfES and DoH 2006).

The major policy driver following these legislative changes, *Every Child Matters*, sought to ensure that the 1989 Act was fully implemented. It defined five goals for children which were to be a focus for all local authorities' children's plans. These related both to children's rights, as expressed in the European convention, to be safe from harm, and to their developmental needs, physical, social and educational; that is, to 'be healthy', to 'enjoy and achieve', and to be involved in decision making, 'make a positive contribution', and to be helped to find further education or into employment, 'to achieve economic independence' (DfES 2004).

Locally in the period between 1998 and 2006, the council, following national trends, reorganised its services from a children and families division in a generic Department of Social Services, to a Children's Trust which included 'Children's Social Care' and Education, under a single director. This major reorganisation of services was accompanied by the introduction of the much-criticised Integrated Children's System, a computerised recording and performance management tool, and by a move to centralised offices, relinquishing the older locality-based and more accessible premises.

The separation of adult and child departments which was a perhaps 'unintended consequence' of these changes was a nationwide development not universally welcomed and has increased some of the problems at the interface between adult and child services. The 'Think Family' initiative, an attempt at ensuring cooperation between these now completely separate bodies with their own identities, represented a belated recognition of the current social reality of family life (Social Exclusion Unit 2008).

Organisational stability or constant change? The impact on staff

While such developments in the provision of services are to be welcomed, Reder *et al*. pointed to organisational change and instability as a significant factor in contributing to the deaths of children as a result of abuse (Reder and Duncan 1999; Reder *et al*. 1993). Cooper and Dartington describe a resulting condition of 'change fatigue' but comment that:

> If the traditional organisational structures, with uncluttered lines of authority and clear boundaries, continue to exist in our minds as knowable entities this

is because they are in part historical containers of values and professional identity. In this sense they are the country we were born and brought up in, from which we are now living in exile. As such they are a powerful influence on us, a source of creative strength in facing an uncertain future, but also of nostalgia and resistance to current realities.

(Cooper and Dartington 2004: 142)

The social context in which health, social care and education professionals work in the borough has always been one of struggle and change, of resources which inevitably fail to match the depth of need, and with a backdrop of loss and trauma. The significant difficulties experienced by families make heavy and unremitting demands on those in public services, which are further increased by a political and organisational climate of constant change. Despite the considerable number of highly committed staff members who have worked there for long periods of time, many of whom remain in 'front-line' or middle management positions, this period of continuous change and upheaval has been accompanied by a high level of staff turnover.

There are a large number of voluntary sector agencies in the borough with an exciting range of provision but their funding and future are invariably short term and insecure. Among all staff, whether in the statutory or voluntary sectors, there is a high degree of commitment and energy, which brings with it valued working relationships that are nevertheless vulnerable to abrupt endings, as services are cut, teams restructured or people simply move on in an effort to replenish themselves. Much effort has been put into the recruitment and retention of qualified and experienced staff. The local authority in particular has recruited from the local community and made professional training available to staff members from different ethnic backgrounds, who have then been able to bridge the cultural, religious and race differences which might otherwise become a source of constant frustration and increasing tensions.

In the course of the restructuring, Children's Social Care gained top 'star' status in government performance ratings at the time. This was important in lifting morale, and facilitating staff recruitment and retention. The joint effort by staff and management which went into achieving this status brought a sense of cohesion, of being part of a robust and committed organisation. This is in contrast with the 'organisational malaise' and 'dysfunctional departments' which Lord Laming criticised so heavily in his report concluding the Victoria Climbié Inquiry (Laming 2003). A similar rating was achieved in adult services, but sometime later, and this may have created an uneven situation in which one section was seen as performing well, while the other could be seen as performing badly, a situation which allows blaming and scapegoating processes to dominate working relations between the two departments. Hinshelwood describes this process as a particular feature of agencies working with mental illness (and one could include personality disorder and substance abuse which form much of the workload of children's services) where

One agency can project the despair and hopelessness into another team within the community services. Different teams then get into the same mutual denigration of each other. . . . Then the service itself becomes fragmented.

(Hinshelwood 1998: 22)

Services become prey to projective processes in which feelings of weakness, incompetence and failure are disowned and lodged in the other partner.

For many nurses the move from hospital ward to community meant a loss of a work environment, of team work with colleagues and feelings of being deskilled, as the new community setting required a different approach. For social workers who had traditionally operated either in single agency teams or in the multi-disciplinary context of the hospital, and who now became part of integrated teams alongside nursing staff with very different functions, the result was a loss of important supervisory relationships, of links across adult and child specialities, and of shared specialist experience and knowledge. Some social workers reported feeling stigmatised by their choice of a specialism in mental health and isolated from their local authority social work colleagues. Integration of these social work and nursing teams into fully functioning community mental health teams including psychiatrists and psychologists was a slow process that was only completed in the mid-2000s.

In this climate of loss of important support networks and relationships the impact upon staff has often been one of constant bombardment bringing new organisational requirements, new policy initiatives, and uncertainty over their contractual status and lines of accountability. It is against this background that mental health staff in particular have been expected to take on what are perceived to be additional responsibilities for children, a task which many experienced as impossible. Woodhouse and Pengelly comment that 'the more threatening the anxiety, the more rigid the defences and the greater the need for a containing environment in which to confront and understand the anxieties and modify the defences' (Woodhouse and Pengelly 1991: 201).

Legislative changes have brought greater complexity, with the human rights of users of mental health services seen to be competing with the rights of the child. Yet

Parenthood is a valued social role. People with mental illness have the same aspirations for parenthood and face the same challenges associated with this role as do other community members.

(McLean *et al.* 2004: 333)

There have been national initiatives to inform professionals in the task of supporting families affected by parental mental illness. In 1998 the Department of Health produced a document *Crossing Bridges* (Mayes *et al.* 1998) which looked not only at the impact upon children of parental mental illness, but also at the needs of parents with mental illness and their children, as part of an interactional system in which parents' health may be additionally affected. The matter was directly addressed by a report from the Royal College of Psychiatrists, *Patients as Parents* (2002), which outlined the risks, and ways in which a psychiatrist might contribute to children's and parents' well-being. Organisations such as SCIE, Barnardo's, the Social Exclusion Unit, the National Children's Bureau and the Princess Royal Trust for Carers have each highlighted the needs and wishes of children and their parents, and importantly have given young people a voice. Others have written about the interface between services and addressed this from a helpful systemic perspective (Reder *et al.* 2000; Daniel and Chin 2010).

However, SCIE, in its report *Think Child, Think Parents, Think Family*, concludes that:

> The context for change is complex. This area of work cuts across a number of sectors and requires a multi-disciplinary response if outcomes for this group of children and families are to be improved. Working in both adult mental health and children's social care services is particularly difficult. Both areas are highly emotive, they attract high levels of media attention and criticism and staff can be wary of stepping outside professional boundaries. Breaking down these professional boundaries is as important as addressing the stigma that exists in accessing services for parents and children.
>
> (SCIE 2009: 14)

We have to recognise that we now live and work in a changed world, the 'networked world' described by Cooper and Dartington (2004). It is a world which demands different skills and different forms of working relationships, and creates different tensions and anxieties. The work described in Part II of this book may be seen as a collaborative effort to gather up the fragments of these old structures, like the broken shards of an old but valued pot, in order to experience again its wholeness and capacity to contain; to build new connections in new roles, while maintaining the link to our history.

References

Ali, R. (2010) *About Me*. Online HTTP: http://www.rushanaraali.org/index.php?id=25 (accessed 12 March 2012).

Bartlett, P. and Sandland, R. (3rd edn 2007) *Mental Health Law: Policy and Practice*, Oxford: Oxford University Press.

Bedingfield, D. (1998) The child in need: Children, the state, and the law. *Family Law*, Bristol: Jordan Publishing.

Butler-Sloss, E. (1988) *Report of the Inquiry into Child Abuse in Cleveland 1988*, London: HMSO.

Coid, J.W. (1994) The Christopher Clunis enquiry. *Psychiatric Bulletin* 18: 449–452. Royal College of Psychiatrists. Available HTTP: < http://www.pb.rcpsych.org> (accessed 6 November 2010).

Cooper, A. and Dartington, T. (2004) The vanishing organisation; Organisational containment in a networked world. In Huffington, C., Armstrong, D., Halton, W., Hoyle, L. and Pooley, J. (eds) *Working Below the Surface; The Emotional Life of Contemporary*

Organisations, London: Karnac. Available HTTP: http://www.karnacbooks.com/ isbn/ 9781855752948, reprinted with kind permission of Karnac Books (accessed 6 November 2010).

Cooper, A. and Lousada, J. (2005) *Borderline Welfare; Feeling and Fear of Feeling in Modern Welfare,* London: Karnac. Available HTTP: http://www.karnacbooks.com/ isbn/9781855759053, reprinted with kind permission of Karnac Books (accessed 6 November 2010).

Daniel, G. and Chin, J. (2010) Engaging with agency cultures in parental mental illness training. *Context 108*: 47–50, Association for Family Therapy, AFT Publishing.

Davis, L. (2009) *The Social Worker's Guide to Children and Family Law,* London: Jessica Kingsley.

Department for Education and Skills (2004) *Every Child Matters: Change for Children*, Norwich: The Stationery Office. Available HTTP: http://www.education.gov.uk/ publications/standard/publicationdetail/page1/DfES/1081/2004 (accessed 12 March 2012).

Department for Education and Skills and Department of Health (2006) *Working Together to Safeguard Children,* London: The Stationery Office.

Department of Health (1990) *Care Programme Approach*, Circular HC(90)23/LASSL (90)11, London: HMSO.

Department of Health (1999) *National Service Framework for Mental Health: Modern Standards and Service Models*, London: HMSO. Available HTTP: http://www. dh.gov.uk/en/Publicationsandstatistics/Publications/PublicationsPolicyAndGuidance/D H_4009598 (accessed 12 March 2012).

Hinshelwood, R. (1998) Creatures of each other. In Foster, A. and Zagier Roberts, V. (eds) *Managing Mental Health in the Community: Chaos and Containment,* London and New York: Routledge.

Hutton, W. (1996) *The State We're In,* London: Vintage.

Laming, H. (2003) *The Victoria Climbié Inquiry*, Norwich: TSO. Available HTTP: http://www.dh.gov.uk/prod_consum_dh/groups/dh_digitalassets/documents/digitalasset/ dh_110711.pdf (accessed 12 March 2012).

Mayes, K., Diggins, M. and Falkov, A. (eds) (1998) *Crossing Bridges: Training Resources for Working with Mentally Ill Patients and their Children – Reader for Managers, Practitioners and Trainers*, Brighton: Pavilion Publishing.

McLean, D., Hearle, J. and McGrath, J. (2004) Are services for families with a mentally ill parent adequate? In Gopfert, M., Webster, J. and Seeman, M.V. (eds) *Parental Psychiatric Disorder: Distressed Parents and their Families,* Cambridge: Cambridge University Press.

National Health Service and Community Care Act (1990) London: HMSO.

Office of National Statistics (July 2004) *Census 2001 Key Statistics. Urban Area Summary Results for Local Authorities* (Table KS21), London: The Stationery Office.

Office of National Statistics (January 2007) *Indices of Deprivation and Neighbourhood Statistics: Tower Hamlets*, Norwich: The Stationery Office.

Reder, P. and Duncan, S. (1999) *Lost Innocents: A Follow-up Study of Fatal Child Abuse,* London: Routledge.

Reder, P., Duncan, S. and Gray, M. (1993) *Beyond Blame: Child Abuse Tragedies Revisited*, London and New York: Routledge.

Reder, P., McClure, M., and Jolley, A. (2000) *Family Matters: Interfaces Between Child and Adult Mental Health,* London: Routledge.

Royal College of Psychiatrists (2002) *Patients as Parents: Addressing the Needs, Including the Safety, of Children whose Parents have Mental Illness,* Council Report 105, London: RCP.

Social Care Institute for Excellence (2008) *Research Briefing 23: Stress and Resilience Factors in Parents with Mental Health Problems and their Children,* London: SCIE. HTTP: http://www.scie.org.uk/publications/briefings/briefing23 (accessed 12 March 2012).

Social Care Institute for Excellence (2009) *Think Child, Think Parents, Think Family: A Guide to Parental Mental Health and Child Welfare,* London: SCIE. HTTP: http://www.scie.org.uk/publications/guides/guide30 (accessed 12 March 2012).

Social Exclusion Unit, Office of the Deputy Prime Minister (2008) *Reaching Out: Think Family,* London: Cabinet Office.

Summerscale, K. (2009) *The Suspicions of Mr Whicher,* London: Bloomsbury.

White, C. and Edgar, G. (2010) Inequalities in disability free life expectancy by social class and area type: England 2001–03. *Health Statistics Quarterly* 45 (Spring), Crown copyright: Office of National Statistics.

Widgery, D. (1991) *Some Lives! A GP's East End.* London: Sinclair-Stevenson.

Woodhouse, D. and Pengelly, P. (1991) *Anxiety and the Dynamics of Collaboration,* Aberdeen: Aberdeen University Press.

Yaccub, E. (2007) *Tower Hamlets Adult Mental Health Needs Assessment 2007,* Tower Hamlets Primary Care Trust. HTTP: http://www.towerhamlets.nhs.uk/publications/ ?EntryId4=2788 (accessed 12 March 2012).

Young, M. (1957) *Family and Kinship in East London,* London: Routledge & Kegan Paul.

Part II

The Children and Adult Mental Health Project (CHAMP) 2002–2012

The chapters in Part II describe the project and its development from just one new appointment, the 'interface development officer' (later renamed the 'coordinator for children in families with mental illness'), whose understanding and practice in her role is portrayed in Chapter 6, to the creation of a small team of parental mental health specialist workers located in adult mental health teams.

That this development took several years – the secondment of the teacher happened in late 2008 – could be attributed in part to problems in funding and in part to the nature of organisations. The post of coordinator was agreed by the local authority in response to the findings of a local Part 8 Review following the death of a child (see Chapter 1). This happily coincided with the recently formed group of professionals with a shared interest in the needs of children of parents with significant mental health problems. However, there was little evidence at the time that the authority might have plans for further development in this area of work, although this soon became central in the thinking of the project group. Thus the initiative for development, while in tune with the national agenda for early intervention and identification of vulnerable children, came from a group of clinicians, front-line staff and middle managers, rather than from senior management. The task then was to 'manage up', that is, to ensure that those making decisions about funding were aware of the risks, and of the nature and extent of the difficulties faced by families and by the teams working with them. This was a new experience for those involved and required much learning.

Local authority funding plans and decisions involve a complex process of budget cycles, prioritising and elected council members' decision making. Budget cycles are different for different parts of the organisation. This had the effect that while the adult social care senior management team might agree to prioritise our proposal for their budget in one year, the children's social care management team, operating to a different timetable, might not come to the same decision at the same time, and a decision would be deferred until the following year, when other priorities would have arisen in the adult services, creating a 'see-saw' effect. While each agency supported the initiative, in practice there was no mechanism to bring them together to overcome this obstacle and make change happen.

Matters were simpler when just one agency could act singly. This occurred with the first additional post to be created, that of the perinatal mental health worker, which is described by child psychotherapist Sandra Nathanson in Chapter 7. The coordinator became aware at an early stage of a number of infants put at risk because a parent's – usually a mother's – mental health needs were not recognised or there was a failure of communication across the children's and adults' services. One such example involved a young woman who had been referred to a CMHT from Accident and Emergency, having taken an overdose. As this was a first incident, the referral was not prioritised and remained in a file awaiting allocation for several weeks. What had not registered in the minds of the receiving team was that this woman had, at the time of referral, a six-week-old baby. This, among other examples, brought unacceptable anxiety in the coordinator and her senior, which was both passed up the management hierarchy and worked into a convincing proposal. Together with effective arguments for early interventions in such situations, which are clearly demonstrated in Sandra Nathanson's detailed work, this strategy led to funding being found for the perinatal post.

Funding for children's specialists in the CMHTs however remained a source of constant frustration and lack of progress. It is in this situation that external seed funding can be critical in giving new initiatives and projects an opportunity to demonstrate both need and effectiveness. Fortuitously, this was found in 2006, and in Chapter 8 Rosemary Loshak begins with an account of the expectations of the external funders, and of the thinking behind the way in which the pilot children's specialist post with its supervision and management structures was set up. It goes on to show how the appointee took up this new role, working to engage with the CMHT, and bringing his own particular skills from his voluntary sector background.

These posts have two key aspects to the role. One is the direct work with children and families which may take many forms, and the other is the cross-agency work facilitating communication between adults' and children's services and developing relationships between them which can be sustained. In both aspects there are many pitfalls to be avoided or managed. Problems of over-identification with one or other service's point of view are, among others, highlighted in Chapter 9 by Philip Messent and Noah Solarin, who bring systemic thinking to a complex piece of work with a case which was a source of conflict between the two services who had taken up polarised positions.

The project had had strong links with education services from its earliest days, as among child mental health services staff contact with schools is frequent. However, this is not the case among adult mental health staff for whom schools are part of a child's world and may be thought of as having little relevance to their clients' health and well-being. The final chapter in Part II, written by two educationalists, challenges this view. Peggy Gosling's contribution shows the forward thinking among senior education staff behind the idea that parental mental health is something that schools should know more about, and it describes the development of this idea into a proposal to create a specialist post linking education and adult mental health. Unfortunately, Peggy Gosling's retirement occurred before funding became available, leading to some loss of her expertise when the teacher's secondment was eventually agreed. However, at the time of writing, this development was unique in the country in establishing a formal link between specialist adult mental health and social care services on the one hand, and the universal services provided by schools, the context in which children and young people spend the majority of their waking lives, on the other.

Louise Gallagher, the specialist teacher seconded from the Behaviour Support Team, brings her varied life and extensive teaching experience to bear upon the challenge of this new role. She vividly describes the work over nearly three years, using case examples to demonstrate the key themes that arose both with the young people and their families and in building and sustaining effective multi-agency support, with the challenges, frustrations and rewards this has brought. She remains conscious of the boundaries of her own role as teacher, and thus avoids the danger of taking on responsibilities which belong to others. In this way she managed to do just

> [w]hat is necessary and sufficient, to get the ball rolling, and keep it rolling until change can be sustained independently. Otherwise, programmes are unfocused, ad hoc, get bypassed, agreements and commitments get forgotten, participants become frustrated, and again these failed programmes are blamed on children.
>
> (Gosling 2001)

This has been ground-breaking work from which much can be learned about setting up such a service, and managing the inevitable difficulties. The determination of each of the authors to make a difference to vulnerable children through an innovative but demanding new project stands out.

Reference

Gosling, P. (2001) Partnership for Change: Effective Practice in Behaviour Support. PhD Dissertation, London: Institute of Education.

6 Making a difference
The role of the coordinator

Rosemary Loshak

'What can one person do?' Response of a child care team manager to the appointment of the coordinator (2002).

In the late 1990s and before the Part 8 Review described in Chapter 1, there already existed a climate for change in the borough, reflecting increasing national awareness. Family Action, then the Family Welfare Association, had launched a 'Building Bridges' project to support families with mental illness, and had done much to raise awareness both nationally and locally (see Chapter 11); in 1996 senior colleagues in mental health and childcare organised a conference in the borough about parental mental illness and its impact on children which was well received by staff, who were clearly aware of the gaps; and some 'cross-over' training by an external trainer had been commissioned. However, no one senior manager or clinician had sufficient capacity in their existing workload to take these necessary developments forward.

CAMHS sought to maintain long-established working links with adult psychiatry, now disrupted by the change to community teams, by initiating links between CAMHS and the acute adult admissions ward, and also with the co-located community mental health team. This arrangement did not lead to increased referrals to CAMHS of children known to the adult services. Cardwell and Britten (2002) have described how in setting up the Parkside Parental Mental Health Service their initial interventions and approaches did not result in the expected referrals of children. They report that naming the lack of success in previous collaborative efforts was an important step in thinking about a joint service which would do things differently and 'avoiding a familiar trap of focussing on who must change' (Anderson-Wallace *et al.* 2000 quoted in Cardwell and Britten 2002).

However, the relationships formed in these two links led to the emergence of the small group of professionals identified in Chapter 1. Tasked initially with gathering data on numbers of children affected by parental mental illness and drawing up a protocol for joint working following the Part 8 Review, this group became the steering group behind the coordinator post and subsequent developments. Through the necessary work to produce a protocol, group members, including team managers from adult and child services, a voluntary sector project manager, an adult psychiatrist and myself, discovered shared concerns about children, but that they spoke different languages, and knew little about the services that each other's teams provided or how they were organised. Curiosity was aroused and dialogues began to take place as all learned more. We identified a starting figure of 200 children of parents known to the community mental health teams, a number which was subsequently to treble. As early as 1999 the group asked itself: 'Are we looking forward to a time when we have specialist childcare workers in the community mental health teams?'

Setting up the coordinator role

Briefly, this group was formally linked into the management structure of the local authority, reporting to a joint divisional meeting which then included both adult and childcare divisions. This promising start came to an abrupt halt when adults' and children's services became divided both nationally and locally, and thereafter a satisfactory jointly managed service structure proved more difficult to achieve.

A decision about where the post of coordinator for children in families with parental mental illness might most appropriately be located and managed was made on the strength of existing relationships with adult social care and staff of the mental health trust. The strong evidence that such families do not easily seek help from CAMHS partly due to a fear of labelling their children as mentally ill, and that their dominant fear is that their children will be removed from their care by child protection services, led to a decision that the post would be best located in adult mental health services (Cowling 2004). The mental health lead's knowledge of adult mental health structures enabled the newly appointed coordinator to become quickly familiar with these, and was invaluable in developing trust and confidence among staff. The new post was advertised nationally and the internal CAMHS social worker was appointed. Her eighteen years of experience in the borough meant that she was well known to staff and across professional networks, and was able to build on a foundation of trusted relationships. The brief for the new post was to facilitate joint working across services, and it included an important development role. While funded by children's services budgets it offered a direct service to adult mental health teams as well as working across services to facilitate joint working. A spirit of enquiry and a readiness to learn about the other service were essential.

Work started with two initiatives. Learning from the experience of the Parkside team we made a programme of visits to community mental health teams (CMHTs), to childcare teams, and to their team managers, to explore their expectations of the new role. We then launched the service through a series of events to introduce the new joint working protocol. These brought the adult mental health and childcare teams based in the same localities together in pairs, in order for them to meet face-to-face and get to know each other free from the pressures of a case in crisis.

It is important to recognise that at this stage there existed a degree of unevenness between the services: while the 'children and families' function within the local authority already included a large number of specialist teams in addition to the front-line assessment teams, in mental health such developments were yet to take place, and specialist provision was limited. The breadth of the gap between children and families and mental health services was indicated by the social workers in the mental health teams who reported feeling cut off organisationally from former social work colleagues in childcare teams. Despite sharing the same employer (the local authority), they felt isolated and marginalised, as if stigmatised by their work with the mentally ill. We hoped that joint informal events might begin to repair this split.

Team responses

Moving from team to team across these two services, the coordinator was able to identify shared concerns from each about the lack of resources and budget limitations. Such comments about the lack of external resources are an essential aspect of staff members' role in identifying unmet need but can also function as a displacement of greater anxieties about exploring the unknown, and about their capacity to make full use of their internal resources. Mental health staff members repeatedly told us that they had little knowledge of what might be available to support children, of how to access such support, or how to talk to children about their parent's illness, while many childcare workers noted their ignorance of mental health provision, of how to talk to someone who is mentally ill, and their fears. We responded concretely to the expressed need for information while keeping in mind the underlying anxieties.

While some mental health staff responded directly to my tentative enquiries about children on their caseload – 'don't make me more anxious than I am already, I have enough' – others spoke honestly of their *fear* of engaging with children. Many concerns reflected real worries about the extent to which they felt able to help particular client groups, for example, adolescents, or how to assist both carers and families, as well as service users. A frequently expressed concern was that the rights of children and the statutory duties to safeguard them were in conflict with their duty of care and their responsibilities under human rights legislation towards their adult patients. This view of a world in potential conflict may be understood as a reflection of their clients' fears of separation and perception of themselves as vulnerable to attack or persecution. It was important for the coordinator to acknowledge the complexities of the task while also demonstrating how early low-level interventions might forestall problems.

As she crossed service boundaries it seemed that the coordinator 'carried not merely information, but the possibility of understanding and knowledge of the other. I am a "go-between", bridging the culture gap between these services and helping them slowly establish more direct links themselves' (Loshak 2007).

Both groups of teams were well aware of the communication problems between their services, which they attributed very concretely to their separate locations and buildings. Communication was felt to be much easier where teams found themselves housed in the same building. They recognised that as 'children and families' and as mental health workers they only met at points of crisis in their clients' lives and deplored what was felt to be a lack of option to consult the other team, that each had to 'raise the tariff' with the other service in order to ensure a referral would lead to action.

Anxiety could at times be much more split off, as became evident in the apparent *absence of concern* among mental health staff who told me that 'we deal with the mentally ill adult' or that 'there are no concerns about the children'. This suggested a more rigid defence system and a denial of reality, echoing the responses of their service users.

> On one occasion my gentle questions after such a reply to my having enquired 'how are the children?' led to the discovery that two under-five children were not registered with a GP and a 6-year-old was not enrolled in school.

Staff may readily become identified with their clients' feelings of hopelessness in relation to their responsibilities as parents and their difficulties in carrying out these responsibilities. Staff members might also be aware that parents did not always want them to know about these things, and were fearful of their communicating with children's and families' services.

In the course of these early encounters the fears that underlie such responses became very evident.

- The fear of breakdown – a fear belonging to the adult but felt powerfully by the mental health worker and the organisation. It is the fear of madness and its stigma, as described by Hinshelwood: 'It is the fear of something going quickly out of control. This may be experienced as either madness or violence, a mind going out of control' (Hinshelwood 1998: 20). It implies possible separation from family, children, home and community. This fear could be displaced onto any children and family professionals who could be seen as having a potential for doing harm, destabilising a patient by raising difficult problems. Talking could be seen as dangerous.
- The fear of losing contact with vulnerable patients who may harm themselves or others. The psychotic defence of splitting the external world into good and bad brings risks that the precarious engagement between staff and the mentally ill adult can without warning suddenly be fractured as the professional is experienced as a persecutor or betrayer.
- The fear of children! This might be better expressed as a real anxiety about talking to children and parents *together* about the illness. Bailey describes the risks in work with a bipolar mother and her child when the child becomes able to tell his mother what her illness feels like to him (Bailey 2010). Yet it is also a fear of the hope, the liveliness and the unexpected that children contribute. It is an expression of guilt and self-blame of the destructive and despairing tendencies inherent in mental illness, and is sometimes framed as a worry that children will inevitably become mentally ill themselves.

The way in which such underlying fears as well as feelings of distress, and despair at the inability to make things right, can interfere with communication between teams and thinking together is demonstrated in the following example.

I arrived at a CMHT one afternoon in the midst of a battle. The team was angry because the children and families team were going to court the following day about one of their service users to ask for an interim care order in relation to her baby. Although the two teams had worked closely together throughout this woman's pregnancy and the first few weeks after the baby's birth, they were now refusing to exchange court reports, accusing each other of high-handedness, and not cooperating.[1] With the help of the team manager I brought the two workers and their managers together and asked them to tell me what had happened so far. I resisted being drawn into their complaints or taking sides, but simply listened. I found myself reminded of my own early days in child care and the unbearable feelings aroused by having to remove an infant from its mother. I spoke about the painful but necessary decision that now had to be made and acknowledged a shared guilt that we had not been able to support this woman better with her baby. My comment seemed to help the workers be in touch with the pain of this separation, rather than to get rid of, or project, it by blaming their colleagues; they began to look at and speak to each other. Suddenly the atmosphere had changed and plans were being made about how to manage the practicalities of the situation together in a way that ensured both infant and mother would be properly cared for, and contact between them sustained.

(Loshak 2007: 34)

In this case it was the ability to reflect on and make use of one's counter-transference in the meeting that enabled movement to occur. Hinshelwood and Skogstad have shown how helpful such self-reflectiveness can be in understanding otherwise incomprehensible responses in mental health settings (Hinshelwood and Skogstad 2000). During the early visits to teams, such responses were sometimes those of despair, or of rejection and abandonment as in the following examples.

At the first of what were to be regular visits to provide consultation to one team:

A nurse asked to speak to me. He told me about Mr A, who had attempted suicide but had failed and had been left with serious injuries and a disability. Mr A had young children who had been at home when this happened but their mother had subsequently left him and he now had no contact. I understood that this nurse was not asking me to advise him, to do or change anything, but simply to bear witness to the pain and despair felt by his patient and himself.

In another team:

I arrived and the room was almost empty. A group of three or four nurses were talking at one end of the large room. They barely acknowledged my presence. The senior said she had something to do now but would speak to me later in the afternoon. She left the room. I sat and waited and nothing happened. I felt abandoned and hopeless. I tried to find ways to occupy myself. Nobody spoke to me. At the end of the afternoon the senior returned and began closing the filing cabinets, apologising to me for having had no time. As I made my way home I passed a newsagent's stand with headlines about a recent murder. Only then I remembered that the murder had been by one of the clients of the team I had just been in. I understood my own 'forgetting', the deadness in the room that day, and my feelings, as those of a child who is being kept in the dark, neglected.

Without a theoretical framework for thinking about and understanding such feelings of despair and hopelessness, the work would surely become intolerable. At an early stage it became clear that in each of the teams one worker was on long-term sick leave. In the first six months of contact with the CMHTs, the services had one murder and three suicides; the impact of these events is felt across all the CMHTs and becomes part of a shared culture, rarely talked about. For an outsider developing a new role in the teams, to maintain a regular pattern of contact, to keep going back and thus to survive these onslaughts on one's emotions and thinking, is essential. A natural tendency is to wish to distance oneself. The pattern of fortnightly visits for each team, that is, two teams each week, felt as much as I could manage. Again Hinshelwood's comment is fitting: 'We tend to pull away from our patients. We reach for a kind of emotional distance from them, as if they are not properly human; or not properly alive' (Hinshelwood 1998: 20). It is likely that this is a not uncommon reaction among children's services staff members, whose contact with and previous experience of mental illness is often very limited. They should not be blamed or criticised for an understandable reluctance to become closely involved.

It was useful as coordinator to hold her old team in mind as a container for such feelings. Henri Rey suggested the concept of the institution as the 'brick mother', providing a secure base, and Urwin described a similar use of the concept in difficult outreach work from her CAMHS base with mothers and babies in a local housing project. Similarly the coordinator consciously kept in mind her years in the multidisciplinary CAMHS team as a container for the disturbance she was encountering (Urwin 2005: 130).

The first four years

The request from the mental health teams was for regular consultation with a focus on the needs of children. It was agreed that the coordinator would spend half a day with each of the four teams once a fortnight. A more limited service was available to children's teams due to the large number of teams involved, and the more established structures for supervision and managerial support. Front-line childcare teams were at this time subject to tightly maintained targets for their workload. Here, a different approach was offered, responding to individual requests for consultation on a case-by-case basis, highlighting cases where there were substantial concerns about children, facilitating relations with mental health staff, and slowly building inter-agency links.

Telephone consultation was also made available, and was taken up by a wide range of professionals from a variety of settings across the local authority, health, education and voluntary sector.

Initially many mental health team staff sought advice in completing referral forms, an apparently basic task but one that required them first to obtain agreement from the ill parent to make a referral which was below the threshold for child protection. This often created anxiety among staff members and could lead to inertia. However, one team specifically requested help as a team with this aspect. A workshop for the whole team was offered, led by a worker from the children's assessment team, together with the coordinator and a family therapist. Through practice in role plays they gained confidence in approaching a parent.

Mental health staff also needed to understand the way in which the children's and families' assessment teams were required to manage their high volume of referrals. First requests were logged as contacts unless clearly urgent. If a number of such 'contacts' indicating a threshold of concern may have been reached, the case would be allocated. This gatekeeping proved to be a major obstacle, as CMHT staff members, thinking they had made a referral, received no immediate response and concluded that nothing was happening, and that they had engaged in a pointless exercise. A blaming process – 'they never answer the phone', 'they don't do anything' – could be quick to follow. This response, based on a failure to grasp the very high workload coming into children's services, is common to many other professions, but the lack of understanding and communication among social care staff is remarkable. It suggests systems at breaking point where individuals under pressure are no longer able to recognise and take into consideration the point of view of the other, as described by Halton (2004).

Mental health staff, used to filling in forms detailing the problems faced by their adult service user, now learned to frame their referrals in terms of the child's needs, and to be clear about possible risk or harm. With this they needed help in identifying children's developmental needs.

As their trust in a new way of working grew, and when they were unsure about which service might best help a family, mental health staff asked the coordinator to see families with them.

One such visit involved a woman with limited English, who was on home leave, about to be discharged after a short admission for her depression. There had been concerns about her threatening the children but these had not reached a threshold for action from the children's team. The latter may have assumed that as she was receiving treatment and there was another 'protective parent' at home, this was sufficient. Her care coordinator[2] remained anxious. When we visited, the mother readily told us of her fears of hurting her children as she was hearing voices which instructed her to harm them, something she had not been able to communicate in a ward round with her husband present. We relayed this to her psychiatrist and to the children's team, and I accompanied a children's social worker to the ward round. Her medication was changed and the plan for discharge revised. The children's worker told me that this was the first time she had been in a psychiatric ward, and she had not known what to expect, or how to contribute. She might also have been fearful of making a home visit. For the care coordinator the idea of raising with this gentle but troubled woman the possibility of her harming her children may have been unthinkable.

It was often the case that very modest and minimal interventions were sufficient, as they might represent something more significant. In resisting the 'expert' role, while remaining neutral and interested, the coordinator could provide containment, enable others to think and alleviate the pressure for action (Loshak 2007: 30).

Professionals' meetings

A second important strand to the work was the chairing of 'joint working meetings' in situations which did not reach a threshold for statutory involvement. These sometimes included the service user but more often were attended only by professionals. For children's services staff this may be counter to the practice of working in partnership with parents. However, where a parent is unwell such meetings add to the distress, as one mother related about an informal meeting in school:

> I didn't remember you from the first time, I was so worried about the meeting, that there was something wrong, that I didn't take it in, who was there. And also when you have got a mental illness you see so many people you can't remember them all.

When a parent has a thought disorder or is psychotic, the effect on professionals' ability to think must be considered, and a separate meeting about the task of working together (which the psychotic part of the patient will unconsciously attack) is necessary (Lucas 2009).

'Joint working meetings' functioned to ensure a coordinated response, as a 'getting to know each other' process in unfamiliar networks, and sometimes as a way of gathering fragmented 'bits' of information located in different agencies to build a holistic picture and assess the level of concern. They helped resolve conflict, build relationships and increase mutual understanding.

> A mental health nurse, recently moved from a ward to a community team, was at a loss to know whom she should be in touch with concerning a mother and new baby about to be discharged from the mother and baby unit. There were concerns about how much care of the baby the mother would assume, or her family would allow her; how to balance her needs to get better, and the nurse's monitoring role, with the needs of the baby for an emotional bond with her mother; how to ensure the baby had adequate stimulation, and consistency of care. A group of professionals were ready to be involved, the health visitor, and a psychologist, with children's social care somewhat in the background deeming the baby safe in the care of the extended family.

Two network planning meetings acted as forums for 'getting to know you'. After the second meeting they were clearer about roles and responsibilities and able to design a visiting plan which would be supportive to the mother while allowing her some space, as their shared anxieties had been tested against the real situation. The baby and mother had an opportunity to get re-acquainted without overwhelming anxiety.

The nurse commented on having been previously quite unfamiliar with this network or with such meetings. Discharge meetings do of course take place on wards, but it may be that these are pressured, decision-making environments, often with a large number of people present. Not only service users but also professionals may feel daunted, so that they are rarely places where such 'getting to know you' and building relationships can take place.

Other meetings can remove obstacles to working together and modify some of the distorted perceptions of 'the other' that so easily build up.

A care coordinator consulted me about a young woman with a personality disorder, often overlaid with depression and alcohol use. Her small child was subject of a care order and long-term decisions about placement were being made. The worker felt 'out of the loop', unaware how contact between mother and child was going, and very concerned that the children's team might have an unrealistic view of this woman's parenting capacity. She had been told that the childcare social worker had been advised not to speak to her, as the case was in legal proceedings and she was deemed to be an advocate for the parent. I suggested an informal meeting between the child's social worker and herself at which I would be present. This took place in due course and I introduced the aim of the meeting, 'to understand each other's roles and find appropriate ways to share information'. I confined myself to asking questions, to clarify what was being said, or to raise particular points I thought may be being overlooked. The two workers were able to recognise that they had a shared concern about the parenting of this child, and the care coordinator was relieved to hear what the actual thinking of the children's team was. The child's social worker was able to explain that she needed to present the mother's views to the court, and needed help in doing this. The care co-ordinator was able to advise her of the risks this woman might present not only to her child but also to staff. My presence was no longer needed as both agencies were able to cooperate toward an appropriate recommendation to the court.

Misunderstandings, workload pressures and the anxiety created by the case had caused a block in communication between these two experienced social workers. However, they were absolutely clear about their respective roles, and the boundaries between them and their agencies.

Others are not so clear, and difficulties can occur when roles appear to be exchanged, with workers tending towards omnipotence, suggesting they know best how the other agency should be performing its role. In such cases reflecting aloud on one's own confusion about who is supposed to be doing what can bring about a pause for reflection and a shift in position. At other times such an interaction might suggest a similar dysfunction in the family. In rare circumstances discussion with the supervisor may be needed to disentangle over-identification on the part of a worker.

The decision in the case above was clear to both workers. In the following case there were strongly divided opinions. Not all meetings will need to involve children's social work teams, but may involve schools, or other health professionals for whom there is no containing structure and who may be frightened by mental illness. Such meetings can deal with the problem of no one agency holding responsibility for coordinating a case.

> A care coordinator had in his care a young woman who had a pattern of admission, followed by discharge when she was under family pressure to care for her two children. This led to a pattern of repeated breakdown and re-admission. The parents were in the process of divorce, and the agencies divided about which parent should be supported to care for the children. Eventually children's social workers became involved and after an assessment supported father as permanent carer, with mother having contact. Over a long period there was a need for close cooperation between the care coordinator, the school, the health visitor and a speech therapist to monitor these young children's progress and to regulate their visits to their mother, with close attention paid to their well-being as well as hers. Regular meetings about this family continued over more than a year ensuring everyone knew what was happening, was able to communicate easily to others involved and had a place for their anxieties to be thought about. These were also forums for learning, as each professional noted.

The comments of staff about such meetings were invariably ones of gratitude, often for having had the opportunity to share their worries with colleagues and to plan together, and for the learning that can take place. Following the impromptu meeting of two staff and their managers about the mother and baby about to be separated, described above, one worker said that both teams had had very fixed ideas and the coordinator's role as facilitator had created a space for their differences to be recognised. Working with difference is part of the territory (Foster 1998). Other staff who consulted about their cases commented that they never usually had an opportunity to think about one case in such detail, and valued this. Thus the question 'what can one person do?' is determined by a theoretical understanding which allows an experience of containment and makes space for thinking.

Developing services

A significant part of the coordinator's role was that of developing services to this client group and to the staff. Parental mental illness and its possible impact on children, together with the needs of young carers, were recognised at government level and given a high priority nationally. The *Every Child Matters* programme of the then Labour government of 1997 to 2010 attempted to ensure that vulnerable children were identified at an early stage, and offered interventions so that their emotional, educational, social and developmental needs would not prevent them from achieving and reaching their potential (DfES 2003). The children of parents with mental illness are not always in need of protection from abuse or neglect but are vulnerable along these developmental lines, and often fail to reach their potential. It was therefore an opportunity to develop new forms of prevention and early intervention as well as seeking best practice in 'joined-up working'.

Essential to any development is the gathering of information about levels of need. This was problematic from the outset. The 200 children known to the staff of the four CMHTs in the borough and identified at an early stage quickly trebled when children's specialists were finally appointed to be a physical presence in the CMHTs.

However, staff members were initially resistant to such information gathering; fears were that it might be passed to children's services, thus breaking confidentiality, or that they might be held responsible for a child. Often the information simply was not available and families would have to be approached, an action that it was feared might cause a break in contact or trust. Persistence and care with the way such information was stored and used resulted in staff gradually relinquishing their anxieties, making files available and being more open. In time the information proved to be of use to mental health staff themselves, when new staff took on a parent's care, or when they wished to know who else might be involved with the family. When given timely and appropriate knowledge and support, staff readily overcame their fears and could recognise their obligations under the Children Act 2004, that children are indeed part of their responsibility.

It is now a standard requirement of mental health trusts to record details of children routinely. Despite this, collecting such information in statistical form for planning purposes remains a challenge. It is hampered by necessarily separate IT systems for the local authority and the mental health trust, or possibly by a residual organisational resistance rooted in a perceived need to protect users from unwelcome intrusion.

The essential aspect of developing any new role is that of building relationships and networks. This was achieved in a variety of contexts with different agency networks; we set up a parental mental health interest group predominantly in education but including adult mental health, CAMHS and voluntary sector staff; we were represented on the Safeguarding Children's Board in the mental health trust and worked closely with its safeguarding nurses; with support from the National Children's Bureau we held a trust-wide conference for senior clinicians, health and local authority managers, and importantly, commissioners, to facilitate the exchange of ideas and information at a senior level.

In an educational role we offered workshops at the request of individual teams on a topic that was important to them. This tailored approach encouraged continuing discussion within the teams. To reach a wider group of staff, parental mental health and the impact on children was incorporated into existing programmes such as foundation and post-foundation child protection courses, and CAMHS courses for childcare staff. We also taught on post-qualifying childcare courses about parental mental health. In-house we were in a position to facilitate or support brief observation placements, to make use of temporary secondments to CHAMP and exchanges between teams.

One of our first and most popular initiatives with families resulted from a generous 'gift' by the King's Fund through a Millennium Grant of £2000. The King's Fund offered a short course to potential 'social entrepreneurs', the majority of whom were mental health service users, to set up a project while learning about leadership and project management from King's Fund staff. This extraordinary opportunity and expression of trust provided an experience of working directly alongside service users, and in the process learning something of their experience of professionals. The learning was of direct relevance to the project and the monies were used over three years to provide a programme of day trips for school-age children of parents who were service users in our CMHTs. This is described in an appendix (see p. 199).

Notes

1 The matter was in legal proceedings, and they had interpreted legal advice in this way.
2 The term 'care coordinator' refers to any member of the CMHT who is responsible for coordinating a 'Care Programme' for a service user. A care coordinator may belong to any of the mental health professions, but is commonly a nurse or social worker. The term is to be distinguished in this volume from 'the coordinator' which refers to the 'Coordinator for children in families with mental illness'.

References

Anderson-Wallace, M., Blantern, C. and Lejk, A. (2000) Advances in cross boundary practice. In Taillieu, T. (ed.) *Collaborative Strategies and Multi-Organisational Practice* (ch. 4).
Bailey, D. (2010) 'If we value our children, we must cherish their parents'. *Context* (April): 53–56.
Cardwell, A. and Britten, C. (2002) 'Whose baby is it anyway? Developing a joined up service involving child mental health teams working in an adult mental health trust'. *Journal of Adoption and Fostering* 26: 76–84.
Cowling, V. (2004) *Children of Parents with Mental Illness 2: Personal and Clinical Perspectives*. Melbourne: ACER Press.
Department for Education and Skills (DfES) (2004) *Every Child Matters: Change for Children*. Norwich: The Stationery Office. Online. Available: http://www.education. gov.uk/publications/standard/publicationdetail/page1/DfES/1081/2004 (accessed 12 March 2012).
Foster, A. (1998) 'Integration or fragmentation: The challenge facing community mental

health teams'. In Foster, A. and Zagier Roberts, V. (eds) *Managing Mental Health in the Community: Chaos and Containment*. London: Routledge.

Halton, W. (2004) 'By what authority? Psychoanalytic reflections on creativity and change in relation to organisational life'. In Huffington, C., Armstrong, D., Halton, W., Hoyle, L. and Pooley, J. (eds) *Working Below the Surface: The Emotional Life of Contemporary Organisations*. London: Karnac. http://www.karnacbooks.com/isbn/9781855752948, reprinted with kind permission of Karnac Books.

Hinshelwood, R. (1998) 'Creatures of each other'. In Foster, A. and Zagier Roberts, V. (eds) *Managing Mental Health in the Community: Chaos and Containment*. London: Routledge.

Hinshelwood, R. and Skogstad, W. (2000) *Observing Organizations: Anxiety, Defence and Culture in Health Care*. London and Philadelphia, PA: Routledge.

Loshak, R. (2007) 'There is a war on! Someone is going to get killed'. *Psychoanalytic Psychotherapy* 21 (1): 20–39. The Association for Psychoanalytic Psychotherapy in the NHS. Taylor & Francis.

Lucas, R. (2009) *The Psychotic Wavelength*. Hove, East Sussex and New York: Routledge.

Urwin, C. (2005) 'A Sure Start Rapid Response Service for parents and their under fours'. In Launer, J., Blake, S. and Dawes, D. (eds) *Reflecting on Reality: Psychotherapists at Work in Primary Care*. London: Karnac.

7 Perinatal Crisis Service

Psychotherapeutic work with babies and their families at a time of crisis

Sandra Nathanson

Introduction

In this chapter I will present work with perinatal patients in a Crisis Intervention Service. This service, which is part of CHAMP (Children and Adults Mental Health Project), was set up aiming at closing the gap between children and adult services and allowing a more inclusive view of the needs of mothers and babies. I will present the service, discuss the different types of intervention and illustrate with a case presentation.

Pregnancy and becoming a parent can be seen as a natural, developmental crisis demanding a shift in ways of being. This crisis can be aggravated by social difficulties such as housing, loss of income and various changes in levels of support from the community, but also by difficulties of an emotional nature: old conflicts brought up by the developmental aspect of the crisis, which have not been worked through in other developmental stages, or which need reworking. More often, it is a conflation of different aspects that brings the patient to the service: a psychosocial crisis. Winnicott emphasises the idea of a holding environment at different levels which complete the system in which the mother and the baby can exist and flourish. Crisis occurs when some of these elements are absent or disturbed.

The impact of the above stresses on parents or parents-to-be is great, and can impinge upon their relationship with the baby. Parents can become less available for their children and harsher in their responses to their children when pressurised by stressful live events (Schore, 2010).

Distressed or suicidal patients, perinatal or otherwise, often mention their children as protective factors. Developing an alliance with the parent part of the patient in perinatal work is of the essence, as is attending to the other parts of the patient that may be getting in the way of allowing the parent part to do its best. At these times, there is very often a great investment in change.

Early intervention is key

Often babies are not seen as thinking and feeling entities, and their care can mostly be thought of at the physical needs level. Consequently, the mental health of babies can be dismissed, and the impact of the parents' states of mind and feelings towards the baby often discounted, except when child protection concerns are raised. This lack can be reflected in the system of help around the baby and mother. Their needs are frequently considered independently and when something goes wrong, it is difficult not to side with the baby or with the mother, but instead to consider them as greater than the sum of the parts. Systems which operate reactively with their emphasis on crisis management do not often foster the necessary thinking.

Very early on, from pregnancy, meaning is given to the relationship between parents and baby. Gestures or manifestations of the baby are often linked with temperament and intentionality: a vital aspect of building the relationship between parents and baby. What if this process is clouded by ghosts of the past or even of the present (Fraiberg, 1975)? At times, parent and baby struggle to find their way to one another without help. An extensive body of research indicates that early disturbance in relationships leads to further disturbance in later relationships and problems with mental health and achievement.

When parents are in crisis, the fundamental aspects of early motherhood such as reverie (Bion, 1962), basic containment (Bion, 1959) and primary maternal preoccupation (Winnicott, 1956) are interfered with and impinged upon (i.e. a very preoccupied parent would not be free to think about the baby and his or her emotional needs). The consequences for the real baby and for the baby in the mind of the parent can be tragic. Babies who are not thought about struggle to thrive. Winnicott (1949) shares a metaphor used by one of his patients describing how the individual is like a bubble to illustrate the importance of external and internal pressures on development. If the external pressure does not adapt to the internal pressure, the environment rather than the individual becomes important and consequently individual development suffers. Early intervention is aimed at bringing the parent and the child to the best start possible, to avoid the development of pathological ways of relating, an important step for the mental health of both parent and child.

Crisis Intervention Service (CIS)

CIS is a psychiatric service offering assessments and brief therapeutic interventions to patients in psychosocial crisis. Many of the patients are suicidal and present via A&E, or are referred by their GPs. They are patients who want to explore their problems through talking therapy.

The team consists of nurses, psychotherapists, a clinical psychologist and a consultant psychiatrist. There are junior doctors on rotation at different stages of their training. There is a referral coordinator who receives and triages the referrals which are then discussed with the team before being allocated.

There are two clinical weekly meetings, three psychological discussion group meetings on a monthly basis and a monthly core team meeting. These forums enable a multi-disciplinary approach and are a space for reflection on the impact of the patient on the service and the wider network. They are crucial in containing the high risk these patients carry, as is weekly supervision.

The team integrates a psychiatric/medical approach with a psychodynamic one, and works in a brief model offering up to twelve sessions post assessment. A post-crisis group is a recent addition to the work offered.

Within this team there is a perinatal post, set up within CHAMP eight years ago, and currently shared between a child psychotherapist and a nurse therapist. The remit of this post is to work with perinatal cases including pregnant women and their partners, and new mothers and their partners with children up to the age of 2 who present in psychosocial crisis or who have difficulties in bonding with their babies. These are patients who are too complex for interventions in community-based services, patients who present with significant but not severe and enduring mental health difficulties. Referrals to this part of the service come mainly from the Perinatal Psychiatry Team and gateway midwifery as well as from GPs, A&E and health visitors.

The perinatal work

This section will address both the type of difficulties for which patients seek help and the types of work undertaken. The work offered is within a brief model and therefore I would like to comment on issues pertaining to the timing of the treatment, the definition of its focus, the therapist's stance and the different levels of work which may be needed on a case.

Work fundamentally aims at helping parents and often other professionals to look at the world through the eyes of the babies and to have a sense of them as feeling and thinking human beings. This enables parents to separate their own difficulties and preoccupations from the baby's emotional needs. For example, helping a mother notice how her baby gets entangled in her internal conflict can enable her to free her baby from it.

Presenting problems

Loss and bereavement: These can be late pregnancy losses, or terminations in the case of chromosomal abnormalities. I have also worked with terminally ill babies, and cases where one of the twins died in utero and the other survived. There have been a number of cases where the birth of a baby coincides with bereavement in the family, at times the death of a parent.

Reworking of childhood conflict and mothers' difficult relationships with their own mothers: An important section of referrals are mothers who have experienced severe difficulties in their relationships with their own mothers and felt rejected and unloved or treated cruelly. Often these patients find it difficult to distinguish their baby from themselves as babies, and themselves as mothers from their own mothers. Daughters of mothers with severe mental health difficulties can find the process of becoming a parent anxiety-provoking as they might fear becoming mentally unwell. A number of these patients have great difficulties with intimacy which can also lead to or manifest as difficulties in bonding with their babies or in accepting their pregnancies.

Identity: Working out the fit between old identities and the new mother identity can be challenging and there is a section of referrals of professional women, often the main breadwinners for the family, who are torn between their need to return to work and their need to remain at home with their baby. These difficulties often arise at a time when the baby is at a developmental stage where separation is key.

Breakdown of relationship/domestic violence: Pregnancy has been identified as a time when domestic violence can start or be increased. The adjustment necessary to accommodate another in a relationship is sometimes too much, and this is a particularly vulnerable time for relationship difficulties to increase or take centre stage.

Often cases present with these different aspects in different combinations and degrees at different times.

Consultation

A number of referrals require professional discussion rather than a direct intervention by our service. This includes cases where another professional has a relationship with the patient and needs support in thinking about and holding the increased risk. For some patients a brief intervention can be contra-indicated and they can be encouraged to engage with a service that can offer longer-term support, at times with consultation from CIS.

Worrying cases at times trigger a scattergun approach in which the family is referred to a number of services simultaneously which does not perform a containing function but rather offers a sense of abundance in deprivation, as these families tend not to engage with any service and fall through the net. Often the work required is one of liaison, to help create a containing space for the parent and baby and to facilitate thinking. Developing relationships with other agencies allows for a triangular space in which thinking can occur to be delineated (Britton, 1989). This is also an important aspect of most pieces of work in which the communication with the GP, midwife or health visitor, Children Centres, Children's Social Care Services, etc. is of the essence in order to assist the creation of a milieu in which the family can flourish. In this instance, the connection and communication between agencies can perform a parental function and be experienced by patients as containing in the same way that Winnicott (1954) talks about the holding environment. About a quarter of referrals are inappropriate, for consultation only, or are referred to other specialities.

Assessment

The assessment includes a state-of-mind assessment focusing on risk and looking out for symptoms of mental illness, such as depression among others, as well as the assessment of the willingness and capacity of the patient to benefit from the work offered.

The assessment is at times the only therapeutic intervention needed. Telling their story, finding their narrative and piecing the fragments together can be very helpful for patients. On occasions, it becomes clear that the patient does not want it, or is not ready for further exploration. The issue of timing is crucial here, as referrals can be premature. Patients are at times re-referred later on when they are ready to engage in psychological work. Some patients are referred to other specialities and others do not respond to be seen or drop out at this stage.

Treatment

One-third of all referrals seen for assessment complete their treatments. This can be supportive work aiming at helping the patient go back to the pre-crisis position, bolstering defences and helping the patient function again. Containing anxiety tends to be the main feature and although transference feelings are acknowledged they are not emphasised, and interpretations are used sparingly. Often, they are therapist based rather than patient focused. The work encompasses the recognition of the nature of their experiences (whether current or resurfacing due to the crisis). Crucially it is adapted to each patient.

There is another section of patients who allow for deeper exploratory work to be undertaken.

Case presentation: Katia and Max

In this section I will present a case to illustrate some of the work conducted. This is a complex and anxiety-provoking case, as are most of the cases referred, and illustrates the need for different levels of involvement. There was an intervention in the realm of the network, an intervention in the realm of the family, an intervention with the mother and an intervention at the level of the mother–baby relationship with an emphasis on facilitating the communication and contact within this dyad. Of course, in practice all of these aspects were not separate but interweaved. However, throughout different periods of work, different aspects were more prominent. The engagement was not straightforward: the mother did not engage in the first referral, broke off the work in the second but returned for a third time to complete the work she had started. This intermittent contact with the service reflected her struggles with closeness and separation and with hopelessness and hope. Her gradual emergence from layers of violence enabled her to finally discover her son and reach out to him. I will deliberately focus on work with the mother.

After an initial referral which did not come to fruition when baby Max was 11 weeks old, Katia was re-referred via A&E when Max was 6 months old, following yet another incident of self-harm. She remained suicidal but denied any thoughts of harming her baby.

Katia, Max and his father were living on the twelfth floor of a council tower block. Katia was claustrophobic and had been unable to use lifts since childhood. This was now particularly crippling because she could not leave the house unless the father was there. They felt trapped and hopeless.

Assessment

In the first meeting the family attended together. There was a sharp contrast between the tense gauntness of the parents and the unfocused roundness of baby Max.

Katia spoke in a barely audible voice: problems had started when she became pregnant. The father lost his job; she hurt her back and also stopped working. They lived in shared accommodation and she was frightened, as other male residents drank and she felt unsafe. They were evicted from this accommodation after the baby was born but the temporary accommodation they were placed in was equally frightening. Katia had an emergency caesarean and felt that the anaesthetic had not worked, and she claimed the doctors had not listened to her.

As the parents told their story, it became clear that Max was peripheral to the main concerns and was not seen as a separate person. The violence in the parents' upbringings came to the fore:

> Katia remembered her father asking her to come into the lift, saying that he could fix it if they got stuck, but she did not want to. Father was alcoholic and would come home drunk at 3 a.m., get all the children up and tell his wife to serve him dinner just to complain it was cold. A row would ensue and he would become violent towards mother. Father would try to convince the children that mother was bad. He wanted them to see it.

Katia was able to connect her claustrophobia to the violence in her childhood and to lacking a benign parenting model. In her mind, baby Max turned into a tyrannical baby, similar to her father: demanding, disapproving and never satisfied. Her guilt for not being able to satisfy Max's needs fuelled her sense of him as persecuting her and exposing her as a bad mother.

> Having no money for electricity Katia felt she could not feed Max because he does not like cold milk. She wanted to make him happy and felt terrible that she could not give him what he needed. Katia felt told off by the baby. Some days she would become increasingly upset: it started with a little thing and she could not let go. It then became a bigger problem and she would explode and harm herself.

Katia managed to explain how by self-harming she got rid of her negative feelings and persecutory states of mind. A common theme emerged: she felt claustrophobic when she could no longer placate the dangerous inebriated/highly emotional men (her father, her housemates and later on her husband and her baby) whom she felt depended on her. Only an aggressive ejection (i.e. self-harm) could resolve this unbearable tension. The baby was invited to take his place in the long queue of men before him. He was not seen as an emergent person in his own right but was given an old dog-eared script to read from and enact. Growing up as a boy seemed dangerous and malignant.

> Katia had a nightmare the night before her session: Max was walking, but he was huge, being hardly able to get in through the door. She was unable to explain what it was that made the dream so scary.

We can see how this dream echoes Katia's feeling that males are powerful and destructive. The difference between the baby in her mind and her real needy and helpless baby is apparent.

Enjoyment was clearly missing in Katia's relationship with her baby and crystallised their difficulty in connecting, thereby impairing Max's development. Max could not see himself in his parents' eyes, clouded as they were with the visions of their past. In fact, he tended to present as disconnected and in dissociative states: not looking at people when they picked him up, offering very little eye contact and oscillating between being quietly out of focus and jumping about when held under his arms in a mechanical, excited yet lifeless way. These two restricted modes of being were his response to stress. This is in line with research quoted by Schore (2010), indicating that hyperarousal and dissociation are an infant's reactions to severe stress.

In this first part of the work, my focus was on creating a sense of containment, piecing all the fragments together and offering back a meaningful narrative. The emphasis was on recognising the nature of their experience as parents, acknowledging the terrible time they had had, and helping them put into words the bleak colouring of their internal worlds. In tandem, sitting by their side and helping them look (through my perspective) at their story created a space between them and these events and allowed for a third dimension to emerge: a space in which thinking could start to develop. For example, Katia was able to recognise the onset of her suicidal states. Slowing her down and allowing her to notice the steps in the process was helpful in bolstering her sense of agency when faced with a process she felt was inexorable. She started resisting enacting these states. Difficulties and power struggles within the couple relationship emerged. This thinking space allowed Max to be seen as he really was. However, at this stage I still had to be the one holding Max's interest in mind.

Balancing an open stance with containing the risk was only possible with the knowledge of there being a multidisciplinary team and a network of professionals, especially the health visitor and the GP at this stage, to think with. Having their thoughts and back-up was crucial in helping me manage the risky feel of this family and to keep all the family members in focus, especially Max, who did not have much of a voice at this stage. Our good communication gave Katia a sense of a net that could hold her at times when she felt unable to care for herself and for her son. Children's Social Care Services were consulted but were unable to provide support at this time. This network also provided me with a sense of partnership which helped me keep my focus on the parent–infant relationship rather than actively managing all their other needs. Collaborating on defining the focus enlisted the family in seeking change more proactively.

Unfolding

> Katia went to see the fireworks in the park and had been scared, terrified; unable to breathe. However, she remained until the end of the display. I asked her what had helped her manage her anxiety and she pointed at Max. Thinking about the firework experience, Katia recounted how she once was on a crowded floating platform on a beach with her sister and she got a panic attack, despite the fact that she knew how to swim. Her sister hit her. I commented on her worry that people might react to her distress with anger and violence.

Katia had been able to withstand some anxiety and felt she had done it for Max, aware that he would benefit from her not falling apart. Yet, the hope of improvement soon turned into a sense of failure as she berated herself for having felt anxious and expected to be punished for what she saw as a weakness. Katia went on to talk about the difficult birth and the emergency caesarean section for which she had not been given appropriate anaesthetics. The sense of pain being overwhelming and impossible to bear was quite clear, as was the dilemma that for Max to be born and become his own person overwhelming pain would have to be faced, and with insufficient support. In parallel, her partner revealed his depression and dependency: his daily nightmares and chronic panic attacks came increasingly to the fore, as did his difficulties with alcohol, which he used as medication. He was referred for individual work and dropped out from our own work as the couple started to disintegrate. Katia began to fight for her son. Despite still feeling suicidal, she resisted acting on her feelings.

> Katia was very close to taking another overdose. She lined up all the tablets on the table, with a glass of water. She stopped herself as she remembered the doctor saying she would be admitted if she tried to harm herself again. She feared Max would be taken away.

This moment crystallised the turning point in the treatment. Katia decided to be a mother to Max. She fought herself and attempted to manage her feelings, mostly successfully. I felt increasingly that she had engaged in the work. Katia reconnected with her family, signalling her commitment to recovery. Addressing the impact of the domestic violence which she continued to deny was still impossible and restricted the help she could get at this point.

Building the mother–baby relationship

During the sessions, Katia discovered that she would need to play a much more active role in her interactions with her son, balanced with increased receptivity to his states of mind. She knew this would be a lengthy process. Despite making progress, she struggled to share Max with another person as she felt shut out, and cut off contact. If he showed interest in others, she felt rejected and gave up on trying to engage him. Her belief that he loved and needed her was fragile.

Katia talked about having 'bad days' when she switched off. Schore (2010), talking about the neglectful care giver, highlights how when there is relational trauma parental figures can be unavailable, inaccessible and rejecting of the infant's communications of negative emotions. Importantly, they do not assist in the regulation of stimulation and arousal and become unpredictable to the infant. Consequently there are few opportunities for repair in the relationship and the infant is left to deal with its stress alone, which is beyond its capacity developmentally.

At times when she switched off, Katia left Max in an excruciatingly difficult position. Knowing Max's suffering was painful and holding onto hope was a challenge. Once more, the network and the team provided invaluable containment. There was a sense that a network where Katia and her baby could exist and belong began to take better shape, with her family of origin now being added as an extra layer to the professional network, who despite failings (changes of health visitor and intermittent communication between services) provided some holding. Katia felt she could now turn to services for help and that services communicated among themselves, contrasting with her initial feeling of services as persecutory and misunderstanding. It was as if her mind was no longer arid and populated by persecutors. Some friendly figures found a place there. This reinforced her resolve to connect with her baby. However, paralleling his mother's efforts, Max tentatively seized hold of his vitality and became more defined and 'in the world'.

> Max was curious about the toys in the room and seemed to be eager to learn about them. He reached for them and vocalised a lot more. He made big, sustained efforts to crawl.

There were struggles ahead as Max came out of his amorphous state. Katia's difficulties in managing her own aggression impaired her ability to differentiate between strength and the pleasure of having a sense of agency on one hand and feeling powerful and the power of rage and anger aiming at hurting others on the other. She struggled to give Max an image of himself as a benign, strong little boy.

> Katia followed Max with her eyes with visible enjoyment, smiling at him and offering him toys. Max responded, taking things from Katia, banging them together and then taking again what she was offering. Max was playing quite vigorously and trying to crawl. He would give short exclamations – 'AAH!' – which seemed to express his sense of effort and power. Katia grew silent. As I talked to her, she explained that she felt Max was angry. In the same conversation she recounted that Max had been able to stand up by himself in his cot and she felt he was trying to escape.

Katia linked this thought with her own first memory.

> She was playing on her own and made a blanket knotted onto a stick, which she carried over her shoulder, as if leaving.

As our work came towards the end, after ten sessions, the domestic violence which had been taking place was finally revealed. Two sessions before the end of our work, after returning to her country of origin to visit family, Katia disappeared. What I did not pick up in the session was Katia letting me know about what was going to happen. We made contact and she was leaving. The case was closed.

Second contact

Katia self-referred to CIS a few months later. She explained she had tried to return to her country of origin but had not been able to extricate herself from her relationship with her partner. When he hit her again she went to the police and was currently in temporary accommodation. Children's Social Care Services were now involved. She wanted help with Max who was now 1 year old and difficult to manage, easily frightened and hard to calm down, tending to lash out and to head bang. He was not communicative, was not pointing, nor did he babble much, seeming to have very poor modulation of his emotions and restricted capacities to tolerate frustration. We agreed another brief piece of work which focused on Katia helping Max modulate his states of feeling. Katia still found it difficult to believe that she could access her son in a benign way and it was easy for him to become the untameable monster she expected most men to be. Creating an image of a benign strong male figure in her mind was the challenge she faced in order to help her son. A great part of the work was to address with Katia how her inner perceptions, her beliefs about the world and her harsh relationship with herself had an impact not only on her parenting, but directly on Max's perceptions of himself and the world. We highlighted the risk to her and Max were she to remain locked in thoughts of violence and mistrust. With Katia's help, Max began to better tolerate frustration and to make links between sessions more obvious as he tried every week to unlock my desk, valiantly working at getting the small key in the lock. As he improved, he became more tenacious in his attempts, showing us how hard he was also working. He became curious and interested in the world around him instead of mainly reacting to events and feeling overwhelmed. His language developed as he began to realise that there was someone who wanted to hear what he had to say. There was a greater sense that he went on being (Winnicott, 1956) rather than being jolted from one state to another.

Another crucial aspect of the work at this stage was to manage the numerous agencies that became involved simultaneously and to contribute to their good communication. This was not always straightforward, and at times the split between the parents and the paranoid and accusatory dynamic between them was reflected in different parts of the network. Core group meetings were very useful in keeping the network communicating and providing containment to the family.

Katia was greatly helped by the refuge she went to. She linked up with other mothers and made friends. Her key worker was instrumental and supported our work. The link with the father was not absent and he remained in the minds of professionals not only in a persecutory way, as often happens, but as a central figure to Max's life. Supervised contact was arranged at this stage, which turned into overnight unsupervised contact. Katia managed this transition without becoming paralysed or dominated by her fears for herself and Max.

We worked hard on the ending of our relationship and at the pain of saying goodbye when there was still so much to do. Max contributed as he played mainly with the phone, trying to call his mother, being able to say hello and goodbye. This time, Katia managed to come to the last session and even consent to share her experience with others so that they could also benefit from the help she felt she had received.

Conclusion

I hope Max's case offers a flavour of the work conducted at the Crisis Intervention Service. It contains the main facets of cases here: the assessment and management of risk as well as the focus on relationships and the importance of the network. Working in this way is a balancing act but can be very helpful to families at a stage when new beginnings ask for reworking of difficulties which can be chronic. The developmental shifts of the perinatal period present as a window of opportunity before unhealthy patterns crystallise. Early intervention is key.

As in Max's case, often the aim of the work is to allow for the real baby to be seen and related to, and for the parent part of the parent to be able to do as best as he or she can: enabling communication and facilitating development.

Work usually involves knitting a network around the family and enabling the family to make use of this network. Often, there is a progression from an initial focus on containing the anxiety to a more challenging approach as patients find their strength. Accessing the enjoyment in the relationship with the baby is crucial to this process. This is reliably what allows the connection between parent and baby to become real, and allows the baby to become more assertive and have a sense that it has an impact in the world.

It has been interesting to consider the impact of the perinatal post on the team, and how the experience of birth, the fact of being a parent, etc. have become more thoroughly discussed in the team meetings in cases where the presenting problem is not perinatal. Being able to consider the importance of the impact of experiences on babies has shed added light on the understanding of adult patients and how their early experiences might be present in later crises. This is not something new, and yet the day-to-day reminder of this known fact has brought a valuable contribution to the work in the team.

References

Bion, W. (1959) 'Attacks on linking'. *International Journal of Psycho-Analysis* 40: 308–315; republished in Bion, W. R. (1993) *Second Thoughts: Selected Papers in Psychoanalysis*. The Maresfield Library. London: Karnac, pp. 93–109; and in Bott-Spillius, E. (ed.) (1988) *Melanie Klein Today: Developments in Theory and Practice. Volume 1, Mainly Theory*. New Library of Psychoanalysis. London: Routledge, pp. 87–101.

Bion, W. R. (1962) 'A theory of thinking'. *International Journal of Psychoanalysis*, 43.

Britton, R. (1989) 'The missing link: Parental sexuality in the Oedipus complex'. In Britton, R., Feldman, M. and O'Shaughnessy, E. (eds) *The Oedipus Complex Today – Clinical Implications* (ch. 2). London: Karnac.

Freiberg, S., Adelson, E. and Shapiro, V. (1975) 'Ghosts in the nursery. A psychoanalytic approach to the problems of impaired infant–mother relationships'. *Journal of the American Academy of Child Psychiatry*, 14(3): 387–421.

Schore, A. (2010) 'Relational trauma and the developing right brain: The neurobiology of broken attachment bonds'. In T. Baradon (ed.) *Relational Trauma in Infancy* (pp. 19–47). London: Routledge.

Winnicott, D.W. (1949) 'Birth memories, birth trauma and anxiety'. In Winnicott, D.W. (1975) *Through Paediatrics to Psycho-Analysis* (pp. 173–193). New York: Basic Books.

Winnicott, D.W. (1954) 'Metapsychological and classical aspects of regression'. In Winnicott, D.W. (1975) *Through Paediatrics to Psycho-Analysis* (pp. 278–294). New York: Basic Books.

Winnicott, D. (1956) 'Primary maternal preoccupation'. In *Through Paediatrics to Psychoanalysis*. London: Hogarth Press.

8 The children's specialist in the adult mental health team

Rosemary Loshak

This chapter describes the important development of the project from a position where there was just one person, the coordinator, in post, to one in which, after a pilot period, we were able to place children's specialists in one, and then two of the four adult mental health teams in the borough, and thus expand our aims.

Setting up the post

In 2006 the tentative ideas of the 2002 steering group became a reality. The steering group submitted a successful bid to the Children's Workforce Development Council (CWDC) which brought £60,000 into the borough for a one-year pilot placing a children's specialist in an adult community mental health team (CMHT). This central government body was especially interested in 'hybrid' staff who could work across traditional agency boundaries and it sought 'New Types of Worker' (NToW) to explore the skills and knowledge needed for these new roles. The NToW programme encouraged recruitment from a wider field than would traditionally be considered, and we were able to appoint from the voluntary sector a worker with local experience of managing a family support project for families referred by the mental health teams.

The primary aims of the role of children's specialist were to ensure early assessment, with the active involvement of the parent, to enable children and parents to access appropriate community resources, to prevent multiple assessments by different agencies, to divert families when possible from needing statutory involvement, and to reduce the child and the parent's social isolation by facilitating their participation in social activities. These aims were shared by the Primary Care Trust (PCT) who commissioned mental health services and had the needs of the local population and the wishes of service users very much in mind. After the CWDC 'seed' monies and a positive external evaluation of the pilot (Paget 2009) the PCT agreed to additional ongoing funding to allow a second worker to be appointed. The service was commissioned from Children's Services, who held the budget for the two posts and that of the coordinator, while the PCT proved a consistent and valued partner whose aims of socially inclusive practice, working with other sectors, equality of access, of early intervention and prevention were also those of the project. This chapter first outlines the structures put in place to provide appropriate supervision, containment and support for the new posts, then reviews the ways in which we approached the primary aims of the project.

Structures for management, supervision and support

In 2008, with the appointment of a second children's specialist (NS), the co-ordinator became 'team manager' for the project, providing regular supervision to its staff. However, the 'cross-agency' nature of the roles between CMHT and children's social care demanded that joint working be incorporated into management and supervision arrangements for project staff. At practitioner level this meant that a joint supervision involving the children's specialist, the CHAMP team manager (RL) and the CMHT manager met three times a month to review the role and the work. This reflected the existing arrangement in which day-to-day management and supervision of the team manager was provided by an adult mental health (social care) lead while inter-agency and strategic matters were dealt with in three monthly joint meetings with both the adult mental health lead and the children's social care fieldwork lead together. These ensured joint accountability to both services, a continuing dialogue, reflection and awareness of the other's point of view and an opportunity for early resolution of differences.

The triangular nature of this supervision arrangement was vital, mitigating over-identification with one service or with a service user. In any supervision the service user is also present in the mind of the staff member, while a supervisor has to keep in mind agency requirements. Thus pairs form in the minds of the participants, influencing their responses and actions, and leaving one person vulnerable to exclusion. When this happens task-focused thinking and effective working are compromised.

The importance of the joint management arrangement for the coordinator and for the children's specialists is evident, allowing these staff members to see the two representatives of the distinct adult mental health and child care agencies, so often in conflict about the management of cases, engaged in a working relationship of their own, quite independent of the staff members' relationships with each other as individuals. Such an arrangement provides a degree of containment of the anxiety inherent in the work.

For the children's specialists based full-time in two adult mental health teams, isolation from child-focused colleagues was an important factor. In this situation the children's specialist may become drawn into the prevailing culture of the team, which may include blaming other agencies, and an inappropriate identification with the service user (see Chapter 9). The position is potentially vulnerable to misuse by authority figures within the CMHT who may see the children's specialist as an extra pair of hands, someone who can cover duty, or who can 'hold' some cases awaiting the arrival of a new mental health worker. A child trained worker does not have the necessary background of skills or knowledge to perform such a task.

It was important for the children's specialists to have a formal connection with children's services to maintain and develop their own child-focused practice. This was achieved by setting up regular sessions within the Child and Adolescent Mental Health Teams (CAMHS). One children's specialist chose to attend referral meetings and a family therapy workshop (described more fully in Chapter 9) while the other attended 'Bring Back' meetings in another CAMHS team at which newly assessed families were discussed. He undertook some joint work with CAMHS colleagues seeing families who were also known to the CMHT. These regular links brought direct benefit to families by avoiding the need for repeated assessment, ensuring that work done in the CAMHS setting could be better integrated with CMHT care planning, and enabling more families to access the service. A CAMHS colleague noted that his presence in sessions with the family 'brought the illness into the room' where it could be talked about.

Engaging with the adult Community Mental Health Team

The CMHT is a second-tier service accepting referrals of those with 'severe and enduring' illness; that is, service users who have usually already had one admission, who may have a psychosis or mood disorder. Important threshold criteria are that they may be considered a danger to themselves or to others, or that their illness is further complicated by significant social problems. Teams are large, complex and multidisciplinary, including psychiatrists, mental health nurses (some of whom have had little experience of working in the community), social workers, occupational therapists, psychologists and sometimes bilingual assistants. The pilot children's specialist coming into such a team felt initially something of an interloper, an uninvited guest, despite best efforts at preparation. While he was clear what he had to offer the team, the initial response of staff was somewhat distant. The children's specialist felt as if regarded with suspicion. Such feelings can best be understood as counter-transference, as he was attuned to the team's resistance to a new way of thinking, and their fears about what would be demanded of them on top of their already heavy caseload. At an unconscious level the team reflect their clients' anxiety in the face of change.

At the beginning the children's specialist found himself underused, and, for the pilot especially, under some pressure to demonstrate the value of the project by the end of the twelve-month funding. One response to these pressures was to engage in manic activity. In the first few months he made himself busy establishing contact in the wider network outside (rather than within) the team, gathering data from files on numbers of children, and seeking grants for families struggling with basic needs. This was a useful activity, widening knowledge of the project locally, and demonstrating a willingness to help team members. It could also be seen as a defensive response to an atmosphere of hopelessness and despair within the team which was hard to bear (Hinshelwood 1998). An alternative but also defensive response might be that of linking with the team and becoming identified with the prevailing culture, unable to maintain a different and separate professional identity.

Early intervention and assessment

The CMHT, like the children's social care teams, operated a process of screening referrals for appropriateness before completing a full assessment. It was at this initial stage that we hoped the children's specialist could become involved, assisting in identifying parenting difficulties, and assessing children's needs. However, mental health staff members' readiness to accept this role could not be assumed; the adult was their primary client and some staff expressed fears that his presence would be experienced as threatening by the service user, thus compromising their own assessment of mental state. More often practical difficulties were indicated, as such assessments, and often most subsequent contact with the service user, were typically arranged during school hours to reduce the possibility of children being present at all. In the context of working with 'severe and enduring' mental illness, staff have felt it important to gain as much understanding as possible of the service users' emotional and mental health with as much privacy as can be managed. There can also be a wish to protect children from the painful reality of their parent's illness. It should be noted that young people's response to this is to comment that they live with the illness on a daily basis and they want to be asked what they see and know (Barnardo's 2009).

Parents also wish to shield their children from knowledge of their illness and it is not unusual for one parent to be admitted to hospital without the children knowing where she or he has gone. An important role for the children's specialist has been – with the agreement of the other care giver – to explain to children where their parent is, the possibility of visiting, and the fact that the illness is not their fault.

Contrary to staff fears, in practice most families welcome the support when they understand that what is offered will be matched to their own perception of the help they need.

CMHT staff acknowledged finding it anxiety provoking to be confronted with concerns about their service users' children. The children's specialist demonstrated his interest in families by asking ordinary questions about a service user's children. This prompted staff to recall relevant information given by parents or to think about ways in which parents' mental health problems might be affecting their children. When initial visits to families were made they were always made jointly with the care coordinator (the team member of any profession who is the designated worker for a particular service user), and the children's specialist made it clear that he was available to all service users who have children, thus hoping to remove the parent's fear of being singled out as a 'failed' parent.

Improving access to community resources

It is not unusual for professionals to refer families with parental mental illness to CAMHS, but few such referrals may be taken up. A parent's worst fear is that their mental illness will be inherited by, or passed on to their child as a result of their own 'bad' parenting. The referral arouses guilt and anxiety. Young people, particularly adolescents coping with the changes brought about by puberty and anxieties about their future, share these fears, which they feel are now confirmed by such a referral. The close working relationship between CAMHS and the CMHT, facilitated by the children's specialists, enables such fears to be managed appropriately and further help provided.

Important community resources are those that are available and accessible to all families without referral, such as children's centres, which offer opportunities to meet other parents, to make use of resources such as baby massage, breastfeeding support, and more intensive individual family support if needed. Both children's specialists made themselves known to the children's centres, to health visitors, and to the local network of children's agencies to introduce the new role. There is a slow process of relationship building which will come to benefit not only parents and families but also mental health staff themselves. Ultimately this fosters more joint working between CMHTs and community-based child-focused resources. This process of bringing services which have much to offer each other together is described by Solarin (2012) in a paper resulting from four years of working with parental mental health.

It is important to recognise that this is a new way of working for many staff in the CMHT who may not have previously worked in the community, and for whom the complex network of children's services is quite unfamiliar. In the evaluation of the pilot phase CMHT staff reported valuing the children's specialist's knowledge of and ability to access a range of resources to support their clients as parents.

Supporting children's educational achievement

In an earlier small local survey to establish what kind of help parents might value, help with homework for their children, help with their contact with school, and help in involving their children in after-school activities were frequently mentioned. These are aspects which the children's specialists are able to put into place either directly, by liaising with the school, accompanying a parent to a school meeting, or organising or contributing to a Team Around the Child (TAC: see Chapter 10).

The long-term aim in each case is to encourage care coordinators to be involved in such contact themselves provided the parent is in agreement with this. For some very fearful or paranoid parents this may not be appropriate, and it is better if school involvement is a separate function, for which the children's specialists are ideally placed. Their continuing presence in the CMHTs and in children's lives means that they can hold knowledge of the child's progress through school, particularly from primary through secondary, which a parent is unable to sustain. Children of parents with a mental illness may be especially vulnerable to what for other children are accepted developmental changes, such as starting school and the transition to secondary education. These involve increasing degrees of separation and independence from a parent for whom the child may feel responsible as a young carer, while the parent may feel excluded, having difficulty in seeing their child as separate from themselves and with their own developmental needs. The children's specialists can ensure that any difficulties are identified quickly before they lead to behaviour problems, poor attendance and poor achievement.

Children have sometimes expressed their gratitude for this kind of support as they may be acutely aware of the anxiety caused to their parent by negative reports from the school, feeling that their difficulties have contributed to the parent becoming ill.

With the later appointment of the specialist CHAMP teacher whose working knowledge of local schools is very important, more extensive work with schools and with individual children in the school setting became possible (see Chapter 10).

Reducing social isolation

During the pilot the children's specialist came to know a number of parents who had barely ventured beyond the end of their street. This may have been an effect of their ill health, lack of energy and motivation, depression, paranoia, and awareness of the stigma within the community. Social problems also contributed: being in temporary housing, knowing no one, living in poverty, not speaking English (see Chapter 12). Whatever the reason, this meant that children also did not go outside and felt unable to bring friends home. Before the appointment of the children's specialists the coordinator had arranged day trips out during half-term and school holidays for school-age children only. The purpose was to provide some respite at difficult times for children and their parents, to widen the horizons of the child, and to give them the opportunity to meet other children in similar circumstances to themselves. One only child with two unwell parents had asked previously: 'Is there anyone else like me?'

With his voluntary sector background the pilot children's specialist had a strong commitment to provide such opportunities for the whole family. These might start from introducing toys and games into the home which parent and child could enjoy together. This often represented a learning experience for parents who had probably not had knowledge of such play as children themselves.

In time, the specialist was able to introduce individual families to easily accessed neighbourhood facilities, such as libraries, sports and leisure centres and local parks, anticipating that in time they might feel more confident in accessing these facilities themselves or in allowing their children to do so. For some, the prospect of trying something new and the fear of failing proved too daunting. It was important to organise activities which parent and child could enjoy together. One mother, for example, spoke nostalgically about playing table tennis during childhood and, after the children's specialist accompanied her and her child to a leisure centre where this activity was available, she was able to return again without help. Much further help might be needed before a parent could show interest in and encourage a child's own choice of activity.

Families were also offered 'days out' as part of a group of families visiting a popular destination further afield. The benefits may be hard to measure; we might speculate that for children to see their parents in a relaxed context enables them to add to their personal store of positive family experiences, while for parents, attendance demonstrates that they can cope with an experience they might previously have found overwhelming, but whether families would repeat such experiences on their own is unclear. Anecdotally, however, a CMHT care co-ordinator suggested that her service users who were parents had fewer crises in the period leading up to the school summer holidays, as the families knew there would be some structure, some plan of activities for their children to look forward to. The borough also runs a very extensive 'Summer University' of two-week courses for children, in which more of the children known to CHAMP have been enrolled each year. Once enrolled, the organisation contacts the child directly the following year so that children acquire a sense of belonging to something in their own right that is not connected with mental health services.

Children of single mothers

Difficulties in the relationship between parents are consistently associated with post-partum psychotic breakdown (Marks 2002: 100), and a considerable part of the CMHT workload consists of single women with children, having separated or been abandoned by the child's father at an early stage. The child who lives alone with a single parent who is mentally unwell and socially isolated from family and community is at greater risk of developing a disorder later in life. The pilot children's specialist observed the tendency of these children especially to form an intense attachment to him, as someone who has demonstrated an interest in engaging with them and listening to their views perhaps for the first time in their experience. It is significant that he is a man, while the children's own fathers are strikingly absent, not only from day-to-day life, but from the mother's mind and active memory.

The importance and particular role of fathers in children's lives has in recent times received greater attention. One part of the father's role is that of providing emotional, and financial, support to the mother particularly in the period of infancy (Etchegoyen 2002). The healthy mother encourages the infant's interest in others, particularly in the father, and even a small baby quickly becomes aware of his presence, then later of his contact with a separate world outside the home. It is this quality of 'otherness', distinct from the mother, which is important for the developing child. Target and Fonagy suggest that the most important aspect of the father's role is that of fostering the child's autonomy, individuation and independent functioning, that is, 'having a mind of one's own' (Target and Fonagy 2002). The father is in a position to help the child reflect on his relationship with his mother, and to see it as separate from his experience of himself. This confirms and elaborates earlier findings about the factors protecting children with a parent with mental illness from developing problems themselves later in life, the presence of an 'alternative care giver' being important.

Working across statutory agency boundaries

The children's specialists do not carry statutory duties, although should a clear need for these arise they will certainly involve the appropriate Children's Social Care Team, or support the care coordinator in so doing. However, in addition to the project aims of early intervention and preventive work a central aspect of the role is to facilitate work across this interface. Where possible the aim is to initiate a joint assessment and planning process from the outset. Some case examples demonstrating the kinds of communication difficulties which can arise appear elsewhere in this book (see Chapters 6 and 9). A first task for the children's specialist in relation to a new referral to the team is that of cross-checking available information records to establish which other agency might already be involved with a family.

Mental health services maintain digital records of service user information. This will include personal history, previous illness, diagnosis, medication, and all assessments and plans made under the Care Programme Approach (CPA), for all of which medical confidentiality must be observed. It is also a requirement that details of the family and any children of the service user are included in all CPA records.

Information held by Children's Social Care (CSC) is also governed by confidentiality, but the nature of the information is somewhat different. All contact with CSC and from external agencies will be recorded, such as school concerns, health visitor concerns, and in particular police reports of incidents of domestic violence where children are in the household. These latter are not routinely passed to health agencies. Thus it is possible for a CMHT care coordinator to remain unaware of domestic violence incidents affecting his client. The children's specialist needs to be able to access this system to confirm children's names, ages and relationship to the service user, and to establish if CSC have any current involvement. Where this is the case, or where there have been child welfare concerns, he or she needs to alert both workers and ensure they are communicating with each other. Sometimes significant child protection concerns may be involved.

> One of the children's specialists was contacted by a primary schoolteacher concerned about a pupil who had a very poor attendance record and whose single parent was thought by the school to have a mental illness. Initial checks showed that the case had recently been closed by Children's Social Care following completion of a core assessment. This had concluded that there was no further role for Children's Social Care given that the parent was accessing support from mental health services and the child had been referred to CAMHS. During the closing visit the children's social worker had asked the parent about a reported incident of possible child abuse, but which had confusing cultural aspects. The parent accepted this had happened, and it was not followed up further.
>
> Subsequent checks in the CMHT showed that although the parent had recently had a first appointment with a psychiatrist, there had been no

previous long-term engagement with the CMHT. However, the psychiatrist had recorded that the parent had reported having disturbing thoughts of harming the child. Follow-up appointments had failed and there had been no communication at that stage between the two agencies about possible risk to the child, perhaps from a delusional belief held by the parent, whose mental state had yet to be fully assessed.

Further checks in CAMHS established that the offer of their support had been declined as no longer required, information not then relayed to Children's Social Care.

This was potentially a case in which the multi-agency involvement of services may result in an assumption that the other agency is responsible and taking action (see Chapter 1). Reder *et al.* had noted that 'the knowledge that someone is doing something reduces anxiety for other members of the network and the case becomes less of a priority for them' (Reder *et al.* 1993: 67).

It may also demonstrate the way in which someone in the grip of a psychotic delusion can quite skilfully keep this hidden from relevant professionals, while the school had been aware of something unusual in the parent's presentation (Lucas 2009).

Conclusion

Often the work may be slow and unrewarding as progress is then followed by a retreat by parents back to older, safer ways of functioning, or the capacity for change may be limited. It is essential that the assessment process and the sub-sequent work with children is not determined by the needs of a very unwell or heavily medicated parent, but maintains a child focus. The children's specialists, while seeking a more holistic approach, need to maintain close working relationships both with psychiatric colleagues and with Children's Social Care to ensure that assessment includes a discussion of parenting capacity, the likelihood of change, and the real risk of neglect to some children.

Those working as 'children's specialists' or as 'parental mental health workers' will bring a variety of life experience, professional training and theoretical approaches to this field, enabling the CHAMP team to provide a greater range of responses. Effectiveness has yet to be measured but what has taken place in the four years of the team's existence is a cultural change within CMHTs where staff new to the team now take the services of the children's specialists for granted, and existing staff members in both mental health and children's services make regular use of their presence for advice and consultation about the needs of children. Many CMHT staff members are increasingly confident in making direct referrals to children's services, whether statutory or community resources.

For a six-month period in 2008 an experienced childcare social worker was seconded to CHAMP. Unfortunately funding was not available to make this a permanent arrangement. Nevertheless, her return to a front-line integrated multi-agency assessment team in Children's Social Care has ensured that the presence of mental illness in the family is given due weight and attention at an early stage, and that inter-agency communication, planning and assessment is increased, avoiding multi-agency uncoordinated contact such as occurred in the case example in Chapter 1. Such secondments enable a greater exchange of knowledge, ideas and skills to take place.

Children especially value the role and the continuity of relationships which is available through these posts. With high staff turnover in statutory teams it can happen that it is the children's specialist who now holds the knowledge of families over time, and can recall past events and ways of coping. The resulting continuity and interest in children and their families goes some way towards mitigating

> the distress children feel at receiving an impersonal service where insufficient time is given to help them understand what is happening to them. They want a social worker who forms an enduring relationship with them and listens to them.
>
> (Munro 2010: 7)

References

Barnardo's (2009) *Keeping the Family in Mind.* Ilford: Barnardo's.

Etchegoyen, A. (2002) Psychoanalytic ideas about fathers. In Trowell, J. and Etchegoyen, A., *The Importance of Fathers: A Psychoanalytic Re-evaluation.* Hove, East Sussex: Brunner Routledge.

Hinshelwood, R. (1998) Creatures of each other. In Foster, A. and Zagier Roberts, V. (eds) *Managing Mental Health in the Community: Chaos and Containment.* London: Routledge.

Lucas, R. (2009) *The Psychotic Wavelength.* Hove, East Sussex and New York: Routledge.

Marks, M. (2002) Letting fathers in. In Trowell, J. and Etchegoyen, A., *The Importance of Fathers: A Psychoanalytic Re-evaluation.* Hove, East Sussex: Brunner Routledge.

Munro, E. (2010) *The Munro Review of Child Protection: Part One – A Systems Analysis.* London: Department of Education.

Paget, B. (2009) *The Children and Adult Mental Health Project, London Borough of Tower Hamlets and East London and City Mental Health Trust, Organisational Case Study Final Report January 2009.* CPEA.

Reder, P., Duncan, S. and Gray, M. (1993) *Beyond Blame: Child Abuse Tragedies Revisited.* London: Routledge.

Solarin, N. (2012) Going beyond: Collaborative work between a community mental health team and a children's centre. *Context* 120 (April). Association for Family Therapy.

Target, M. and Fonagy, P. (2002) Fathers in modern psychoanalysis and in society: The role of the father and child development. In Trowell, J. and Etchegoyen, A., *The Importance of Fathers: A Psychoanalytic Re-evaluation.* Hove, East Sussex: Brunner Routledge.

9 How systemic work can contribute towards the development of collaborative work between child and adult mental health services

Philip Messent and Noah Solarin

Of the two authors of this chapter, NS is a member of the CHAMP (Children and Adult Mental Health Project) team located within two of the borough's Community Mental Health Teams (CMHTs). Trained as a social worker and systemic practitioner, he also maintained a link within one of the local CAMHS teams where the other author (PM) worked as a family therapist, participating with him in a family therapy clinic there. Particularly complex cases that NS came across within his adult mental health service context, where children or young people were experiencing problems in their own right, were referred to the CAMHS team and where deemed appropriate by the multidisciplinary team were then seen within the family therapy clinic. This chapter describes the systemic approach that we have developed through making use of our joint membership of this clinic to addressing the needs of such young people and their families, using a case example as an illustration. It begins with a consideration of factors making such collaborative work problematic, then it uses a case example to illustrate key systemic practices which have helped us to overcome such obstacles.

Factors making collaborative work problematic

Reder *et al.* (2000) described the factors which have traditionally emphasised the differences between mental health services for children and those for adults (and therefore acted as barriers to collaborative work between them) as the theories and knowledge bases which have dominated the different specialities; the organisational structures of the different services; and the ways that professionals in the different services are trained.

Daniel and Chin (2010) give a more elaborated description of the differences between the two organisational cultures and the dominant explanations for problems:

> The adult team, serving those with 'severe and enduring mental illness' advocates a bio-psycho-social model with a large emphasis on the 'bio'. Interest in the adult's experience often begins at the onset of their 'symptoms' . . . Priorities include stabilising symptoms; securing housing and providing meaningful daytime activity. . . . Such an approach leaves little space for

thinking beyond the individual, and the needs of involved children can become marginalised outside of basic child protection requirements. In CAMHS there is a much lower threshold for accessing services, there is more of an acknowledgement of relationships and the effect of these on the presenting problem but within this culture parental mental health can be marginalised, as the child's perspective is privileged and parenting (rather than the parent's well-being) becomes the highest context marker.

The establishment of CHAMP was an attempt in one borough to dissolve such organisational barriers, to build common theoretical understanding and to provide joint training opportunities by locating staff within adult mental health services whose role was to raise awareness about and address the needs of the children of parents with mental health problems. This group has been found to be especially vulnerable to experiencing problems of their own. Rutter and Quinton (1984), for example, found in a four-year follow-up of the children of psychiatric patients that one-third showed no emotional or behavioural disturbance, one-third showed transient problems and one-third exhibited persistent disorders. Other studies since have also reported findings that children whose parents have mental health difficulties are at substantially greater risk of developing mental health problems later in life (Andrews *et al.*, 1990; Beardslee *et al.*, 1998; Farrell *et al.*, 1999; Shiner and Mormerstein, 1998; Weissman *et al.*, 1997; Zubrick *et al.*, 1995). However, Hall (2004) has concluded that the high rate of psychological disturbance in children of psychiatric patients relates more to psychosocial factors than to the illness itself, making such problems more amenable to change. We would not wish to imply that the experience of being brought up in families with a parent who is experiencing mental health problems is necessarily a harmful one, for fear of perpetuating unhelpful stereotypes; Denborough (2010) has described a 'memory project' which actively seeks to undermine such a view, highlighting the 'special understandings, learning and appreciations' linked to histories of growing up in the context of parental mental health struggles.

Key systemic practice one: 'joining'

Establishing liaison links through Child and Adolescent Mental Health Service staff members visiting adult mental health services and advising colleagues there has been one relatively well-established way (e.g. Maitra and Jolley, 2000) of making sure that the needs of such children are highlighted, but such approaches may have only a limited impact on such a different organisational culture. CHAMP involved workers with a training and interest in children's welfare being based *within* adult mental health teams, participating in every team meeting, and ensuring that the needs of the children of service users were thought about consistently and reliably. Being physically located within a service provides myriad opportunities for making sure that staff working within adult services feel that their point of view is being grasped, recognised and appreciated. This allows for a process of 'joining' as described by Minuchin and Fishman (1982); they describe this as the way in which a therapist needs to make sure that family members feel that their point of view has been understood before he can begin to introduce new perspectives. Similarly here with fellow professionals, physical co-location has allowed NS to understand and make use of the language and ways of understanding clients' behaviour which are prevalent within CMHT contexts, and this has then given him opportunities to introduce new perspectives. Daniel (2010) describes in a similar way the significance of sharing a physical space, highlighting the usefulness of sometimes simply sitting in the CMHT staff area, where consultation and joint working with care coordinators can happen more naturally.

There is evidence to suggest that despite their vulnerability to difficulties of their own, the children of users of adult mental health services may not be referred to specialist services (Weissman *et al*. 1997) and, when they are referred, they may not actually attend. Parents with mental health problems may be particularly anxious about the stigma associated with services and wish to protect their children from involvement. Fredman and Fuggle (2000) describe an example of a mother with mental health problems who initially refuses an invitation to bring her daughter along to a meeting to help clarify what sense the daughter can make of her mother's situation, insisting that her daughter was a 'good child' and had 'no problem'. Having a practitioner permanently based within adult mental health services and also attending a CAMHS family therapy clinic meant that not only were children of mentally ill parents who were experiencing problems appropriately targeted for such an intervention, but it also made it more likely that such families would actually take up such help. NS was ideally situated to ensure that any similar anxieties that parents and young people had about attending were addressed, starting to 'join' and building a relationship of trust with them before making referrals, then reminding them of appointments, and thereby maximising the likelihood that such families would attend appointments and engage with the help that was offered.

> A Bangladeshi mother (P) with long-standing mental health problems (and a diagnosis of schizophrenia) was seen by a Looked After Children social worker as risking the placement stability of her 8-year-old son C, who had been living with his maternal uncle and his wife and family for the past eighteen months, by her demanding and aggressive behaviour towards them when seeking contact with her son. The social worker made a referral to NS almost simultaneously with a referral from P's CMHT case worker, who felt that the child's social worker was unfairly prejudiced against the mother and that she should be given 'a chance' to regain the care of her son, despite her ongoing mental health problems.

It is often the case that there are splits or different perspectives between adult and children's services and that the result is not helpful in reaching a multi-agency agreement about how parents with mental health problems can still exercise some parental responsibilities, and the requirement on the other hand for their children's needs to be adequately protected. Buchanan and Corby (2005) found in a study of the views of the different workers involved with drug-abusing parents and their children that Drug Dependency Unit workers, whose primary focus was the welfare of parents, were more optimistic about the potential of drug-abusing parents to care reasonably for their children, with social workers whose focus was the needs of the child more circumspect, and health visitors, who had the least sustained contact with parents, least positive about their potential as carers. This case exemplified an exactly similar difference in view: staff most involved with the parent wished her to have more opportunity to play a role in her son's life, while staff responsible for ensuring the child's well-being were anxious to protect the boy from an involvement with his mother which they saw in largely negative terms.

With parents who experience mental health problems, Daniel and Chin (2010) suggest that most practitioners are grappling with the dilemmas created by, on the one hand, a strong wish to help parents to overcome the shame and stigma that so often accompany psychiatric distress and to develop self-esteem in their parenting tasks and, on the other, the need to assess whether children, despite their loyalty to their parents, are simply 'having to manage too much'. They suggest that holding and reflecting on these dilemmas and tensions in ways that do not become polarised and blaming between different services or professionals can itself in quite profound ways have an effect on families, diminishing anxiety and creating confidence in them about the possibilities for freer and more enabling talk.

It is our experience that both family members and professionals are likely to be more on the defensive and less open to new ideas when they are not on their own territory. Actually visiting families and agencies in their own homes and offices is sometimes necessary in order for family members and professionals to feel that their perspective is being acknowledged and appreciated, and once they have had this experience, they will become more able to entertain other points of view. Where differences of view have become polarised, a phone call or an email will not be sufficient for clients or fellow professionals to be brought together in a coherent way.

Key systemic practice two: the 'both/and' approach

One strength of the CHAMP model whereby a worker with responsibility for highlighting the needs of children is placed within the CMHTs is that it provides an opportunity to include and recognise both perspectives: seeking to maximise a parent's capacity to parent while also recognising the needs of children and seeking to find ways of addressing these needs creatively. A systemic approach helps to provide a framework for such a 'both/and' approach to the work, as Hoffman describes in a similar role that he occupies:

> In working systemically, one allows for multiple perspectives and truths. This has enabled me to respect the many different discourses eg psychodynamic, CBT and psychiatric in the multi-disciplinary context.
>
> (Hoffman, 2010)

This move away from an 'either/or' approach in which one perspective is a true representation of reality is one part of the postmodern movement as elaborated by Andersen (1992), with its central idea that we relate to life based on our perceptions, descriptions and understandings of the world, and that therapeutic conversations involve keeping alive multiple ways of understanding rather than aiming at 'truth'.

Tate *et al.* (2010) describe how even within their joint adult and young person family clinic working with these same families, a team can become divided, taking up positions of seeing things from either the adult's or young person's perspective. Once this has been acknowledged and explored further within the team, however, this has usually led to a more 'encompassing' response, drawing upon both perspectives.

In our work with C, his mother, carers and the professionals involved with them, it was important for us to maintain such a multiple perspective, recognising both the validity of P's wish to maintain her relationship with her son, and the risks that her contact introduced into the safety of his placement. It was only by keeping both of these legitimate perspectives in mind that all parties to this situation could remain connected, and open to ideas about new initiatives and ways forward.

During one phase of the work NS found himself starting to believe that P might indeed be able to resume taking a greater responsibility for C's care and might even once more become his main caretaker. He was coming to this view through his contact with P and with her care coordinator in the CMHT who saw her as being unjustly treated, through his own powerful commitment to the fair treatment of parents with mental health problems, and his belief in the fact that such parents are often unfairly stigmatised as not being able to provide parental care. In systemic work practitioners are encouraged to be explicit about such orienting beliefs and values, so that the team of which they are part can reflect about their likely impact upon the work, and introduce other perspectives (Fredman, 1997). In this way practitioners can remain reflexive about their own beliefs and open to other ways of thinking about a situation.

Other members of the family therapy clinic team were more sceptical about P's capacity to take on more of a parental role, given her own continuing mental health problems, and urged caution about encouraging P to adopt an increasingly active role in her son's care. This helped NS to not get too enthusiastic about urging the family and other professionals to take further steps in this direction. Such scepticism was proven justified when there was an incident in which P was violent towards C's aunt with whom he was placed.

Key systemic practice three: a multi-systemic approach

As a way of helping to include these different perspectives which are held by different agencies involved in such cases, we have developed a multi-systemic approach to the work, something akin to that developed for the treatment of young people with conduct disorder (Hengeller and Lee, 2003). The original version of this approach, multi-systemic therapy, aims to address problem-maintaining factors within the multiple social systems of which the young person is a member: the self, the family, the school, the peer group and the community. A unique intervention programme is developed which targets those 'subsystems' that are seen as most responsible for the maintenance of difficulties.

In a similar way the intervention offered within our CAMHS clinic is only one part of a wider systemic approach, aiming to find ways of understanding the perspective of the different family members and agencies involved and helping them towards a coherent and cooperative way forward, in which both the child's and the parent's needs and aspirations are recognised and responded to. In this case, through ongoing discussions in the clinic, NS was able to formulate and gain support in putting into action a plan involving all elements of the system represented in Figure 9.1.

At the heart of this diagram P and C are intersecting through their continued contact with one another. The main agencies are represented showing their primary focus of intervention: the CMHT mainly concerned with P, the other agencies mainly concerned with C. The journey that NS needed to repeatedly make during the course of his involvement as a part of his multi-systemic approach is represented by the arrowed lines, sometimes literally visiting, and always connecting with all the parties involved.

Described below are the different elements of the multi-systemic approach as applied with P, C, their extended family and the agencies involved with them, and the key systemic practices involved: the steps involved in NS's journey around the family and professional system mapped out in Figure 9.1. This is not a straightforward journey: the point of the approach is to be responsive to events

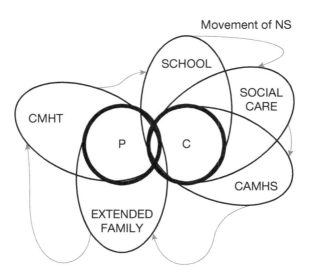

Figure 9.1 Systems involved with parent and child

and NS had to weave back and forth between agencies and contexts in order to stay connected, working towards a coherent goal with the different parties involved. In order to keep focused on such a goal NS needed to maintain a 'meta-perspective' on how he could make best use of his efforts to influence the different parts of the family and professional system, and his membership of a family therapy clinic was essential to this.

Key systemic practice four: the use of the family therapy clinic

Both of us belonged to a family therapy clinic team within a Child and Adolescent Mental Health Service, a group of colleagues of different disciplines working together for three hours every fortnight, dedicated to offering children and families a systemic family therapy service, and to developing the skills of workers involved in this treatment modality (Messent *et al.*, 2011). One very important way in which the family therapy clinic was helpful in this work was in providing a space for NS to reflect upon the complex situation in which he was being asked by two separate parties, the child's social worker and the CMHT worker, to become involved. Workers within the professional system had very different views stemming from their different perspectives, and it was important for the development of a coherent plan about what was going to be the best way forward, that NS was able to maintain a therapeutic flexibility, not getting drawn too much into one point of view and rather seeking ways of seeing the validity and usefulness of all points of view in order to bring all parties together. In order for anyone to retain such flexibility it is going to be necessary to have access to a reflective space and the family therapy clinic was ideally suited to fulfil this role, dedicating time for NS to bring us all up to date with progress and his movements around the family and professional system, to offer our different perspectives about what sense to make out of such developments and to come to a plan about his next steps.

Another use of the clinic was for NS to interview members of the family there, using other members of the clinic team present to maximise the impact of such contacts. Unusually, C himself was never seen within the family therapy clinic or indeed within CAMHS. This was because he was not actually symptomatic in any way: the concerns of the different agencies were about the long-term implications of his contact with his mother rather than C's immediate psychological well-being. In order to discuss the nature and frequency of such contact with his family and the agencies involved it was of course important to ascertain C's views, but it was not seen as necessary or desirable to invite him into the service to meet a new group of workers to do so directly. C had already made clear his wishes to social workers from Children's Social Care, and stayed consistent in his views throughout the period of our involvement that he wished to continue to live with his maternal uncle and his family, and to have some contact with his mother. Where we felt that some direct involvement with C would be beneficial this was through his involvement in group work delivered by CHAMP, and a piece of individual work delivered by a learning mentor at his school, both described below.

The clinic was used instead as a venue in which NS could meet with the main adults involved in C's care to explore their views about the nature and frequency of such contact, and how it could best be managed. When P was interviewed in the clinic over the course of several months, she presented as very focused and preoccupied with the idea of being able to resume the full-time care of her son. While her thinking about this wasn't always very coherent, she was able with encouragement to formulate a plan whereby she could hope to begin to convince the agencies involved with C that she was now more able to care for her son, signing up for and attending a parenting class, and keeping consistently to the routine of her weekly contacts with C, collecting and returning him to her brother's household.

In meetings with the uncle and aunt subsequent to P's attack upon C's aunt, the clinic used a reflecting team (Andersen, 1987) approach whereby team members would emerge from behind the one-way screen where they had observed NS interviewing the family members, to describe their different perspectives on what had transpired during the interview. This technique carries the implicit message that there are many different views about family lives and relationships, and it is inherently equalising, suggesting that there is no one professional truth about any family situation. During these meetings members of the clinic team were able to acknowledge in this way the difficulty of the uncle and aunt's position, in their desire both to encourage and make possible P's continuing contact with C, and at the same time to protect their household from P's unpredictable behaviour, which could sometimes be very hostile and intrusive. Their need especially after this violent incident to maintain boundaries about the nature and quantity of contact was recognised and reinforced by members of the clinic team, with P's contact with her son from this point taking place elsewhere. The uncle and aunt told the team how important it was for them to feel that NS and the team appreciated how challenging and problematic P's behaviour could be, having often felt frustrated in their attempts to communicate their concerns about P to staff involved in her care in the CMHT (where staff members will often be seen as reluctant to engage with such concerns of relatives, due to feeling bound by rules about maintaining the confidentiality of their patients).

Key systemic practice five: fostering good inter-professional relationships

In order to ensure that P was supported as much as possible in her attempts to take on more of a role in the parenting of her son and to ensure C's continuing well-being, NS also needed to stay connected with the different agencies involved with both. With P this was other members of the CMHT, the care coordinator and psychiatrist responsible for her care. With C this was his social worker and school staff. NS's commitment to supporting P's rights as a parent helped in ensuring that her care coordinator was able to feel that her patient's potential was being appreciated and recognised, and this helped the care coordinator to also acknowledge the importance of ensuring the safety and stability of C's placement. In a similar way NS's commitment to attending to C's needs ensured that agencies primarily involved with him, having begun from a position of being fiercely critical of P and seeing her as a threat to C's well-being, were able to become more sympathetic to her situation, recognising that C would need to preserve a relationship with his mother of some sort into the future, despite her continuing mental health problems. If it is clear to us that another worker is taking our point of view seriously, we are going to feel less duty-bound or 'positioned' (Campbell and Groenbaek, 2006) to put that point of view forcefully, and more willing to consider other points of view. By visiting the agencies involved, having arranged meetings with the relevant staff, NS was able to bring about a softening of the positions taken by staff involved with mother and son so that they were able to move from polarised positions to joining in working on a coherent plan which involved (initially) testing the capacity of P to build her relationship with her son, dependent upon P's continuing to comply with her medication regime, while carefully monitoring any adverse impact upon C and his placement with his uncle and aunt.

Multi-agency meetings are helpful arenas for reaching such a consensus, though these need to be chaired skilfully to encourage a dialogue in which all participants' contributions to the discussion could be acknowledged and included, without entering into unhelpful polarisations, with their associated ascriptions of blame and responsibility for causing problems. Tate *et al*. (2010) have stressed how by keeping conversations non-blaming, participants in such meetings can feel more able to take part and to discuss potential difficulties such as making plans for what to do if a relapse occurs. *Team Around the Child* (CWDC, 2009) which later also became *Team Around the Family* (DfE, 2011) meetings, recommended as part of The Common Assessment Framework (CAF) process to gather and assess information in relation to a child's needs, are ideal frameworks for such conversations, in that both carry an implicit assumption that in order to provide well for children and young people's welfare, it is going to be necessary for professionals and family members to come together and reach an agreement about how they can best work together. In contrast to similar meetings convened under child protection procedures, there is no inherent need in such meetings to assign blame or responsibility for difficulties, which allows greater freedom for creative collaboration. We have found that convening and chairing such meetings has on occasion been an extremely effective way of developing and maintaining such a consensus.

Key systemic practice six: 'externalising'

Many of the practices of social care and mental health have the unintended consequence of service users coming to internalise their problems, seeing themselves as identified with the problems for which they are seeking help. White (1989) has developed practices for encouraging service users rather to objectify problems as external to them, to encourage a sense of agency in combating and resisting the influence of such problems upon their lives and relationships. NS also supported and encouraged a learning mentor in C's school in undertaking a piece of individual work with C over a period of several terms at his school as a way of ensuring that he had an opportunity to reflect about the impact of the changes in his life in a context which was not going to be stigmatising or disruptive to his continuing education. NS introduced the learning mentor to the 'Tree of Life', a method drawn from narrative therapy (Ncube, 2006), which is an externalising approach to discussing with a child or young person the impact of potentially traumatic events on their life, emphasising the strengths and resources they have been able to draw upon in ensuring that they have been able to survive and succeed. With the guidance and support of the learning mentor, C drew a tree to represent his life to date, including all of his strengths, abilities and supports, before going on to talk about the impact of 'storms of life' that he had encountered, and to describe how he had withstood such difficult times. This approach provided a context for C to talk about the changes in his life with a trusted and familiar adult, and he produced a beautiful and creative piece of work, which reinforced a sense of himself as someone with resilience and the ability to survive difficulties and to succeed in his life. P was able then to witness and admire her son's creation, and to take in its clear message that while in the future he wished to continue to have contact with his mother, he saw himself as remaining in his uncle and aunt's care: '*I love my mum but I want to live with my uncle.*'

Key systemic practice seven: utilising all available resources to effect change

While family therapy early on in its development emphasised using resources within the family, as it has progressed to including the wider system as its focus, it seeks to identify potential positive influences wherever these may be found. Apart from NS's contact with P in our meetings at the clinic, he was also active in attempting to promote and support her contact with C in other ways. He arranged for a Bangladeshi female colleague to see P for some individual sessions, in which his colleague was able to explain to P more effectively than NS or any professionals previously involved in her care her rights in relation to C, the different roles and concerns of other professionals, and how she would need to conduct herself in order to reassure professionals that she was able to sustain a positive relationship with her son.

NS also included P and C in joint family outings organised by CHAMP, and C participated in holiday group work activities led by a drama therapist, aimed at encouraging the development of his self-confidence and his ability to communicate and work together with other young people, developing with them a performance then witnessed by his aunt as part of the audience.

NS also made sure that he was available to speak with C's uncle and aunt whenever they had concerns about the behaviour of P. This was probably crucial in sustaining the placement: in the clinic they repeatedly said how important it was to feel that someone understood and appreciated how very intrusive and disruptive C's mother's behaviour could be, and took seriously their concerns about her well-being and the need to protect themselves at times from the risk of her more challenging and outrageous behaviour.

Conclusion

After one further relapse resulting in a period of inpatient care, P has resumed a pattern of having regular contact with her son through phone calls and meetings at a contact centre which she has arranged and paid for herself. His uncle informed us that it was now C who had become expert at letting his mother know when her phone calls had gone on for too long, telling her that he had other things to do! C is now settled at secondary school, and P more acceptant of the part she has to play in her son's life.

This case example illustrates elements of a systemic approach which have proven helpful in undertaking work with parents with mental health difficulties and their children. This approach both encompasses the complexity of the family and professional network that becomes involved in such cases, and provides sufficient therapeutic flexibility to engage with family members and professionals with different and polarised points of view. At the heart of the approach is the use of a family therapy clinic team in ensuring NS's continuing effectiveness as he navigates his way around this network, helping to ensure that family members and professionals are able to remain part of a coherent and consistent treatment and placement plan.

References

Andersen, T. (1987) The reflecting team: Dialogue and metadialogue in clinical work. *Family Process, 26:* 415–428.

Andersen, T. (1992) Reflections on reflecting with families. In S. McNamee and K. Gergen (eds) *Therapy as Social Construction*. London: Sage, pp. 54–69.

Andrews, B., Brown, G.W. and Creasey, L. (1990) Intergenerational links between psychiatric disorder in mothers and daughters: The role of parenting experiences. *Journal of Child Psychology and Psychiatry, 31*: 1115–1129.

Beardslee, W.R., Versage, E.M. and Gladstone, T.R.G. (1998) Children of affectively ill parents: A review of the past 10 years. *Journal of the American Academy of Child and Adolescent Psychiatry, 37*: 1134–1140.

Buchanan, J. and Corby, B. (2005) Problem drug use: A new conceptual framework. In R. Cornwell and J. Buchanan (eds) *Effective Practice in Health and Social Care: A Partnership Approach* (pp. 163–179). Maidenhead: Open University Press.

Campbell, D. and Groenbaek, M. (2006) *Taking Positions in the Organisation*. London: Karnac, pp. 13–22.

Children's Workforce Development Council (2009) *The Team Around the Child (TAC) and the Lead Professional. A Guide for Managers.*

Daniel, K. (2010) The dance of attempting to break down barriers: Working with children and families where a parent is experiencing mental health difficulties. *Context, 108*: 56–59.

Daniel, G. and Chin, J. (2010) Engaging with agency cultures in parental mental illness training. *Context, 108*: 47–50.

Denborough, D. (2010) To come to reasonable terms with one's own history: Children, parents and mental health. *Context, 108*: 63–65.

Department for Education (2011) *Team Around the Child (TAC)*. Available at http://www. education.gov.uk/childrenandyoungpeoplestrategy/integratedworking/a0068944/team-around-the-child-tac (accessed 6 September 2011).

Farrell, G.A., Handley, C., Josephs, A., Hanke, A. and Hazelton, M. (1999) *The Tasmanian Children's Project Report: The Needs of Children and Adolescents with a Parent/Carer with a Mental Illness*. Hobart: Tasmanian School of Nursing and the Department of Health and Human Services.

Fredman, G. (1997) *Death Talk: Conversations with Children and Families*. London: Karnac, pp. 100–114.

Fredman, G. and Fuggle, P. (2000) Parents with mental health problems: Involving the children. In P. Reder, M. McClure and A. Jolley (eds) *Family Matters: Interfaces Between Child and Adult Mental Health*. London: Routledge.

Hall, A. (2004) Parental psychiatric disorder and the developing child. In M. Gopfert, J. Webster and M. Seeman (eds) *Parental Psychiatric Disorder: Distressed Parents and Families*. Cambridge: Cambridge University Press.

Hengeller, S. and Lee. S. (2003) Multisystemic treatment of serious clinical problems. In A. Kazdin and J. Weisz (eds) *Evidence Based Psychotherapies for Children and Adolescents* (pp. 301–324). New York: Guilford Press.

Hoffman, E. (2010) New perspectives in working with parental mental health. *Context, 108*: 51–52.

Maitra, B. and Jolley, A. (2000) Liaison between child and adult psychiatric services. In P. Reder, M. McClure and A. Jolley (eds) *Family Matters: Interfaces Between Child and Mental Health*. London: Routledge.

Messent, P., Pearson, A. and Skillicorn, I. (2011) Practitioners' experiences of family therapy clinics. *Context, 113*: 38–41.

Minuchin, S. and Fishman, H.C. (1982) *Family Therapy Techniques* (pp 28–49). Cambridge, MA: Harvard University Press.

Ncube, N. (2006) The Tree of Life Project: Using narrative ideas in working with vulnerable children in Southern Africa. *The International Journal of Narrative Therapy and Community Work, 1*: 3–16.

Reder, P., McClure, M. and Jolley, A. (eds) (2000) *Family Matters: Interfaces Between Child and Adult Mental Health*. London: Routledge.

Rutter, M. and Quinton, D. (1984) Parental psychiatric disorder: Effects on children. *Psychological Medicine, 14*: 853–880.

Shiner, R.I. and Marmorstein, N.R. (1998) Environments of adolescents with lifetime depression: Associations with maternal depression history. *Journal of the American Academy of Child and Adolescent Psychiatry, 37*: 1152–1160.

Tate, S., Perry, K., Fox, A. and Matthews, S. (2010) Making links: The reality of a CAMHS and adult mental health venture. *Context, 108*: 59–63.

Weissman, M.M., Warner, V., Wickramaratne, P., Moreau, D. and Olfson, M. (1997) Offspring of depressed parents, 10 years later. *Archives of General Psychiatry, 54*: 932–940.

White, M. (1989) The externalising of the problem and the re-authoring of lives and relationships. *Dulwich Centre Newsletter*, Summer Special Edition.

Zubrick, S.R., Silburn, S.R., Garton, A., Burton, P., Dalby, R. and Carlton, J. (1995) *Western Australian Child Health Survey: Developing Health and Well-being in the Nineties*. Perth, Western Australia: Australian Bureau of Statistics and Institute for Child Health Research.

10 A specialist teacher in the Children and Adult Mental Health Project

The growth of an idea

Louise Gallagher and Peggy Gosling

Introduction

This chapter aims to describe and reflect critically on the contribution of a specialist teacher within a multi-professional team such as the Children and Adult Mental Health Project (CHAMP). It describes the historical, theoretical and political context in which this development arose, and sets out the intended aims and objectives of the development in facilitating better outcomes for children of parents with mental illness.

Part one: Background to CHAMP in education

The long-standing history of immigration, coupled with acute poverty and continuing social and environmental deprivation, in this borough has been discussed elsewhere in this book (see Chapter 5), providing considerable challenges both for children and families residing in the borough and those providing services.

The demography of the borough is reflected in its school population. In 2009, owing to larger than average family size, 71 per cent of school-aged children were of black and ethnic minority families, with 57 per cent of Bangladeshi origin. The majority of these had English as a second language. Fifty-three per cent of children in the borough were entitled to free school meals, reflective of the levels of deprivation, and 23 per cent had special educational needs.

Since coming to work in education in the borough in 1994, I observed that there was growing commitment in schools to working closely with the local authority and other agencies, to ensure that these challenges were addressed, and that disadvantages to children and young people were minimised.

This is a small, densely populated borough with just over 100 schools in total. In 1994 only 18.7 per cent of secondary pupils had achieved five GCSE passes at grades A*to C in the borough, compared with a national average of 43.3 per cent (results from individual schools ranged from 11 to 33 per cent). By 2009 45.9 per cent of pupils achieved this standard, closer to the national average of 49.8 per cent for all schools (DCSF 2009). During the intervening years, by actively engaging and investing in local and national strategies and initiatives, including a programme of considerable refurbishment of schools, we were succeeding in raising standards of teaching and learning, and consequently making a very significant difference to a generation of children.

The education background – meeting the challenge

The Behaviour Support Team (BST), which I had the privilege to lead from 2001 up until my retirement, made a strong contribution to this outcome by helping schools and families to prevent and/or address problems of behaviour and disaffection and consequently maintain low levels of exclusion relative to comparable boroughs (DCSF 2009). In 2008/9 the rate of permanent exclusion was 0.16 per cent, comparing favourably with the average rate in surrounding boroughs. Disruptive behaviour, the most common cause of permanent exclusion, was not the sole focus of the BST. There was also a focus on social withdrawal and non-attendance, which similarly led to educational failure.

The BST was established in 1979, part of the veritable explosion of behaviour support services nationally resulting from widespread concern about the seemingly impossible problem of behaviour in schools. In contrast to the dominant pupil-focused model of the time, the BST adopted a school-focused approach developed by Lane (1978) in a nearby urban borough. Using this model, one focused on problems within the school context where they occurred. Topping's (1983) international evaluation of systems of support for disruptive pupils demonstrated that in contrast to 'pupil-focused' approaches (e.g. offsite centres, EBD schools) which were at best unproductive, at worst counter-productive, school-focused support teams, especially those employing behavioural approaches, could be effective in bringing about positive change for children within mainstream education, thus reducing disaffection and exclusion. Lane (1990) further elaborated this approach and its strength was supported by UK practitioner research (Harper 1987; Gosling and Gurney 1989; Crombie and Noakes 1992; Crombie 1995).

Having worked with Lane previously, I found a 'professional home' when I joined the BST in 1994 and brought a strong desire to extend his theoretical model, by exploring the nature of effective school-focused support: What did this model mean in practice? What were the necessary knowledge and skills which effective practitioners brought to their work? How were these developed and maintained? These questions formed the basis of my doctoral research (Gosling 2001), carried out on a part-time basis alongside a day job as a specialist teacher and manager. The findings were informed by the work and that of colleagues, and subsequently informed the development of practice within the team and with multi-agency partners.

They not only provided answers to these research questions, but suggested that effective working practices are underpinned by key values and principles reflected in both casework and in-service activities. At the most general level, these findings suggest a theory of contextual support, with context relating not just to the location of casework, but providing its central focus.

Two key values of partnership and evidence-based approaches supported practices and skills which enabled key adults to overcome aspects of school culture described by Miller (1996) as the '*debilitating*' isolation of staff, combined with '*conflicting feelings, beliefs, and attributions about behaviour*' which inhibited change. By building trusting relationships, effective practitioners enabled participants to attend to emotional and perceptual issues, while at the same time bringing evidence-based, reflective perspectives to problems.

This process was characteristic of the 'scientific practice' later described by Lane and Corrie (2006; see also Corrie and Lane 2010). On the basis of observations and other sources of information, such practitioners were able to formulate hypotheses that were creative and unconventional, and often 'risky' or intuitive. However, they were prepared to discard these hypotheses if they did not stand up in the light of evidence. They drew on a range of theoretical perspectives, which enabled them to elaborate participants' narratives, understand them in a new light, or change them to create different futures. Within partnerships operating with a commitment to evidence, they promoted shared ownership, understanding and expectations, objectivity, and the capacity to plan, reflect and evaluate.

One of the most interesting findings to emerge from this research was that these key values were also reflected in the in-service context where collegiality and a commitment to an evidence-based approach within the team supported competent and effective practice.

Expanding partnership – multi-agency working and early intervention

On completion of the research I took on the dual role of Head of Behaviour Support and Lead Officer for Social Inclusion. Determined to see the findings of my research realised, I began to elaborate the notion of context by extending it beyond the school gates into the wider context of home and community in which children lived their lives. These aims aligned closely with strategic priorities for this local authority which joined with partners in the health authority in forming a Children's Trust. At managerial level these principles were realised through the Social Inclusion Panel (SIP), a monthly meeting of service managers who considered cases of children and young people identified at risk of exclusion on account of their behaviour or attendance, or both. The SIP aimed to identify the agencies and actions that were required to prevent exclusion and promote good outcomes for vulnerable children. At operational level these priorities were promoted through the Multi-agency Behaviour and Social Inclusion Network (MABSIN), established in order to promote rapid and effective multi-agency responses to vulnerable children and young people in the borough. Through termly events, frontline professionals from education, CAMHS, social care, youth justice, voluntary and community agencies came together to share information about their work, to put faces to names, to liaise on current casework and new initiatives, in short – to oil the wheels of multi-agency working.

When the Coordinator (RL), appointed to work across adult and children's services, presented information at MABSIN suggesting that up to one-third of the service users of the community mental health teams, that is, 400 to 500 families, were then known to be parents caring for children and young people under age 16, there was a simultaneous recognition within the SIP of the existence of a group of children living with parental mental illness, who were presenting problems in schools ranging from withdrawal and social isolation on the one hand, to aggressive and antisocial behaviour on the other. What was particularly striking was that prior to the emergence of quite severe problems in learning, behaviour or attendance, the fact of mental illness in a particular child's family was often entirely unknown by schools, or 'known' in a way which was unhelpful and defensive, reinforcing unhelpful and emotive 'typifications' of problem pupils and their parents which inhibited change. Minor or temporary problems in learning, behaviour or attendance often went unnoticed and the additional special needs of these children remained hidden.

Children's social care was not then identifying these children as 'children in need'; nor had they, for the most part, met the threshold for child protection, while adult services did not then see children as their responsibility. In addition, the families themselves were anxious about the involvement of statutory services and did not readily or easily access community, other health or statutory supports.

From 2002 onward an informal link was established between the Coordinator, MABSIN and the SIP, enabling them to identify some of these children and ensuring that their needs were addressed before they became severe and entrenched. This early link led to my joining the steering group for the Children and Adult Mental Health Project.

A senior colleague from the Education Social Work Service, together with two behaviour support specialist teachers, subsequently played an important role in the Parental Mental Health Interest Group. This was a less formal but regular meeting of frontline practitioners from CHAMP, CAMHS, education and voluntary sector agencies. The group shared experiences of complex situations and came to focus on developing training and resources designed to raise awareness and understanding in schools. The group, which continues to meet, serves as a wider forum for discussion and exchange of information about CHAMP's work and that of other agencies.

This joint involvement brought an educational perspective to the development of CHAMP. It supported local research to ascertain the views of parents who were users of community mental health services, on the needs of their children. The two members of the BST, already engaged in CAMHS-funded postgraduate training in mental health, assisted in the collection and analysis of these data, which clearly indicated parents' wish for someone to help them access other agencies, to befriend their children, and help with homework.

In 2007 CHAMP had secured external funding to appoint children's specialist staff in the adult mental health teams, and a proposal for the inclusion of a part-time specialist teacher within this new CHAMP team was formulated. The local authority, recognising the importance of this development, identified funding to support a part-time teaching post in 2009, and this support continues, despite massive cuts in government grant in April 2011.

The aims and objectives of the specialist teacher post

The overall aim of the post was to maximise educational attainment for children living with parental mental illness, by working with multi-agency partners within the CHAMP team, to promote the broader *Every Child Matters* (ECM) outcomes: children's safety, their physical and mental health, their participation in education, and their economic well-being (see Chapter 5). ECM was the key driver of policy and practice in Children's Services from 2004 onward. While keeping a primary focus on these outcomes, specific objectives for the specialist teacher were defined as follows:

1 To promote effective working relationships between schools, multi-agency partners and parents/carers to assess holistically and meet the needs of children and young people referred to CHAMP. To ensure an early assessment of referred children's additional needs the Common Assessment Framework (CAF) then being rolled out nationally as part of the ECM agenda was used by members of the BST who found that by bringing their specialist knowledge of behaviour problems in schools, they could make it work. Making it work was described in a subsequent study (Gosling 2010).
2 To assist the school and partner agencies in developing plans to meet identified needs by taking on the role of 'lead professional', at least initially, to ensure that such plans were delivered, and to monitor outcomes for children and families. She would provide group interventions as needed to children and young people in schools as well as other settings. These might include interventions addressing bullying, bereavement and loss, raising self-esteem, easing transitions to and beyond secondary school, and supporting children in their young carer roles.
3 To introduce an educational perspective into adult mental health and children's social care settings and foster effective professional relationships across settings for the benefit of children and families. She would develop skills in working across traditional professional boundaries, identifying the skills, knowledge and qualities needed to make such work possible, thus enabling clear identification of training needs across the children's workforce.
4 To disseminate the knowledge and skills gained in such a way that the challenges of cross-agency working at the interface between adult mental health and children's services are understood and lead to more informed ways of working and improved services to families. The ongoing Parental Mental Health Forum provides one arena for this.

In Part two there follows an account of my co-author LG's pioneering work as the specialist teacher on the CHAMP project. This account describes the reality and the challenges of working contextually, of extending the focus beyond the school gates to the wider context of children's lives in their home and community. It also highlights the knowledge and skills she brings to this task.

A number of themes emerge from LG's account, many of which reflect themes that are consistent with my earlier research findings (Gosling 2001, 2010) reported above, but which, significantly, also emerge from other chapters in this volume.

- **Establishing trust through meetings and conversations** with children, families and inter-agency colleagues is a recurring theme running through this account and examples drawn from her casework illustrate the immense skill she brings to this task.
- Another recurring theme is a fundamental commitment to **building strong inter-agency partnerships**, networks of support for vulnerable children and families.
- She does what is **necessary and sufficient** to get the ball rolling, and keep it rolling until change can be sustained independently.
- Her **tenacity** in pursuing this goal is striking. However, it seems that theoretical, structural and professional differences sometimes present obstacles to effective partnership. **Supervision and the values and culture of the CHAMP team** are seen as crucial in overcoming these obstacles and preventing potential additional risk to vulnerable children.

Part two: A specialist teacher in CHAMP

Already a specialist peripatetic teacher in the BST, I (LG) was appointed to this new role on a part-time basis in 2009, bringing extensive experience of work within the borough across both primary and secondary provision and an unusual set of skills derived from a varied early working life. These included working as a secretary, as a nature reserve warden, in an adolescent residential setting, in a claimants' union, and teaching motor vehicle repair skills to young offenders. Such life experience possibly developed the creative and unconventional approaches outlined below.

The child spends the larger part of her waking life at school, and staff members already have a level of knowledge and insight into the child's emotional and academic well-being. Many professionals such as social workers and mental health professionals seem not to be aware of or appreciate this area of expertise and knowledge within schools. Therefore it may be helpful to explain the school scenario before showing how the involvement of an experienced borough peripatetic teacher can enable a fuller picture to be obtained in liaison with the parent, school and agencies, so that the most appropriate way to resolve difficulties can be agreed through teamwork.

The child's experience in school

For a child with difficult home circumstances, school is a very different reality from home. The predictable school timetable can provide a desperately needed structure for some children's lives, particularly those children who experience a chaotic or traumatic home life due to domestic violence, drug use by adults, or problems stemming from chronic parental mental illness. Whereas home can be a mixture of fearfulness, unpredictability and responsibility, school can provide sanctuary, rest, fun and a sense of achievement. In such circumstances children can flourish in school, experiencing the joy of childhood, with friendships and some real academic success. However, the reverse can be true; a child of a parent with mental illness may, in the school community, become known as the child of a 'mad' or 'weird' parent. Children can then suffer social isolation or ostracism throughout their schooling at a subtle level quite unsuspected by their teachers. The school may have cause for concern due to absenteeism or neglect, overt or withdrawn behavioural issues, with academic studies suffering due to the child's preoccupations with a stressful home life.

The school and its staff

Schools can seem rather inaccessible places, especially to parents and other professionals. The school environment can be rather a pressured one for teachers, proscribed by the teaching day, by assemblies, and five to six lessons per day, interspersed by break times and lunchtimes. Even during these periods teachers have to carry out break-time responsibilities, complete report cards, prepare for lessons, and deal with issues arising. Meetings take up valuable teaching time and are therefore extremely time limited and precious. After-school staff meetings often focus on developing all areas of pedagogy. A major feature of teaching is regular monitoring and assessment, with expected methodical intervention in support of children with lower levels of progress. Strategies to support a child's learning and well-being should include scrutiny of both academic issues and relevant home circumstances. However, there is rarely enough time for adequate ongoing pastoral care. In particular, where secondary school heads of year take on a pastoral role, many of them become frustrated by the lack of time available to do justice to the task. Given this full timetable, there can be a real difficulty for non-education colleagues in accessing relevant staff. The peripatetic teacher, however, has a certain 'right of entry', with prior knowledge of many of the staff across the borough's schools, and importantly of the school ethos or 'mindset' which can vary from school to school, each having different priorities. Awareness of these priorities is essential to the task of identifying pupils' immediate needs, and negotiating ways in which they might best be met. Some schools, for example, are able to recognise and accommodate greater difficulties accompanying children in families under significant stress, while others might maintain a 'zero-tolerance' approach to behaviour.

The advisory teacher for CHAMP: working with the school

Experience in the behaviour support team, supporting a range of difficulties in schools, has developed my understanding and sensitivity towards the most vulnerable and challenging pupils. Teaching across primary through secondary provision is also invaluable, particularly where children perform and achieve over a wide range of levels, struggling to reach National Curriculum targets. Children's cognitive skills may be adversely affected by parental mental illness (see Chapter 3), while others may have special educational needs. I work with children from nursery (approximately 3 years of age) through to GCSE level (15 years of age) and beyond, even including older siblings who might be unemployed and NEET (Not in Education, Employment or Training) or attending college. Family dynamics and caring responsibilities may result in enormous stress for this age group. Often their own emotional and mental health problems will never have been previously recognised or considered.

While some school staff may have experiences of mental illness among their own family or friends, others may share the fears and prejudices of wider society about mental illness. Such factors may prove an obstacle to the business of forming a mutually trusting and useful relationship with the parent. Essential to my role is ongoing formal or informal training and support for school staff, so that both child and parent are supported rather than exposed to added stress.

Some families suffer an embarrassment of agency input. A major element of the advisory teacher role is to draw together and rationalise the disparate agencies for a Team Around the Child (TAC), usually located within the school, with the school senior manager given the task of lead professional. Ideally, at this excellent and focal meeting the parent is securely supported by her or his CMHT worker, the child is involved where appropriate, and the team will agree the specifics of concern, and interventions to target support. Individuals take responsibility for specific outcomes within an agreed time frame, thus ensuring that agencies work in tandem. The aim is that the team continues to monitor and review, thus ensuring secure progress. I support the 'lead professional' to ensure that a holistic approach is sustained over time, that regular review meetings take place and that relevant agencies continue to work together. In this way the school and statutory requirements are adhered to, and all parties can feel confident within the procedure in which parent and child are participants, and the child's needs and welfare continue to be protected. The following case example demonstrates such teamwork:

> Secondary-aged Mandy was violent towards peers, and confrontational towards staff, unable to focus on her school work or even to see its relevance or importance to her in her immediate situation. She placed herself at risk of permanent exclusion from school. Her own fears about protecting her younger siblings from elements of her father's illness were affecting sleep and eating patterns. With my support, a school-based team of attendance welfare adviser, school social worker and school police officer provided a safe haven in their tiny office for her gradually to voice and address her fears, so that she could reflect upon and understand her behaviour and attempt to slowly change her behaviour – and be empowered to act more positively.

Working with the Community Mental Health Team (CMHT)

For a specialist teacher, despite much experience of multi-agency work, the move into the mental health professional field can still be difficult. It can take time to develop confidence in this field of new acronyms, parameters and language. Insensitivity in one's contact, whether with child, ill parent, school or mental health staff, could easily result in misunderstandings and a closing of possible avenues of engagement or negotiation.

For example, taking part in a parent's care plan approach (CPA) meeting can be daunting in the face of a very busy and powerful psychiatrist used to meetings taking a proscribed route. Feeling able to influence this scenario, as well as inform discussion with children, parents, teachers and other related agencies, is a delicate skill enhanced by previous multi-agency experience. However, there is an acute awareness, in this sensitive field, of the impact of one's actions having possibly serious repercussions. Such concerns can easily be immobilising, but for myself, excitement at being part of this important project, strong professional commitment, a high level of supervision and a dogged determination to persist until a means of change may be found for the children, help address feelings of doubt.

Hard-pressed CMHT workers are unused to working with children and schools, yet developing sound working relationships between mental health workers and school staff is crucial. Awareness of and respect for each others' expertise, workload and possible insecurities or defensiveness need to be addressed. CMHT staff workload is heavy, demanding and sometimes dangerous, and a move into unfamiliar territory can be tough. Yet their input is crucial in supporting the joined-up work between school and the possibly apprehensive parent in developing confidence in their parenting role, and trust in their child's school. Given the opportunity, I can often help CMHT staff to realise how helpful and relevant a CHAMP teacher can be to their work with service users who are also parents. Ideally, the CMHT care coordinator will have a relationship with the parent, and can respond to information about difficult school–parent relations, to help the parent in engaging more confidently with the school. Where CMHT staff, consultant and manager have understood the importance of such support to service users and their families, they will directly approach me with worries about service users' children. For others who have less experience of community-based work, this can be more problematic.

> When 10-year-old Faisal couldn't get his mother to wake up in the mornings (due to her erratic use of medication) he was too fearful to leave the house to go to school. Mother colluded with his wish to stay at home, citing his spurious illnesses. Significant absenteeism continued through primary school until CHAMP's involvement meant he was able to discuss his fears about his mum. The school was persuaded to allow him to arrive late without censure and to phone home during the day, thus alleviating his worries, resulting in improved attendance. The resilience of this very able boy also led him to ask me for information about his mother's illness, and then to make real academic

progress, enjoying school. Often the child doesn't understand the nature of the illness. In this case the CMHT care coordinator was the ideal person. Comfortable in conversation with the child and the parent, she explained and reassured Faisal about various aspects of the illness, and the possible impact on the family.

In these complex situations, it is crucial to be able to maintain confidence in one's own professional identity and perspective as a teacher, while remaining open, flexible and cooperative in work with a range of other professional and non-professional colleagues, irrespective of differences in their views, attitudes or theoretical approach from one's own. When sound, such work can effect real improvement in the quality of children's emotional health, educational achievement and lives overall.

Working with parents

This new role required that I develop a trusting relationship with parents, addressing more sensitive, private and often hidden areas of their lives. Teachers' lack of statutory powers mean that they are not feared in the same way as are social workers. One particular parent told a social worker that, whereas she would not meet with her, she would speak to the CHAMP teacher.

When working with disempowered and often distrustful families one needs to maintain a scrupulously high level of confidentiality while still keeping open lines of communication with other relevant professionals. Using the important clues to feelings and states of mind provided by non-verbal communication and body language is important.

It is crucial to encourage a parent to trust the school with information about the family's and the child's circumstances and needs. This has to be balanced by the staff's need to know, and protected within a closely guarded circle of confidentiality.

Kamal was a challenging reception-age pupil who became at risk of permanent exclusion. The domineering father would not allow the mother to assert behavioural management of any kind, and as a result she was bullied by her 4-year-old child. After an agreed home visit I learnt that an older brother had been reluctant to meet but quickly showed his distress, not having had an opportunity to discuss worries about his ill parent before. He asked for help in applying to college, perhaps a first step in requesting further help if needed.

Working with the child

A variety of issues may prompt a parent, the school or CMHT staff to request my involvement in supporting more vulnerable children in school. The examples below show ways in which the home situation can lead to significant absenteeism from school, instances of bullying or being bullied, the inability to form peer relationships, poor concentration, low self-esteem and behaviour likely to lead to exclusion. Without early intervention such difficulties can have long-term consequences for the child's emotional, social and academic development.

It is important to broach discussion with the young person non-intrusively – for example, favourite or difficult lessons or teacher relationships, friendships, and their own hopes for change. Children can only feel comfortable about broaching family issues if they have a high level of personal resilience, or if they feel they can trust the adult involved. The adult requires the confidence and ability to respect and listen. Within the school environment, I might employ and support a relationship of trust which already exists between a child and a member of the school staff. Children's own experience and worries are often unspoken and unsought. They may be affected by their parents' fears, which may represent a much-distorted worldview. Sometimes this will be the first time anyone has broached a parent's illness with the young person, and has wanted to listen to what the child has to say in a safe and confidential way. Children are aware of the prejudices in society, the impact of their parent's illness behaviours on the local community. In many cases, children accept their, often secret, life as representing normality (see Chapter 3). The fears the child has about their parent's illness can include guilt over their shame, fears that they have caused or contributed to the illness, that they too can become ill or taken into care, or that their parent will go into hospital.

> Ten-year-old Tanya made very poor progress at school, and was very isolated. The ostracising of Tanya had continued since nursery and she had not developed the social skills or the inner resources to ask for help, or to resist the attraction of inappropriate friendships, so eager was she to be included. Her mother was well known in the community; her bizarre appearance offending other parents. Tanya was drawn into negative company, and was involved in bullying a much younger child, with the result that she was excluded from school. It transpired that she was fully aware of the reasons for her isolation among her peer group; she was embarrassed by her mother, not understanding her condition. With my intervention she received outside agency support, small group involvement in school as well as learning support, aimed to enable her to explore her feelings, and develop the social skills to help build her independence. Following this intervention she received opportunities to catch up with her studies before moving to secondary school, where support was to be continued.

A family approach which recognises the impact of individual needs and behaviours on the rest of the family sometimes leads, in large families with a wide age spread, to my becoming involved with much older siblings, to bring about helpful change. Significant pressure on responsible older siblings (aged between 19 and 21) can result in a considerable risk to their own mental health.

In the case of 4-year-old Kamal, it was only his eldest brother, Soyful, who could assert an influence on him, and he carried a great deal of responsibility within the family. Soyful had completed his schooling, but was not confident enough to begin to look for work or have a life independent of the household. I obtained his agreement to apply for support from a Carers' project, which then helped him to build confidence, to obtain work, and occasionally to say 'no' to his family.

More worryingly, for Chantelle, the eldest daughter in another family, the pressure had led to a suicide attempt. I was able, with her agreement, to contact her university counselling department, where Chantelle now feels able to go for support.

Within these families the older child takes on a caring role, supporting parents. There may be a well parent able to offer the child an alternative experience of care. Some children appear highly resilient (see Chapter 3), though they may be fragile and vulnerable.

A primary-aged child lived alone with her very ill mother. Despite her parent constantly hearing voices and refusing to go into other rooms in the tiny flat because of her fears, Katya had a smile for everyone, was popular at school, and was making progress in her studies. Furthermore, the teacher would ask her to help others in the class, such were her social skills and ability. However, it was agreed with Katya that regular weekly access to a key worker with whom she could feel relaxed meant that she could talk about her worries if or whenever they threatened to become unmanageable. Transition to secondary school does not appear to be a success as yet, despite work. It is clear that this young, 'resilient' person still requires support. Difficulties in secondary transition remind one of the compounding factor of adolescence.

Early intervention of this sort is probably the most important way in which CHAMP can be effective in the work in the school.

Other children find themselves in 'hard to reach' families where effective parenting may be seriously compromised or absent. There may be any number of reasons why a family does not engage – fears of the family being broken up by Children's Social Care, previous unsuccessful or short-lived experiences of support, being intruded upon by staff from multiple agencies who fail to ask relevant questions or to treat the family with respect, telling the parent what she or he should be doing, telling the children (who are probably very experienced with looking after a very ill and unpredictable parent) what to do, or not listening to their views. Sometimes service users feel too depressed or overwhelmed by anxiety to make any contact at all. One parent demonstrated a real desire to engage, but simply could not summon up the energy or nerve to answer the phone or the door for days on end.

Stephen had grown up in a secretive and closed family unit. The alcoholic father had died, leaving Stephen with his severely agoraphobic mother and older sibling. Stephen was the only member of the household who left the house, to go to school alone. As a result he had a limited social experience and a resultant fear of the world. School had never seen his mother, and her CMHT worker who visited regularly was unable to motivate her to do anything. It has proved an incredibly slow and difficult process to encourage Stephen's mother to take on any level of parenting, or for him to get on a bus, then to get on the bus alone – to take on voluntary work, and attend sixth-form college – all encouraging him possibly to see the world as a place he has a right to be and where he can be happy and productive.

I worked to build a trusting relationship with the CMHT worker who knew the family well and was helpful, and who gave relevant and useful background knowledge. She also facilitated access to his mother who, over fifteen years, had had no previous face-to-face contact with education services. This enabled the mother to allow me to work with her son. Over the past two years, another agency has joined the work which has resulted in moving this parent to engage with the services helping her son out of his trapped life, towards college, and possibilities of work.

Conclusions

Skills

Specialist teachers are equipped with a range of tools for helping such vulnerable children, including solution-focused brief therapy, and counselling skills. They will have knowledge of child development and of age-appropriate educational key stage expectations, as well as of significant points in a child's school life where vulnerability is increased, such as transition to secondary, or school leaving. They need also to understand attachment theory, the making of secure maternal bonds between mother and child in early infancy, and the ability to recognise the behaviours associated with poor attachment histories. Teachers specialising in working with parental mental illness will also want to build on their knowledge and take into account new developments in mental health provision, and also, in the field of the neurobiology of the developing brain, to understand the impact of early trauma or violence within the family on children's cognitive, emotional and behavioural development.

Awareness

Children may be more vulnerable by birth and pre-birth experience of their mother's mental illness, and by physical or emotional separation. Children's resilience will vary and it is important to know how best to support it. Some children astonish one with their apparent maturity, positivity and social sensitivity in the apparent absence of emotional support. However, as with Katya, their possible fragility needs to be kept in mind. Where a child is experiencing particularly stressful circumstances and reacting accordingly, their ability to make use of what is on offer from a sensitive, informed and perceptive member of staff means there is a possibility for change and growth. Early damage can still be mitigated in later childhood through good friendships, the care given in a close adult relationship and positive achievements.

Inter-agency work

Multi-agency working is fraught with frustration. The regular inability of agencies to come together, and the effort and determination required to encourage disparate workers to see the benefits of inter-agency working, can be wearing. Despite the mission statement and statutory responsibility of the CMHT to support the whole family, to work in a multi-agency way to support their clients in their parenting role, and despite the CMHT worker's own sometimes long-term relationship with that family, it has been very difficult to persuade them to liaise with schools and children's social work teams. Perhaps this reflects managerial direction or service users' own difficulty in engaging with the complex world. School staff too may feel discomfort in taking on possibly difficult or challenging parents in more therapeutic approaches to their needs in order to support the most vulnerable pupils. However, when there is awareness of this, a non-blame culture can be created, and worthwhile benefits can result for the family. For example, the well-run Team around the Child and Family (TAC) meeting can be a truly useful facilitator of effective inter-agency work with the family.

Finally, this work relates to a significant population within our society. In such entrenched and sensitive situations it moves slowly, requiring patience and persistence over a lengthy period of time. This is important work in progress.

References

Corrie, S. and Lane, D. (2010) *Constructing Stories, Telling Tales: A Guide to Formulation in Applied Psychology.* London: Karnac.

Crombie, R. (1995) 'Managing Behaviour in Mainstream Schools: Changing the Culture', unpublished Ph.D. thesis, Warwick University.

Crombie, R. and Noakes, J. (1992) 'Developing a service to support children with behaviour difficulties in mainstream schools', *Educational and Child Psychology,* 9, 4: 57–67. London: The British Psychological Society.

Department of Children, Schools and Families (2009) *Achievement and Attainment Tables 2009 – Secondary School GCSE & Equivalent,* Tower Hamlets and 'Performance Tables 1994 GCSE' (Internet). Available from http://www.education.gov.uk/cgi-bin/performancetables (accessed 10 March 2012).

Department for Education and Skills (DFES) (2004) *Every Child Matters: Change for Children in Schools.* Norwich: The Stationery Office.

Gosling, P. (2001) 'Partnership for Change: Effective Practice in Behaviour Support', unpublished Ph.D. thesis, London Institute of Education.

—— (2010) 'Every Child Does Matter: Preventing school exclusion through the Common Assessment Framework'. In Corrie, S. and Lane, D.A., *Constructing Stories, Telling Tales: A Guide to Formulation in Applied Psychology.* London: Karnac.

Gosling, P. and Gurney, P. (1989) 'Islington Educational Guidance Service: Evaluation Report', unpublished report to Inner London Education Authority.

Gray, P. and Noakes, J. (1994) 'Providing effective support to mainstream schools: Issues and strategies'. In Gray, P., Miller, A. and Noakes, J. (eds) *Challenging Behaviour in Schools.* London: Routledge.

Harper, T. (1987) 'An Evaluation of the Work of a School Support Team', unpublished Ph.D. thesis, London Institute of Education.

Laming, H. (2003) *The Victoria Climbié Inquiry.* Norwich: The Stationery Office.

Lane, D.A. (1978) *The Impossible Child.* London: ILEA.

—— (2nd edn 1990) *The Impossible Child.* Stoke-on-Trent: Trentham Books.

Lane, D.A. and Corrie, S. (2006) *The Modern Scientist-Practitioner: A Guide to Practice in Psychology.* Hove: Routledge.

Miller, A. (1996) *Pupil Behaviour and Teacher Culture.* London: Cassell.

Topping, K. (1983) *Educational Systems for Disruptive Adolescents.* London: Croom Helm.

Part III

The wider context

The three chapters that follow, as well as describing particular areas of important work with families experiencing mental illness, are part of the wider context, the backdrop, in which the project was set, and it is unlikely that without each of their contributions it would have been able to develop at all. Together they may be said to constitute a part of Winnicott's 'facilitating environment' in which growth can take place (Winnicott 1990).

The Family Welfare Association, now renamed Family Action, set up a Building Bridges project in the borough three to four years before the appointment of the coordinator from a central government specific grant. They raised awareness of the difficulties of families struggling with children and mental illness with both council members and the senior management team within the Social Services Department as it was then known, successfully negotiating a contract to provide a support service for these families. They introduced their service to the community mental health teams and ran a series of lunchtime seminars for all professionals to come together. Notably, as Catriona Scott's chapter demonstrates, they engaged the ethnic minority communities among whom the need appeared greatest. In essence the groundwork for the appointment of the coordinator and later the development of CHAMP had been done by them, making senior management and the mental health teams aware of the level of need and of the (then) new ideas about parental mental health and child welfare.

In the late 1990s the number of psychiatrists in the borough did not reflect the growing population, nor the high levels of serious mental illness. The existing consultant group had experienced, just as had staff in the teams, constant reorganisation including the beginnings of 'care in the community', new management structures, boundary changes, and redefinition of their role in relation to other mental health staff no longer based on the wards. They carried a heavy responsibility for the safety both of their patients and of the public. They placed patient care first, and were, unsurprisingly, often resistant to further demands to think about families and children, whom they would refer to colleagues in CAMHS or to child protection services if necessary. Eleni Palazidou took a particular interest in the minority communities in the borough, particularly women patients who shouldered the burden of childcare, sometimes caring for a mentally unwell partner and sometimes unwell themselves. She was an early member of the project group, contributing an important perspective which she outlines in Chapter 12. She emphasises the essential nature of the relationship between the consultant psychiatrist and his or her patient, a central theme of this book. This relationship is continuous over time, providing a developmental perspective on family life, which is not always recognised by other professionals. She also outlines the changes in relation to the children of mentally ill parents, and the impact these continue to have on psychiatric practice and workload. The newly created Mental Health Trust has increased the number of consultant psychiatrist posts and recruited several young consultants whose training will have included these recent developments in relation to children and parents. They are now based within the community mental health teams, which has increased their accessibility to staff, and allowed far greater exchange with the children's specialists than had been possible earlier.

Finally, Cathy Urwin's chapter describes a piece of outreach work in Sure Start, from the late 1990s, which developed out of an Under-Fives project within CAMHS. She had led an Under-Fives discussion group for some years in which a small multidisciplinary group drawn from the three CAMHS teams and from primary care examined Under-Fives referrals to CAMHS, the outcomes and the pathways these families followed. It was an important forum for sharing thinking, knowledge and ideas for improving the service to this group. Other chapter authors have spoken of the unresolved loss which women and their children may experience when they are separated, either permanently as a result of the child going into the care of the local authority or temporarily through the mother's hospitalisation, and of the impact of such separation on children. Working with two women who had previously experienced a serious post-partum depression, and were at risk of hospitalisation, Cathy Urwin demonstrates that it is possible to work through the difficulties, to listen to both mother and child, attending to the needs of both, encouraging the mother in her parental role, and preventing further breakdown or separations in the long term.

Pregnancy and birth when a mother is acutely mentally unwell is a time of intense anxiety for the mother, the family and for professionals. It is a time of potential conflict among agencies and their staff about whether to admit the mother to hospital and how to provide care for the baby. While both mother and baby need reliable and sensitive care, their needs appear to compete, and this may be played out among agencies, community and hospital based. Eleni Palazidou has described how advance preparation with the mother, the family and with support services in the community can combine with consistent medical care and optimum treatment of symptoms. Cathy Urwin's case example takes this further, illustrating the way in which the bio-medical model of treatment of severe mental illness can combine with a psychosocial model of understanding the psychological processes at work in the mother whose capacities for parenting a baby are overwhelmed by her disturbed state of mind.

Urwin has referred elsewhere to the need for the secure base of the CAMHS multidisciplinary clinic team for such work to be possible (Urwin 2005). She demonstrated there the depth of work that can be achieved in a community setting where factors such as a regular time and space, privacy of sessions, and confidentiality may require constant renegotiation, and cannot be taken for granted. In such circumstances it is

> the traditional organisational structures, with uncluttered lines of authority and clear boundaries, [which] continue to exist in our minds as knowable entities . . . because they are in part historical containers of values and professional identity. . . . As such they are a powerful influence on us, a source of creative strength in facing an uncertain future.
>
> (Cooper and Dartington 2004: 142)

This traditional organisational structure in which there was time for supervision, learning, thoughtful case discussion, and a disciplined evidence-based approach to new areas of work was the same secure base which underpinned the development and growth of the coordinator role and of the child and adult mental health project.

References

Cooper, A. and Dartington, T. (2004) 'The vanishing organisation; organisational containment in a networked world'. In Huffington, C., Armstrong, D., Halton, W., Hoyle, L. and Pooley, J. (eds) *Working Below the Surface; The Emotional Life of Contemporary Organisations.* London: Karnac. http://www.karnacbooks.com/isbn/9781855752948, reprinted with kind permission of Karnac Books.

Urwin, C. (2005) 'A Sure Start Rapid Response Service for parents and their under fours'. In Launer, J., Blake, S. and Dawes, D. (eds) *Reflecting on Reality: Psychotherapists at Work in Primary Care.* London and New York: Karnac.

Winnicott, D.W. (1990) *The Maturational Process and the Facilitating Environment.* London: Karnac.

11 Providing a comprehensive service

A partnership with the voluntary sector

Catriona Scott

Partnership working between local authorities, other statutory agencies and the voluntary sector has in recent years become an increasingly important aspect of public service delivery.

Family Action is a charitable organisation which provides a range of support services for vulnerable and disadvantaged families and children throughout England. It specialises in professional home-based support.

Set up by Octavia Hill in 1869 as the Charity Organisation Society (COS) the charity initially provided financial help in order to relieve poverty and prevent families from having to enter the workhouse. It was soon recognised that what was needed was not financial support on its own and that, to make effective changes to the social circumstances of families, both practical help and emotional support were necessary. Providing a combination of these three elements marked the beginning of 'social casework' and the early establishment of social work as it has become known today. This work with families was originally carried out by volunteers and when it became apparent that training was needed the COS published a volunteer's training manual, and went on to become a pioneer in the professionalisation of social work. Family Action continued to play a key role in the development of social work training.

The COS was renamed the Family Welfare Association (FWA) in 1946 but two years later with the 1948 Children Act most of the social casework it had been providing became a statutory responsibility of the new Children's Departments. The FWA refocused its work on therapeutic support for families who had a range of complex and deep-rooted problems. It organised the first UK Family Therapy Conference in 1975 at a time when family therapy was not well recognised in this country. The organisation developed a new role in designing and delivering services which complemented those of the statutory health and social care services. In 2008 following consultation with service users, staff, commissioners and funders the FWA decided to modernise by changing its name to better reflect its values and standards of service delivery. Consequently FWA became Family Action, and the organisation continues today to provide services that work with complex family situations and that are now commissioned by local authorities and health authorities to do so.

In its early days Family Action campaigned for policy change, and this campaigning role has remained one of the organisation's activities. Through its firsthand experience of working with individuals and families Family Action is able to identify the need for change, provide responsive services which are monitored and evaluated, and use the resulting evidence to influence policy makers about the need for changes in services and welfare.

The other aspect of Family Action's role which has continued from these early days is its financial support to families. The charity continues to make grants to families in need throughout the UK for essential household items, education and training or for much-needed holiday breaks.

Family Action's approach to working with families is based on understanding what it is that *individual* families need, being prepared to work alongside all the family members and engaging the family in the design and delivery of the services they receive. While safeguarding vulnerable adults and children is the organisation's top priority, it uses a whole-family approach, with a focus on relationships underpinned by theories of attachment. In its direct work with families a solution-focused approach is used, with a concentration on building on strengths and working with positives.

Family Action's Building Bridges model

Building Bridges was developed in response to research and Family Action's experience as a service provider to families. Research was showing that adult mental health services failed to take account of the fact that many of the users of their services were parents, and consequently the needs of their children were overlooked. This reinforced Family Action's experience of a lack of communication between the many different agencies working with a family. This was especially so with services focusing on adults' needs and those focusing on the health and welfare of children.

Family Action set up the first Building Bridges project in 1999 and others followed later in various locations across the country. The model uses a range of clinical tools to measure the impact of its interventions. An external evaluation in 2007 noted the very striking positive feedback both from other agencies and the parents who received the service. Only five out of thirty-one parents interviewed expressed any degree of dissatisfaction with the service (Morris 2007). A further evaluation in 2011 amplified this feedback and found the service to be extremely effective in improving outcomes for parents and for their children, and saw a significant reduction in family members' involvement with statutory services (MacLeod 2011).

For example, analysing data from 2004 to 2010 that is England-wide, the 2011 evaluation finds that Building Bridges reduced the need for the Care Programme Approach for Adults by 47 per cent and for local authority care by 70 per cent. Parents reported a statistically significant increase in satisfaction with parenting. While methodologies make clinical scales for children's well-being less straightforward, nevertheless both the 2007 and 2011 evaluations demonstrated improved outcomes in this area as well.

Further validation of Building Bridges as an effective model for working with families affected by parental mental health is that it was featured as a good practice case example in the SCIE Guide 30 Mental Health and Child Welfare: A Guide for Adult and Children's Health and Social Care Services. In 2010 the Centre for Excellence in Outcomes featured Building Bridges in its *Grasping the Nettle* report into effective early intervention models and estimated that every £1 spent on Building Bridges yielded a social return on investment of at least £2 owing to savings generated by, for example, reducing the need for care proceedings and the need for local authority care.

Originally the Building Bridges model was developed to offer an intensive home visiting and support service to families where a parent, or parents, had severe and enduring mental health problems. Gradually this remit has extended to include families where the parent has a wider range of multiple complex needs such as learning difficulties, substance misuse, etc. The same approach is used, though in different local areas the model has been able to be flexible to suit the needs of the commissioners. In this particular area the service is restricted to families where a parent or parents have a severe and enduring mental heath problem. The service is commissioned jointly by the adults' and children's services with the greater part of the funding coming from the adult mental health services, and therefore families can only be referred through them. The majority of referrals are made by the Community Mental Health Teams, and close working relationships are maintained between them and the local Family Action team. This includes Family Action staff accepting referrals and reporting back on a regular basis on the progress of work with a family. The family support worker will attend meetings, case reviews, care planning meetings, etc. regarding the parent and will liaise with other professionals working with the family (e.g. community psychiatric nurses, social workers, health visitors, GPs, etc.), often acting as an important liaison when there are a number of professionals involved with one family.

Indeed, the quality of partnership working was the most common feature mentioned by stakeholders in Mary MacLeod's independent evaluation of the Building Bridges service (MacLeod 2011).

When a family is referred to Building Bridges an initial assessment of the family's needs is made by the coordinator who makes a home visit. It is important at this stage to find out how the family see their needs and what issues they want to address. A family support worker is then allocated to the family and together with the family draws up a work plan with specific goals. Progress on achieving these goals is reviewed regularly throughout the work with the family which may be ongoing for up to a year. At the end of the work, before a case is closed, a final review is held with the family, the family support worker and the co-ordinator. Feedback from these reviews is used to inform the development of the service.

The family support worker is able to help with practical concerns as well as emotional, financial or other issues. Very often the issues identified by the family are practical, and helping with those issues is an important way of building up a working relationship with the family. This enables the worker to go on to address some of the more complicated emotional difficulties the family may be experiencing.

All family members are included in the work and this holistic way of working is at the heart of Family Action's interventions with families who have complex and deep-rooted problems.

Work with the family may include:

- help to improve adult relationships;
- help to improve parenting, relationships with children and children's behaviour;
- work with children to help them understand the mental ill-health difficulties facing their parents;
- accompanying parents to appointments;
- introducing parents to other services (e.g. Sure Start Children's Centres);
- advice and guidance on accessing benefits and other services;
- help to complete forms/make applications for other services;
- liaison with other agencies involved with the family;
- arranging family outings/activities for the children.

The borough-wide Family Action service

The local Family Action team in this area is made up of several different projects each with specific remits, working closely together and complementing one another. At different times and depending on funding initiatives, the projects running include a behaviour support service in schools and an intensive family support service in partnership with Children's Centres across the borough. Working in partnership in this way enables Family Action to reach out to the neediest and most isolated families, and by operating on a home visiting basis the support workers become a vital link between the family and other agencies.

The team has an overall manager with coordinators who manage the separate projects. The coordinators line manage and supervise the staff team of support and development workers. Members of staff are recruited to work in a particular project but when necessary are able to work across projects. This ensures that experience and expertise are shared and it also allows flexibility in being able to match families' needs with workers' backgrounds or particular skills.

Building Bridges, as one of these projects, works closely with the Carers Connect Project which supports those who have caring responsibility for a family member with mental health problems. Carers Connect aims to raise awareness of issues faced by carers and to develop support services for them and their families. As well as providing services for adult carers, the project also runs trips and activities for young carers, many of whom are from families known to the Building Bridges project. A family could be known to more than one of the projects within the team or be referred between projects. Workers in the wider staff team decide who would be the most appropriate worker to engage with the family to avoid duplication. Workers are also able to support one another and sometimes another worker could be called in if, for example, a family preferred to have a female worker when their current allocated worker was male, or vice versa.

In addition to the individual casework provided by the projects the team organises family outings and activities in the school holidays to which all families using the services are invited to join in. These are important for families who may be otherwise very isolated and it gives the family support workers a chance to get to know the parents and their children in an informal setting.

Family visiting project

A further development which followed on from the work of Building Bridges was the Family Visiting Project. It had been the experience of the family support workers in Building Bridges that in many of the families they were supporting, the children's uncertainty and anxieties about mental health issues were a feature. When a parent's mental state had deteriorated to the point where hospital admission was necessary this more than likely would have been preceded by an unsettling or perhaps even a very frightening situation at home. Adult services were not particularly geared up to deal with the problems of the children, and the family may not have been known to Children's Services.

It is well recognised that hospital psychiatric wards are not suitable places for children and can be alienating and cause anxiety. When the psychiatric inpatient facilities of the local hospital were rebuilt, a room was allocated for children and young people to use when visiting a parent in hospital. This set the scene for the Family Visiting Project to develop as a partnership between Family Action and Children's and Adults' Social Care Services. The project aimed to raise awareness among the hospital-based staff of family issues and to promote both the needs of the mentally ill adults to keep in contact with their children and the children's need to see their parents in an informal and homely atmosphere.

The family room was designed to be a safe, comfortable and child-friendly environment within the hospital building. A group of children likely to use the room were consulted as to their views on decoration and furnishings. It is seen as important to keep the use of the room solely for its original purpose, which is a challenge given the inevitable pressure on accommodation within a busy hospital. There have been frequent calls for it to be used as an occasional meeting room or as a quiet room for staff, but this would affect its availability and devalue it as a resource for children.

A Project Coordinator, whose role it is to promote the facility with service users and with both the hospital and community adult mental health staff, ensures the room is kept for its original purpose. The Coordinator works as part of the wider Family Action staff team in the borough which means that, though mainly based in the hospital, she has the support of colleagues in the whole team, as well as supervision from the team manager and access to all the training and development activities which are available for the team members. This ensures that the project is properly linked into the other Family Action services, and families can be referred into the Building Bridges project directly via the Family

Visiting Coordinator. As well as working closely with the Family Action team, the Coordinator provides an important link between hospital and community mental health staff.

Because of her knowledge of the families, she is able to support ward staff with information for family histories and can often provide details of which other agencies a patient may be linked into. For some families a degree of supervision is necessary, and for others some facilitation is needed. This is usually provided either by a member of the ward staff or a family support worker or social worker who is known to the family. The usage of the room has gradually increased and feedback from those who use it is generally very positive. Some members of the hospital staff have expressed the view that patients who use the facility tend to recover more quickly, although there is, as yet, no hard evidence to support this.

The Family Visiting Project has a steering group made up of representatives from the Mental Health Trust and Children's Social Care, as well as Family Action staff. After the initial pilot funding ran out, the local authority Children's Services continued to fund the project and the contract was later combined with that of Building Bridges.

A very important focus of all of the work in the Building Bridges project is raising awareness of mental health issues in a way which can be understood by children and young people of all ages. At the request of the Primary Care Trust who provided the funding, Family Action produced a resource leaflet aimed at children and young people to help identify those who had caring responsibilities for an adult with a mental illness and to ensure that they received appropriate support. Family Action was in a good position to be able to do this as it already ran carers' services, young carers' activities, services linking into schools and young people's organisations, combined with its experience of working with the families in Building Bridges. The leaflet was made widely available through schools and youth organisations across the borough.

Relationship with CHAMP

Given Family Action's reputation in the borough for work supporting parents and their children where the mental health of the parents was an issue, it was fitting that the organisation was involved in the early discussions and planning of the Children and Adult Mental Health Project (CHAMP). Family Action was represented on the steering group which progressed the idea of a coordinated approach within the borough. The children's specialists who were employed as part of the CHAMP initiative were able to refer families to the Building Bridges service when it was considered that they needed intensive ongoing family support.

For Building Bridges the great benefit of having a children's specialist within the adult mental health team is that it ensures families are identified and assessed as being in need of support at an early stage. The children's specialist keeps the child, or children, in mind and is an important link between the Family Action team and the professionals in the adult mental health team.

Working in a culturally diverse borough

The borough is one of the most deprived in the country. Although it does contain small pockets of wealthy areas, overall there are high levels of unemployment and it has one of the highest rates of child poverty in the country. The Campaign to End Child Poverty in their review covering the whole of England reported in 2012 that 52 per cent of children were living in poverty in the borough compared to an average throughout England of 20.9 per cent (endchildpoverty.org.uk).

In addition to being one of the most deprived boroughs, it is also one of the most ethnically diverse, having a long history of a changing population as successive new immigrant communities are attracted to the area. According to the 2001 census figures almost half of the borough's population is made up of different ethnic groups, the largest of these being the Bangladeshi community. There is also a substantial Somali community, though this is not reflected in census figures as there are no subdivisions of African categories.

Among the many different cultures within the borough there are variations in attitudes towards mental health. For example, there is little recognition of mental ill health in the Somali culture. The Somali language does not contain words to describe mental illness and the concept is not understood by many in the community. There was a concern in the statutory services that this community did not access preventive mental health services but rather there was an over-representation of Somali inpatients on the hospital psychiatric wards. Following a needs assessment of mental health in the Somali population carried out by the local Primary Care Trust, Family Action worked in partnership with the statutory agencies to raise awareness within the Somali community of health issues including mental health. Using a video produced by the Trust, Family Action ran workshops and information events to help identify those in need of services and ensure they were able to access services appropriately.

Identifying families in need of support in the Somali community has been a particular challenge. By employing workers from the Somali community Family Action was able to build up trust in the local community and has been successful in identifying those in need of services and engaging them in the work.

Indeed, in its local project Family Action set out actively to recruit workers from the various ethnic backgrounds which make up the population of the borough. The main group is Bangladeshi and the project successfully recruited Sylheti-speaking workers, both male and female, which was important in taking into account the specific needs of the families referred.

When recruited, the majority of those family support workers, though they may have had some experience in health and social care, did not necessarily hold recognised qualifications in working with families. Family Action offered training, specifically NVQ training, to those workers to equip them for the work. The family support workers are closely supervised and supported by senior workers who are both trained and experienced. Each family support worker receives on a fortnightly basis supervision that includes reviewing the work with each family and planning future work.

In addition to regular individual supervision, the team manager and co-ordinators are available on a rota basis to all staff throughout the day for advice and guidance as required. Previously staff attended morning meetings, held every day, to which they could bring any particular dilemma they were facing in their work. These regular meetings, which were facilitated by the team manager or one of the coordinators, were a useful forum for the learning and development of workers but they have had to be discontinued due to pressures of work. As a further training activity full case discussions led by a member of the CAMHS staff are held on a monthly basis. Staff turnover is low, which helps to ensure consistency for the families receiving the services.

Career progression is encouraged and members of staff are able to access both local authority training courses as well as those run by the Family Action Training and Development Department. Staff members are encouraged to take advantage of these training opportunities. They are also encouraged to contribute their knowledge and experience of their own cultures to others in the team. In this way the team has built up its knowledge and skills in working sensitively in an ethnically diverse environment.

Working in partnership with the local authority

One of the great strengths of the voluntary sector is to be able to identify gaps in services and design projects in response to need. Working at a grass-roots level enables staff to gain insight into the needs of those they are supporting, and the voluntary sector can also be more creative and flexible than statutory agencies.

Family Action has worked in the borough for more than ten years and has on the whole enjoyed very positive relationships with the local authority and the mental health trust. The organisation has very strong roots in the community and has developed its service provision by consulting with service users, its local staff team and other professionals from local statutory and voluntary agencies. Family Action participates in many local multi-agency forums and other partnership initiatives. Networking is especially important where there are so many different community groups representing the different cultures of the area. Effective networking and joint working arrangements ensure that the services on offer are relevant and appropriate to the needs of the families who will use them. Family Action has worked extensively with the Bangladeshi and Somali communities, raising awareness of particular health and social care issues which are relevant to the communities and enabling members of those communities to access services.

The main challenge for the voluntary sector is securing the funding of services. It can be relatively easy to attract funding for an innovative idea to pilot a new project but it is usually more difficult to secure continuation funding. This always depends on being able to prove the value of the service and there is now a much greater emphasis on outcomes-based development of services. Proving the value is however complicated for these types of services and there is the argument that the true value may not be shown until many years later.

The level of funding dictates the capacity of the service, and if the funding is low there are often long waiting times between a family being referred to the service and a family support worker being allocated to begin the work. This can cause frustration for those professional workers referring into the service and can have a negative effect on relationships with other agencies. For work with the family it can mean that the workers have to put more effort into establishing a good relationship when they are first introduced to the family who may be disillusioned at having to wait so long. It can also happen that by the time the family is allocated a support worker the family's circumstances have changed such that the service is no longer appropriate.

Local authority and Primary Care Trusts generally want to commission services which have more emphasis on short-term work rather than on longer-term support. In the lives of those accessing the Building Bridges project short-term interventions are not always appropriate, as very often change is slower to take place and more time is needed to really embed the changes into the family's life. Originally the local arrangement was that a family would be supported by Building Bridges for a maximum of six months, but in recognition of this the commissioners agreed to a maximum of one year. Neither do commissioners usually want to see families return for future support after their case has been closed but in some families this 'top-up' support can be beneficial; it can be short term and it can prevent the family from slipping back into a further crisis.

Examples of work with families

The following case examples illustrate how the Building Bridges project has helped families to make changes in their lives. Details have been changed and elements common to a number of families have been included, in the interests of preserving confidentiality.

Case 1

This Somali family was referred by the Community Mental Health Team because the mother suffered from depression and both parents were requesting help with managing their children's behaviour. The family consisted of a mother, father and six children aged 3 to 13.

During the initial visit the parents said that what they wanted was support with taking the children out on after-school and holiday activities and they also identified a need for general support with managing their children's challenging behaviour. The children seemed to enjoy a good relationship with their parents, especially their mother, but when they displayed challenging behaviour she was unable to deal with them appropriately.

Despite the fact that the parents requested help from the Building Bridges project the family support worker allocated to them found that they were very difficult to engage. The worker would attempt to make home visits but the mother would often cancel the visit shortly beforehand. Telephone contact was also problematic as the mother tended not to answer phone calls and it was therefore difficult to reschedule appointments. This meant that it took time to establish a relationship with the family and it required the worker to be persistent in continuing to make contact. The mother's mood fluctuated, which was a key factor in her inconsistency in keeping appointments. The worker established that this was a feature of the family's contact with other agencies, with the result that they were not accessing services. Part of the work with the family became helping them to establish and maintain relationships with other agencies.

From the outset it was clear that the family were not receiving the benefits they were entitled to and they lacked some essential items which would make life easier for them. The worker gave advice and support on Disability Living Allowance and made applications to charities for essential household items. The mother felt the worker understood the family's difficulties. She appreciated the worker's non-judgemental attitude and the fact that she made an effort to see things from the family's viewpoint. Working alongside the mother on managing financial matters helped establish a good relationship between the two.

Early on in the work with the family the worker observed that the mother rarely moved from her bed or the sofa, giving instructions from there to her children. The worker started by exploring with the mother her depressive state and helping her find practical ways to cope on a day-to-day basis. Gradually, building on the relationship she had established with the mother, she was able to help her gain confidence and increase her self-esteem, to a point where the mother was able to take on, together with her husband, a more proactive stance in relation to the children. The parents began to work together on setting and maintaining boundaries for their children and as they became more in control of the children, they became more confident as parents, and more inclined to take their children on outings and activities outside the home. Initially the worker accompanied the family and was able to introduce them to accessible and free activities such as park and library visits. She also encouraged the family to play together within the home which both the parents and the children came to enjoy.

Working with the family in this way helped the worker to build up good relationships with the children too. By discussing with them their likes, dislikes, ambitions and interests she helped improve their confidence and self-esteem. She also helped the children to better understand their mother's mental illness by talking to them, finding out about their understanding of mental health issues and building on this through the use of creative activities. She introduced the children to the Princess Royal Trust Young Carers' Project and encouraged them to attend sessions and activities provided for children and young people who are in a caring role.

An important part of the work with this family was the liaison with other agencies and professionals, such as the local Children's Centre, the health visitor, the community psychiatric nurse and the psychiatrist, particularly around the inconsistency of attending appointments and the impact this was having on the mother and the children.

By the end of the work with this family some very positive outcomes had been achieved. The parents were better able to manage their finances. The mother was more confident in her parenting role and both parents were better able to deal with their children's challenging behaviour. Generally all the relationships within the family improved. The children developed more contacts outside of the family which created for them a wider social network, including supportive friendships with other young people in a similar situation.

Case 2

This family was referred by the Community Mental Health Team who were concerned about the vulnerability of this young Bangladeshi couple, on account of their history of mental health issues. The family consisted of a mother, father, their 3-year-old daughter, and the mother's brother, who lived with them.

The mother suffered from depression and had threatened suicide on several occasions. She appeared to be very detached from her daughter, seeming to be too preoccupied with her own emotional needs to understand her daughter's needs. The little girl was overweight and her development was slightly delayed. The mother's brother, who was 20 years old, mis-used drugs and, because of his erratic and antisocial behaviour, the family were further isolated from neighbours. There had been several violent incidents reported on their estate involving a group of young men to which he belonged. The parents felt intimidated by this young man's sometimes aggressive behaviour but they felt powerless to do anything about it. The father was estranged from his own extended family and said that he had no one to turn to for emotional support.

The family support worker managed to establish a good relationship with this family. Initially she supported the mother's brother by referring him to a voluntary agency which had the remit of supporting those with drug and alcohol misuse problems. He was finally helped to find his own accom-modation, which was a great relief to all concerned. The worker was then able to help the parents concentrate on the practical care and emotional well-being of their daughter, working in close liaison with the family's health visitor and the community dietician. She supported the work of the dietician by encouraging the parents to keep appointments, accompanying them on their first appointment with her. She also accompanied the mother on a food shopping trip, practically helping to raise her awareness of healthy eating, thus reinforcing the work of the dietician. The parents were also encouraged to make regular exercise part of their daily life.

The worker helped the parents to establish routines, especially for the morning and evening. She encouraged them to play with their child and to enjoy making everyday tasks interesting and fun. She supported the mother in understanding the importance of being a role model for her daughter and encouraged her to give her daughter attention and use appropriate language with her.

In order to support the father with the emotional difficulties he was experiencing in caring for his wife and daughter, the worker referred him to the Carers' Project. By the end of the work both parents felt more in control of their home life as the burden of having the additional troublesome family member had been removed. The father felt less isolated as he now had his own support network with people who had similar caring roles within their family. The mother became more involved in the care of her daughter and kept regular appointments with the dietician. The mother and daughter's relationship subsequently improved significantly. The parents and their child began taking regular exercise and all the professionals involved with the family agreed that there was a marked improvement in the child's health and general well-being.

Case 3

This is a Bangladeshi family consisting of a single mother and her three children, aged 10, 6 and 3 years. She had separated from her husband, the father of the children. The family were referred by the Community Mental Health Nurse for support to the mother with her parenting skills and for advice and support around the impact of her mental illness on her children. Although separated from her husband, the mother was still dependent on him and his extended family with regard to the care of the children. She was otherwise fairly isolated, having no contact with her own extended family and no contact with friends or neighbours.

The mother's mental health was adversely affected by the stress caused by the violent marital relationship. She had been diagnosed with bipolar disorder and her frequent relapses necessitated several admissions to hospital, and at such times the children were cared for by their father, with the help of his parents.

The mother's ability to give consistent parenting to her children was extremely limited and the eldest child appeared to be taking on a parenting role within the family.

This mother was not only very socially isolated but also she spoke little English. The allocated worker was able to speak to her in Sylheti and was able to build up a good relationship with her. This enabled the worker to focus on helping the mother to adopt a more active role in parenting her children. The worker encouraged the mother to have more contact with the children's school and to take an interest in the children's achievements.

In working with the children the worker helped them to understand their mother's mental health problems. She took the eldest child along to the Young Carers' Project, introducing her to other young people there. The family needed particular support during the mother's hospitalisation and the worker encouraged them to use the family visiting room facilities at the hospital. On these occasions it was noted by the hospital staff that there was a significant improvement in the mother's mood.

Work with this family achieved some very positive outcomes. The mother was enabled to build up her social network, thus reducing her dependence on her husband. Her parenting skills improved which had a beneficial impact on her relationships with her children.

The eldest child received ongoing support from the Young Carers' Project, widening her social network and helping build her self-esteem. All three of the children were less distressed by their mother's latest hospital admission as they were visiting her regularly and receiving support in understanding her illness.

Work with these families illustrates the importance of the voluntary sector in providing services which complement those of the statutory sector. Family Action's particular model of supporting families where parental mental ill health is an issue combines creativity, a sound knowledge of the local community, and flexibility in its service delivery, while working within a network of other local agencies and maintaining good partnership relationships with the local authority and Primary Care Trust.

References

Ahern, M. (2008) *Mental Health Needs Assessment of the Somali Population of Tower Hamlets.* http://www.lho.org.uk/viewResource.aspx?id=14684 (accessed February 2012).

Centre for Excellence in Outcomes (2010) *Grasping the Nettle: Early Intervention for Children, Families and Communities.* http://www.c4eo.org.uk/themes/earlyintervention/files/early_intervention_grasping_the_nettle_executive_summary.pdf (accessed November 2011).

End Child Poverty Campaign (2012) *Child Poverty Map of the UK.* www.endchildpoverty.org.uk (accessed February 2012).

MacLeod, M. (2011) *Building Bridges: An Independent Evaluation of a Family Support Service.* Family Action. www.family-action.org.uk.

Morris, J. (2007) *Building Bridges Evaluation.* Family Welfare Association. www.family-action.org.uk.

Social Care Institute for Excellence (2009) Guide 30. *Think Child, Think Parent, Think Family: A Guide to Parental Mental Health and Child Welfare.* London.

http://www.scie.org.uk/publications/ataglance/ataglance09.asp (accessed 12 March 2012).

12 Parental mental illness
The adult psychiatrist's perspective and role

Eleni Palazidou

Introduction

About one in five people will experience a mental illness in their lifetime, and 25 to 50 per cent of these will be parents. In the UK at any given time about 10 per cent of women and 5 per cent of men with mental disorder will be parents. The large majority will have common disorders such as depression and anxiety and about 0.5 per cent will have a psychotic illness (Parker *et al.* 2008).

Changes in the approach to treatment and the introduction of Community Care have facilitated a more normalised way of living for people with serious mental illness, making it easier for men and women to enter into relationships and have children. The availability of new generation antipsychotic drugs which are less likely to adversely affect fertility has contributed to an increase in pregnancies. According to a community survey the percentage of women with a psychotic illness who are mothers is as high as 63 per cent in the UK (Howard *et al.* 2001).

The children of the mentally ill are at an increased risk of mental health problems. This is partly related to genetic transmission and partly to environmental factors and the effect the parental mental illness may have on the child's physical and psychological development. On the other hand, the stress of bringing up children may affect parental mental health. Parental illness is often associated with socioeconomic problems and other adversities. Mental illness is commonly co-morbid with substance misuse. For example, men with bipolar disorder are twice as likely to have alcohol problems compared to the general male population and women with bipolar disorder are four times more likely than the general female population to have problems with alcohol misuse (Helzer *et al.* 1991). Women, in particular younger women, with dual diagnosis are also more likely to be exposed to violence from male partners (McPherson *et al.* 2007). These commonly present adversities complicate the life of the mentally ill and add to the burden of disease on the family.

The mentally ill parent

Due to the nature of their illness, mentally ill parents are liable to experience fluctuations in their mental state which affect their mood and behaviour, and these may interfere with parenting. The illness may affect relationships with others and mentally ill parents can be socially isolated. Family support is not always available and at times of relapse single parents may not have access to help other than that of professionals. Women with mental illness are often single mothers and this adds to the difficulties of parenting. The British community survey highlights the loneliness these women experience and their lack of social support; one-fifth of mothers with psychotic disorders who have children at home had difficulties obtaining help with childcare, and over one-third expressed a need for company (Howard *et al*. 2001). Mothers with schizophrenia reported the personal benefits of motherhood such as love, purpose, identity and support but at the same time recognised the negatives; namely stress, exhaustion, poverty, fear of losing custody and fear their children may develop schizophrenia. They noted the need for support, information and therapeutic programmes such as social activities, coun-selling for substance use, relationship and assertiveness groups and family planning advice. Those who had lost children to foster care or adoption described feelings of anger and enduring grief (Chernomas *et al*. 2000; Seeman 2002).

Parenthood, in those with serious mental illness, is not an easy undertaking. It adds to the existing difficulties and the burden of disease not only for those affected but also their families and society at large. They have to battle with the stigma of mental illness, the effects of the symptoms of the illness on their day-to-day life, on their socioeconomic status, the additional impact of substance misuse in many cases and sometimes the adverse effects of medication. They are fearful of failing and sometimes this is the harsh reality they face; a significant number of mothers with psychotic illness lose the care of their children to the local author-ity. Unfortunately, the nature of schizophrenia is such that the people affected have multiple difficulties which may affect their parenting ability if their condition is not well controlled. When controlling for socioeconomic status and marital background, 49 per cent of mothers with schizophrenia and related disorders, compared to 2 per cent of controls, had children in foster care and significantly more of the mothers with schizophrenia who had children in their care, relegated this to others (36 per cent) compared to control mothers (9 per cent) (Miller *et al*. 1996).

Focus group work with mentally ill mothers carried out in Australia identified loss of custody as a major concern in addition to hospitalisation, social isolation, stigma and single parenthood. They also noted the mothers' need for substitute care, better access to community services, consistency in care provision and improved relationships with their children (Bassett *et al*. 1999). Accessing mental health care is not straightforward for mentally ill parents with multiple barriers in the way. These barriers include individual beliefs about help-seeking, knowledge of services (or lack of), fear of losing the care of their children, stigma, conflicting demands on parents, the presence of other stressors and difficulties, and problems with transport and childcare (Beresford *et al*. 2008). The fear of losing custody significantly impacts upon their maintaining or avoiding contact with health services. Very importantly the primary motivating factor to engage in treatment is the ability to maintain the parenting role (Mowbray *et al*. 2001). This needs to be recognised by the professionals and used to the patients' benefit in their 'negotiations' on treatment (see Chapter 7).

Mentally ill fathers

Most of the research into parenthood in the mentally ill has focused on mothers, while mentally ill fathers receive much less attention (Styron *et al.* 2002). Fathers with severe mental illness share many similarities with mothers who have mental illness, although men are more likely to misuse drugs or alcohol. Lone fathers are almost four times more likely to have a common mental disorder than other men (Cooper *et al.* 2007). Paternal depression has been linked to depression and other mental health problems in the offspring. Although mentally ill fathers have been less studied than mothers there is little doubt that both genders need adequate treatment and support to ensure they cope effectively with the demands of parenthood.

In 2008, the then Children's Minister, Beverly Hughes, under pressure from 'fathers' rights groups', launched a campaign jointly with the Fatherhood Institute, titled 'Think Fathers' (DCSF 2008). Its aim was to dispel the myth that fathers are the 'invisible parent'. It posited that the public, health and family services need to go further in recognising and working with fathers and placed a requirement for both individual clinicians and services to recognise the importance of parenting in the fathers' lives and to provide appropriate support and care to enable them to fulfil their parental role. Unfortunately, this programme did not specifically address the needs of fathers with mental illness.

Box 1   What do parents want?

1   Being a parent should come before being a person with a mental illness.
2   Parents feel supported when the needs of their children are met.
3   Professionals to listen more and value a parent's point of view and feelings.
4   Ensure the health and safety of the child without excluding the parent from the decision-making process when other family members are involved.
5   Parental ability should be evaluated before removing children.
6   Professional support is needed for the partner when a parent is acutely ill and education is required to prepare for ongoing treatment, convalescence and recovery.
7   Respect confidentiality with regard to sharing information with family members.
8   The most profound loss for some parents with mental illness is the loss of custody of their children.

---

continued

---

9   Parents want their right to privacy respected.
10   Services should be sensitive to the parents' cultural background.
11   Service providers should be educated to network services and link
   parents into the most useful ones.
12   Parents want to be viewed as persistent and zealous, and working to
   battle prejudice and injustice.

(summarised from 'Parents as Patients': RCP 2011)

Children of mentally ill parents

The children of the mentally ill have an increased risk of developing a mental illness. A variety of factors operate which include genetic predisposition and environmental factors related to the home milieu, and exposure to the effects of parental mental illness in day-to-day life. An additional stressor is the fear of inheriting the parent's condition. The Copenhagen High-risk Study found that 16 per cent of the children of mothers with schizophrenia developed schizophrenia compared to 1.9 per cent of the children of controls (Parnas *et al.* 1993). Interestingly, more psychopathology was found in those children reared apart from their schizophrenic mothers compared to those who stayed with them. This may reflect the fact that those children who were removed from the mother's custody were those whose maternal illness was more severe but it also suggests that staying with the mother, who has schizophrenia, does not necessarily increase the risk of developing the illness. The rate of mood disorders was no different between the offspring of the mothers with schizophrenia and those without (Higgins *et al.* 1997; Parnas *et al.* 1993).

According to several reports, including that of the Royal College of Psychiatrists, the children want to be kept informed. They feel better when they know their parents' unusual behaviour is due to illness. The facts can be shared with them in a sensitive, supportive and clear way, and the level of information needs to be adapted to the age and maturity of the children involved.

A particularly traumatic time for both parents and children is hospitalisation. When action needs to be taken for the parent to be hospitalised either on a voluntary basis or compelled to do so under a Section of the Mental Health Act, the children need to be considered and they want the professionals to pay attention to their wishes and views, and explain to them the course of action to be taken and why.

Article 12 of the United Nations Convention on the Rights of the Child states that children have a right to be listened to and have their views taken into account on matters that affect them (Office of the UN High Commissioner for Human Rights 1990).

The Mental Health Act Code of Practice stipulates that the kind and amount of information that children and young people (especially young carers) should receive about a parent's condition or treatment, as well as the interests of the child or young person, should be balanced against the patient's right to privacy and their wishes and feelings (DoH 2008b). Any information should be appropriate to the age and understanding of the child or young person. Whatever the decision of the assessing team, this should be explained to the children in age-appropriate terms.

Box 2   What do the children want?

1   Introduce yourself. Tell us who you are and what your job is.
2   Give us as much information as you can.
3   Tell us what is wrong with our parents.
4   Tell us what is going to happen next.
5   Talk to us and listen to us. Remember, it is not hard to speak to us; we are not aliens.
6   Ask us what we know and what we think. We live with our parents; we know how they have been behaving.
7   Tell us it is not our fault. We can feel really guilty if our mum or dad is ill. We need to know we are not to blame.
8   Please don't ignore us. Remember, we are part of the family and we live there too.
9   Keep on talking to us and keep us informed. We need to know what is happening.
10   Tell us if there is anyone we can talk to. MAYBE IT COULD BE YOU.

(Barnardo's 2009)

Parental mental illness – the psychiatrist

Mental illness generally presents for the first time at a young age, usually in the teenage years and early twenties. Given the chronic relapsing nature of most psychiatric conditions and the way mental health services are organised to ensure long-term continuity of care, the adult psychiatrist is likely to be working with the individual with mental illness from the time they enter adulthood, through to parenthood, and having a major role to play alongside other agencies in trying to help make this journey as smooth as possible for the mentally ill parent. A relationship of trust needs to develop for this collaboration to be effective and the patient usually perceives the doctor as their advocate, and this is what the doctor also prefers as his or her primary role. In practice this is not always possible, as often the doctor has to make decisions that go against the wishes of the patient, for example, in situations when the Mental Health Act needs to be implemented for compulsory treatment or when there are child protection issues and possible care orders.

Before conception

Work on the welfare of the children of the mentally ill can often start before conception. Adult psychiatrists' work with the mentally ill requires them to have knowledge of their patients' family life, and work on this needs to start as early as the pre-conception period. Discussions on sex education and family planning have to take place with all women of reproductive age as well as men who have serious mental illness. Advice on contraception may be given or the patient may be directed to other appropriate agencies such as their GP for further advice on this. Possible plans for having a family need to be discussed with the patients, particularly women; pregnancy, childbirth and coping with young children can have a major impact on the course and treatment of mental illness, and the NICE guidelines recommend the psychiatrist ensures such conversations take place (NICE 2007). Certain medications may be detrimental to the development of the foetus and pregnancy or childbirth may trigger a relapse of illness. For example, women with bipolar affective disorder are at higher risk of a relapse after childbirth particularly if they have had a recent episode of illness. In the latter case they would be advised to postpone plans for pregnancy until a reasonable period of time has elapsed.

Pregnancy and perinatal period

Pregnancies in women with mental illness, like women in the general population, are often unplanned. If the patient wishes to proceed with her plans of pregnancy, arrangements for monitoring her mental state, and early intervention and crisis plans as necessary, need to be put in place. Modifications in their medications may be required. This is a good time to discuss the impact of parenting on the patient's mental state in the future and the effects of her own illness on her offspring. It should be explored whether there are any family supports and, if not, arrangements for professional support need to be planned. Ideally these plans should be made well in advance of any pregnancy but unfortunately in reality this is not always possible. Women with mental disorders who become pregnant or who are in the post-partum period should be managed in accordance with the NICE guidelines and recommendations. Ensuring safe pregnancies and childbirth and prevention of perinatal psychosis enables healthy bonding with the baby. Continuing effective treatment and support for the mothers as well as monitoring the well-being of the children may decrease the risk of mental health problems in the children.

Unfortunately not all mentally ill mothers cooperate with antenatal and peri-natal care. Women with schizophrenia often do not engage with antenatal care and they have a higher risk of premature delivery and low birth weight which may make the offspring more vulnerable to future health problems.

In more serious cases when severe psychotic illness presents with symptoms which may pose a risk to the offspring, the child protection services need to be informed and usually a pre-birth conference is arranged. This particularly trau-matic experience for the pregnant mother is also very difficult for the psychiatrist and other adult mental health professionals concerned, as the patient's expectation is that they should be 'on her side'. It requires a skilful and sensitive approach on the part of the professionals to ensure their relationship is not damaged and patient trust is maintained through this very difficult period.

Parenting under-age children

Child protection issues may emerge at any time and not only after childbirth, and psychiatrists are asked to provide a report on their patients' mental health and their parenting capacity if the child protection agencies have concerns. In order to do this the psychiatrist needs to have a good knowledge of the patient's family arrangements, the existence of young children and their welfare. Psychiatrists may also have concerns about their patients' mental state which may pose a risk to others and in particular to their children.

Mental health professionals in both acute and rehabilitation adult services have been criticised for not always ensuring they obtain adequate information about the well-being of their patients' children. Some of the attitudes previously pervading the adult mental health services are now successfully challenged and changing in keeping with new policies and guidelines on ways of working. For example, although they recognise the importance of offering support to the children of the mentally ill patients under their care, professionals have not seen this as being the role of the adult mental health services. In addition, a degree of mistrust has existed between mental health professionals and child protection agencies which, as well as professional boundaries, issues of confidentiality and possibly unrealistic expectations has been forming barriers among different agencies (Darlington *et al.* 2005). Mental health professionals – including doctors – tend to see themselves as advocates of the parent, the person for whose care they are responsible. There is a concern among those dealing with adult patients that asking questions around their children and exploring parenting issues may adversely affect their relationship, undermining the patients' trust in them (Maybery and Reupert 2006).

The introduction of Community Care and the Care Programme Approach has led to better continuity of care with ongoing monitoring and support for the mentally ill. The consultant adult psychiatrists remain in post generally until retirement; hence they are usually the clinician the patients have known the longest in the course of their illness and also the professional whom patients see as ultimately responsible for their care. A good, trusting relationship can be built over time which helps the mentally ill parent feel supported and secure, particularly during the difficult times of relapse, hospitalisation or detainment under the Mental Health Act.

As a new consultant in the Trust, in the 1990s, I carried out a domiciliary visit to a woman at the request of her general practitioner who was concerned about her mental health. On arrival I was met by her husband who appeared to be mentally ill himself. It was soon clear to me that both parents had a psychotic disorder. There were three children in the family. They were well presented and although shy, they appeared happy and relaxed around their parents. They clearly were well aware that their parents were mentally unwell. Although the father, despite his condition, was the main care provider for the family, the children shared a substantial amount of these duties. A referral to the local authority children's services resulted in an assessment that the children were not 'at risk'. In the absence of any offer of support from the children's services, arrangements were made for a member of the Community Mental Health Team to be allocated to the children, separate from the clinician allocated to the parents. Medical treatment and support helped improve significantly the parents' condition over time, and they remained stable and in contact with the Community Mental Health Team. The children, now grown up, are doing well, apart from one who also developed a psychotic illness. The positive experience of the mental health services' involvement with the parents enabled this young person to engage well with the services.

This case, which is not uncommon in inner city, multi-ethnic settings, highlights that not so long ago there were limited resources to support the children of the mentally ill if they were considered not to be at immediate risk. Although some input was offered by the adult services in this case, this was not adequate by today's standards, as the professional involved in supporting the children did not have expertise in child mental health and welfare. However, it does also show some valuable benefits. The adult mental health services in working more closely with the parents and the children were able to develop a relationship of trust which facilitated the engagement of the parents in treatment, encouraged discussions around any concerns about the children and access to support as necessary. The one child who developed mental illness in her later teens felt comfortable in seeking help and readily accessing for herself the mental health care she needed.

    This and other cases involving parents and children were instrumental in the formation of a group to agree a joint working protocol, initiated by RL, which consisted of professionals from both health and social care and children and adult services, including a consultant psychiatrist (EP). The adult services were alerted to the need to explore the parent status of their patients and consider their children's welfare. The group was successful in persuading the local authority to fund the appointment of a liaison person to help bridge the gap between adult and child mental health services. The mental health trust subsequently appointed a formally assigned safeguarding team which resulted in the establishment of dedicated safeguarding nurses in each borough. The local authority and the Primary Care Trust later provided additional funding for two 'children's specialist' professionals based in two of the CMHTs. All patients who are under the care of the CMHT and are identified as parents are referred to this children's specialist who makes an assessment, involves children's services as appropriate and is actively involved in CPA reviews.

National regulations, policies and procedures on safeguarding children

In the meantime widely publicised cases of child neglect or abuse such as that of Victoria Climbié have led to the introduction of a series of regulations in the last decade, with the objective to ensure and safeguard the welfare of children in general. These rules, policies and legislations also specifically address the welfare of the children of mentally ill parents.

In their assessment and putting in place a care plan, it is essential for psychiatrists to be mindful of the existence of the children and consider the impact any decision making about the parents' care may have on their welfare. They should remember and be reminded that the children's rights to be safeguarded are paramount, even when they are perceived as interfering with the therapeutic relationship between the adult patient and the professional.

The following series of regulations, policies and procedures introduced nationally together with more specific guidelines by health agencies such as NICE (National Institute for Clinical Excellence) dictated the need and the establishment of comprehensive protocols of care expected from the mental health professionals which formally record and document the process of mental health assessment and delivery of care.

The SCIE (Social Care Institute for Excellence) systematic map published in 2006 identified over 200 interventions related to parental mental health (SCIE 2006). Many of these are population interventions with some being primarily preventive. Of the remainder, some were either parenting or family but specific to children of parents with mental illness. The majority of these were focused on depressive illness. It was recognised that more research was needed to establish which interventions are effective, particularly for mothers with psychosis. Collaboration between health and social services in this area of research may be more productive in the future.

The Children Act 1989 was followed by the Children Act 2004 and guidance, *Working Together to Safeguard Children*, issued in 2006, was reviewed and updated in 2010 (DoH 2010). These documents taken together provided a framework that established local, safeguarding children's boards and clarified the duty of all agencies, including health, to make arrangements to safeguard and promote the welfare of children. Section 11 of the Children Act 2004 requires the strategic health authorities, special hospitals, Primary Care Trusts (PCTs), NHS trusts and foundation trusts to ensure that they safeguard and promote the welfare of children.

The Care Programme Approach. Adult mental health practitioners are expected to routinely record details of patients' responsibilities in relation to children as part of the CPA process. A recent review of the CPA process, 'Refocusing CPA', sets out a new statement codifying the values and principles that underpin good practice in mental health services.

> The approach to individuals' care and support puts them at the centre and promotes social inclusion and recovery. It is respectful – building confidence

in individuals with an understanding of their strengths, goals and aspirations as well as their needs and difficulties. It recognises the individual as a person first and patient or service user second.

Care assessment and planning views a person 'in the round' seeing and supporting them in their individual diverse roles and the needs they have, including: family, parenting, relationships, housing, employment, leisure, education, creativity, spirituality, self-management and self-nurture with the aim of optimising mental and physical health and well-being.

(DoH 2008a: 7)

A joint statement by the Department for Children, Schools and Families and the Department of Health on the responsibilities of doctors and other professionals in investigations of child abuse. Health professionals are expected to be conversant with the risk factors relevant to safeguarding children issues, the risks to unborn children and also the needs of the mentally ill parents, and know where to refer for help (DCSF 2008). They should be open to sharing relevant information with other appropriate agencies, be involved in assessments of parenting capacity, planning for vulnerable children and contribute to child protection conferences, serious case reviews and the implementation of action plans arising from these events.

In order to ensure the implementation of these requirements it is now mandatory for all relevant staff to undergo training in safeguarding and promoting the welfare of children. Mental health trusts are required to appoint either a designated doctor or nurse or a named doctor or nurse with lead responsibility and expertise for promoting good professional practice in safeguarding. Inpatient mental health services must have policies and procedures relating to children visiting inpatients and a designated family room for the visits to take place (DoH 1999). Planning for such visits should always make paramount the best interests of the children involved.

Referral to the local authority children's social care services in relation to child protection or other safeguarding concerns is encouraged via an inter-agency referral form. More recently this has been achieved through a Common Assessment Framework process (CAF).

The National Patient Safety Agency (May 2009) issued a Rapid Response Report which requires all chief executives of mental health trusts providing adult mental health services to ensure a series of actions, as listed in the following.

Box 3 Action

1   All assessment, CPA monitoring, review, and discharge planning documentation and procedures should prompt staff to consider if the service user is likely to have or resume contact with their own child or other

children in their network of family and friends, even when the children are not living with the service user.

2   If the service user has or may resume contact with children, this should trigger an assessment of whether there are any actual or potential risks to the children, including delusional beliefs involving them, and drawing on as many sources of information as possible, including compliance with treatment.

3   Referrals should be made to children's social care services under local safeguarding procedures as soon as a problem, suspicion or concern about a child becomes apparent, or if the child's own needs are not being met. A referral must be made:

- if service users express delusional beliefs involving their child; and/or
- if service users might harm their child as part of a suicide plan.

4   Staff working in mental health services should be given clear guidance on how to make such referrals, including information sharing, the role of their organisation's designated lead for child protection, and what to do when a concern becomes apparent outside normal office hours.

5   A consultant psychiatrist should be directly involved in all clinical decision making for service users who may pose a risk to children.

6   Safeguarding training that includes the risks posed to children from parents with delusional beliefs involving their children or who might harm their children as part of a suicide plan is an essential requirement for all staff. Attendance, knowledge and competency levels should be regularly audited, and any lapses urgently acted on.

www.npsa.nhs.uk/patientsafety/alerts-and-directives

The Royal College of Psychiatrists (2011), taking into consideration the existing legislation and policies and procedures, made a series of recommendations summarised very briefly below.

Box 4

1   All psychiatrists and members of multidisciplinary teams should be familiar with legal and policy frameworks in relation to safeguarding children.

2   Training in safeguarding is essential and attendance, knowledge and competence levels should be regularly audited; and any lapses urgently acted on.

continued

3   All assessment, care programme approach (CPA) monitoring, review and discharge planning documentation and procedures should prompt staff to consider parenting issues.

4   Any assessment should measure the potential or actual impact of mental health on parenting. Remember the children's rights to be safe-guarded are paramount, even when they are perceived as interfering with the therapeutic relationship.

5   Referrals should be made to children's social care services under local safeguarding procedures as soon as a problem, suspicion or concern about a child becomes apparent, or if the child's own needs are not being met. Referrals must be made:

   (a) if service users express delusional beliefs involving their child; and/or
   (b) if service users might harm their child as part of a suicide plan.

6   Be conversant with guidance on how to make referrals to children's social care services, including information sharing, the role of their organisation's designated lead for child protection, and what to do when a concern becomes apparent outside normal office hours.

7   Consider the possibility of unplanned pregnancy and discuss contra-ception as well as the risk of pregnancy. Give culturally sensitive information at each stage of assessment, diagnosis, disorder course and treatment about the impact of the disorder and its treatment, including medication, on their health and the health of the foetus or child.

8   In the community where children may be part of the household, note that the Mental Capacity Act does not have provision for the protection of others. Therefore, if an intervention is needed in individuals who are parents, partly for the protection of children, the Mental Health Act must be used (in Scotland, the Children (Scotland) Act (1995) allows the removal of an adult from the house if a child is going to come to harm at the hand of that adult). When arranging the Mental Health Act assessment, the local safeguarding team should be contacted and any relevant information sought from them.

9   Inpatient settings should ensure that contact between parents and children when a parent is in hospital is actively encouraged and that there are family visiting rooms which are warm, clean and well equipped.

(summarised from 'Parents as Patients': RCP 2011)

Conclusions

The role of the psychiatrist in managing mental illness in parents is very complex. The traditional role of being responsible for the health and welfare of the individual patient and to 'do no harm' as far as that person is concerned is challenged by the realities of parenthood; the life of that individual is inextricably linked to that of others who may be dependent on her or him. The existence of rules and policies imposes additional roles and responsibilities upon the psychiatrist which conflict with this more comfortable role. She or he is expected to 'police' his or her patient's behaviour and report any concerns about risk to others hence 'betraying' confidentiality. This information if shared with other agencies may lead to the patient losing custody of their children temporarily or permanently, possibly irreparably damaging the therapeutic doctor–patient relationship.

However difficult it may be, this task can be made easier if frank and sensitive discussions around parenting and children's welfare take place early on in the management of people of reproductive age. Dealing with problems as they arise, and engaging the patient in an informed and considerate way allows effective working towards prevention of crises and loss of custody. Ensuring good illness control is the doctor's primary responsibility and the best prevention strategy. It has been reported that keeping children's custody is the primary motivating factor for staying in treatment in mothers with mental illness. Patience, persistence and honesty with a supportive attitude, together with optimum treatment of the illness with the very much needed patient's cooperation, can be effective in preventing long separations of children from their parents in most cases.

References

Barnardo's (2009) *Keeping the Family in Mind*. Ilford: Barnado's.

Bassett, H., Lampe, J. and Lloyd, C. (1999) Parenting: Experiences and feelings of parents with a mental illness. *Journal of Mental Health* 8: 597–604.

Beresford, B., Clarke, S., Gridley, K., Parker, G., Pitman, R., Spiers, G. and Light, K. (2008) *Technical Report for SCIE Research Review on Access, Acceptability and Outcomes of Services/Interventions to Support Parents with Mental Health Problems and Their Families*. Social Policy Research Unit, University of York.

Chernomas, W.M., Clarke, D.E. and Chisholm, F. (2000) Living with schizophrenia: The perspectives of women. *Psychiatric Services* 51: 1517–1521.

The Children Act 1989. London: The Stationery Office.

The Children Act 2004. London: The Stationery Office.

Cooper, C., Bebbington, P.E., Meltzer, H., Bhugra, D., Brugha, T., Jenkins, R., Farrell, M. and King, M. (2007) Depression and common mental disorders in lone parents: Results of the 2000 National Psychiatric Morbidity Survey. *Psychology of Medicine* 38: 335–342.

Darlington, Y., Feeney, J.A. and Rixon, K. (2005) Practice challenges at the intersection of child protection and mental health. *Child and Family Social Work* 10: 239–247.

Department for Children, Schools and Families (2004) *Working Together under the Children Act 2004*. http://www.dcsf.gov.uk/childrenactreport/ (accessed March 2012 – archived).

Department for Children, Schools and Families (2006) *Working Together to Safeguard Children: A Guide to Inter-agency Working to Safeguard and Promote the Welfare of Children.* www.everychildmatters.gov.uk or www.ecm.gov.uk/workingtogether (accessed 12 March 2012).

Department for Children, Schools and Families (2008) House of Commons Children, Schools and Families Committee and the Children's Plan, HC 213, House of Commons. London: The Stationery Office.

Department for Children, Schools and Families (2010) *Working Together to Safeguard Children: A Guide to Inter-agency Working to Safeguard and Promote the Welfare of Children.* HM Government. http:www.education.gov.uk/publications/standard/publicationDetail/Page1/DCSF00305-2010 (accessed September 2012).

Department of Health (1999) *A National Service Framework for Mental Health.* London: Department of Health.

Department of Health (2008a) *Refocusing the Care Programme Approach: Policy and Positive Practice Guidance.* London: The Stationery Office (www.dh.gov.uk).

Department of Health (2008b) *Code of Practice: Mental Health Act 1983. 2.43.* London: The Stationery Office (www.dh.gov.uk).

Helzer, J.E., Burnam, A. and McEvoy, L.T. (1991) Alcohol abuse and dependence. In Robins, L.N. and Regier, D.A. (eds) *Psychiatric Disorders in America.* New York: Free Press, pp. 81–115.

Higgins, J., Gore, R., Gutkind, D., Mednick, S.A., Parnas, J., Schulsinger, S. and Cannon, T.D. (1997) Effects of child-rearing by schizophrenic mothers: A 25-year follow-up. *Acta Psychiatr Scand.* 96: 402–404.

Howard, L.M., Kumar, R. and Thornicroft, G. (2001) Psychosocial characteristics and needs of mothers with psychotic disorders. *British Journal of Psychiatry* 178: 427–432.

Maybery, D. and Reupert, A. (2006) Workforce capacity to respond to children whose parents have a mental illness. *Australian and New Zealand Journal of Psychiatry* 40: 657–664.

McPherson, M.D., Delva, J. and Cranford, J.A. (2007) A longitudinal investigation of intimate partner violence. *Psychiatric Services* 58(5): 675–680.

Miller, L.J. and Finnerty, M. (1996) Sexuality, pregnancy, and childbearing among women with schizophrenia-spectrum disorders. *Psychiatric Services* 47: 502–505.

Mowbray, C.T., Oyserman, D., Bybee, D., MacFarlane, P. and Rueda-Riedle, A. (2001) Life circumstances of mothers with serious mental illnesses. *Psychiatric Rehabilitation Journal* 25(2): 114–123.

Office of the United Nations High Commissioner for Human Rights (1990) 'Convention on the Rights of the Child'. New York: United Nations. www.2ohchr.org (accessed March 2012).

Parker, G. and Beresford, B. (2008) *Protocol for SCIE Systematic Review on the Prevalence, Incidence and Detection of Parental Mental Health Problems.* York: Social Policy Research Unit, University of York.

Parnas, J., Cannon, T.D., Jacobsen, B., Schulsinger, H., Schulsinger, H. and Mednick, S. (1993) Lifetime DSM-III-R diagnostic outcomes in the offspring of schizophrenic mothers. Results from the Copenhagen High-Risk Study. *Archives of General Psychiatry* 50: 707–714. 'The Copenhagen High Risk Project 1962–1986, V. 13, No. 3 (1967). http//schizophreniabulletin.oxfordjournals.org (accessed March 2012).

Rapid Response Report NPSA (2009) *RRR003: Preventing Harm to Children from Parents with Mental Health Needs,* May 2009. www.npsa.nhs.uk/patientsafety/alerts-and-directives (accessed 20 January 2012).

Royal College of Psychiatrists (RCP) (2011) *Parents as Patients: Supporting the Needs of Patients who are Parents and their Children.* College Report CR164 January. London.

Social Care Institute for Excellence (SCIE) (2006) Systematic map report 1: The extent and impact of parental mental health problems on families and the acceptability, accessibility and effectiveness of interventions by Salina Bates and Esther Coren. SCIE.

Social Care Institute for Excellence (SCIE) (2009) *Think Child, Think Parents, Think Family: A Guide to Parental Mental Health and Child Welfare.* London: SCIE. www.scie.org.uk/publications/guides/guide30 (accessed 12 March 2012).

Seeman, M.V. (2002) Women with schizophrenia as parents. *Primary Psychiatry* 9: 39–42.

Styron, T.H., Pruett, M.K., McMahon, T.J. and Davidson, L. (2002) Fathers with serious mental illnesses: A neglected group. *Psychiatric Rehabilitation* 25: 215–222.

13 Managing post-partum depression in the community
Who cares for the babies?

Cathy Urwin

Introduction

Factors predisposing mothers to severe postnatal depression or puerperal psychosis at the birth of a baby are now sufficiently well documented to lead to welcome preventative measures or extra support during pregnancy (Leigh and Milgram, 2008; NICE, 2007). Where cases are severe or these measures are insufficient or not available, the increasing availability of mother and baby units provides opportunities for babies to be with their mothers in most cases. Increasingly, visits from family members are encouraged, with accommodation for fathers available occasionally. Attention is given to both reducing symptomatology and developing adequate rehabilitation and care arrangements for discharge afterwards (Friedman, 2010).

With a second or later-born baby, the situation is more complex. The mother not only has the challenge of working out her relationship with her new baby and her sense of herself away from home, there are also the older child's needs to be thought about. That child will, of course, be dealing with a separation from his or her mother of unknown duration and will need to get used to a baby sibling on the mother's return home.

Yet research shows that one episode of puerperal psychosis or severe postnatal depression strongly predicts a second, and that some patient groups, such as bipolar patients, are particularly vulnerable (Robertson *et al.*, 1995). Factors likely to trigger admission include persistent self-harming and/or suicidal ideation, and paranoid delusions that might result in harm towards the baby and/or others. In such cases, the mother's illness has flooded her caring capacities, making it impossible for her to manage both the demands and satisfactions of caring for her baby and her own vulnerability. Another way of putting this is that the mother's need to be cared for, including her need to be 'mothered', must be attended to before she can be effective as a parent herself.

Hormonal shifts and genetic factors have both been identified as contributing to vulnerability to depression through and post pregnancy (Bennett *et al.*, 2007; Brockington, 1996). Yet the operation of these factors is not independent of psychological processes they may trigger and from which they derive their strength, impact or meaning. Furthermore, in recognising the importance of biological processes, it may be easy to miss the massive significance of child bearing and parenthood as psychological challenges, bringing particular vulnerabilities but also opportunities for psychological growth. In a very real sense, parenthood creates developmental opportunities for young adults. Bearing these issues in mind is no less important in supporting families where the mothers have been or are postnatally depressed than families who in this respect have been more fortunate.

Recent qualitative research on mothering and identity carried out in an inner London borough has shown that, across diverse ethnic groups and social classes, having a baby can have profound effects on a woman's sense of who she is (Urwin, 2007). This transition mobilises complex, internally driven emotional and psychological processes, as well as reactions to external circumstances and changes in social status; a mother's place in the workforce may need to be temporarily or more permanently renegotiated, for example. From a psychological point of view, the emotional work of the new parent includes reworking her relationship with her own mother; she becomes not just a daughter but also a mother herself. Also affected are her relationships to her siblings, the other children of her parents. Although most marked in having the first baby, subsequent pregnancies also have the potential for affecting family relationships across generations. This process can release disturbing emotions, even in apparently normal circumstances. For example, it is not uncommon for a mother to be taken aback by feelings of rivalry with her new baby, to feel eclipsed by this new centre of the family's attention, or, as Harris (1987) has described, for a mother to feel jealous of her own baby feeding at her breast.

Harris (1987) has argued from a psychoanalytic point of view that ultimately the mother's rivalry here is with her baby as if he or she is a sibling, her mother's *other* baby in psychic reality, as the intimacy of breast-feeding stirs up feelings from the past. Reworking these feelings, normally in small doses, may bring depressed states of mind or what I have called 'existential loneliness' as the mother experiences anomie, no longer being who she was and as yet uncertain in her new identity (Urwin 2007, 2009). The mother's progress through this period and her increasing sense of competence is greatly aided by the baby's demands and responses which set the pace and the agenda for what the mother needs to achieve. This includes the growth of the baby's attachment behaviour towards her. This preferential treatment is both hugely uplifting and confirms her unique and special position as the baby's parent.

It is a general finding in studies of mothering that managing this period may be associated with a greater closeness or improved relatedness between the new mother and her own mother (Thomson and Kehily, 2011). But for some young women, beginning this process is especially difficult. For example, a traumatic birth that has been life threatening, painful and terrifying for the mother in spite of the delivery of a healthy baby will not easily lead to the mobilisation of her caring capacities unless her own needs for emotional care are attended to. These difficulties will be all the greater if compounded by well-attested psychological processes contributing to severe postnatal depression. These include unresolved loss, trauma and lack of family support (Leigh and Milgram. 2008), and/or situations where the mother's relation to her own mother is already compromised, for example, through her death, her absence or abandonment, or a long history of fraught interactions or disturbed attachment.

Two case studies

In this chapter I describe two mothers with challenging family backgrounds who suffered serious episodes of depression or psychosis in connection with pregnancy and childbirth and who were seen in the context of an Under-Fives service within the Child and Adolescent Mental Health Service (CAMHS), one arm of which was linked to a Sure Start project based in a Children's Centre (Urwin, 2005). Initial concerns were focused on their management of and relationships with their first-born and, at that time, only children. Each mother had suffered some degree of mental disturbance during and following the birth of the first child. In one case this was severe. Both mothers became pregnant for a second time. These pregnancies raised concerns about the mothers' vulnerability to further episodes of mental illness and the advisability or otherwise of hospital or mother and baby unit admission.

I describe the nature of the Under-Fives work that preceded the second pregnancies and continued through their duration, and the processes involved in psychiatric services making the decision to avoid admission in both cases by increasing community support. Further work with each mother, her new baby and the elder sibling followed the new babies' births.

Interestingly, both elder children presented initially with separation problems. In helping children to separate we are enabling them to keep in mind the idea of good, caring parents even in their absence. But mothers also need to be able to separate and to address the emotional experience of separateness. This can be hard. Mothers may feel that they have only just had their children and, already, they must give them up to the nursery or school. One response may be to cling to the child. On the other hand, letting go and enabling the child to move on can be enormously strengthening, confirming identity as a competent parent. Working on these issues, essentially ones of loss and mourning, requires parents to revisit and possibly work through for the first time aspects of their own separation histories.

Nasima and Sami

In traditional Bangladeshi culture, arranged marriage plays an important part in managing the separation of young women from their own families. The literal 'giving away' of the young bride involves her taking up residence in her in-laws' household. Here, her tasks may include cooking and cleaning for the entire family. Traditionally, the new wife is part of the insurance policy for looking after the older generation. In return, she will be afforded protection by their relationship with their first-born son, who will assume responsibility for looking after his mother and any unmarried sisters in the event of his father's death. According to Ramanujam (1992), there is no distinct period of adolescence to *bring about* separation in traditional Indian or Bangladeshi culture; this follows gradually with adult responsibilities that come with marriage. The looseness around separation and the strength of family obligations will have had important functions in a culture where historically there has been relatively little social welfare or health care for the elderly and infirm. But some of these patterns may be less adaptive in contemporary Western urban society. They may cause confusion where immigration and shortage of accommodation have demanded compromises with tradition, or where there are wide differences in experience between first and later generations.

The first case involves a Bangladeshi family and illustrates how the separation problem in the child reflected his young mother's difficulties in separating from her own family and how working through these difficulties eventually contributed to a more satisfying and effective identity as a wife and as a mother.

A first-born child, Sami was referred at 3 years by a health visitor because his mother wanted help in enabling her to leave him at the playgroup in her local Sure Start Children's Centre. Nasima had moved to London at age 16 when she married Sami's father, moving in with her husband, her mother-in-law and her husband's younger brother. The father-in-law had died the previous year. Nasima had grown up outside London and found the East London housing estate strange. Her husband's family were very traditional, while hers had been liberal and easygoing. She missed her own family, especially her mother and sisters.

I first met Sami and his mother in the playgroup itself. Sami was prepared to leave her to go to the water tray, eyeing me closely and scuttling back to speak to his mother if I showed interest in her. 'Look, mermaid', he said, pointing to a mermaid toy with a suitably exposed top. He then showed me a shark with very sharp teeth. I wondered from these communications whether he had experienced weaning and other early separations as particularly savage and if this was contributing to the current difficulties. He allowed me to chat to his mother in a quiet corner and listened as she described his early development.

Nasima had found Sami's birth particularly painful. Despite a normal delivery, she felt that she could not get over it. She had felt lonely and frightened away from her family, and depressed. She did not take medication because she was breastfeeding, which had gone well. Sami had always been close to her and would 'watch me like a hawk'. He had never allowed himself to be left, even with the paternal grandmother.

While Nasima had felt in some ways like a fish out of water in London, it emerged that her husband Hussein also felt displaced. He had married and become head of the family soon after his father's death. He had come to England much later than Nasima and he spoke much less good English, though they 'got on all right'. During this conversation, Sami brought over a book, pointing to a picture of a cow with large udders. Nasima described how the family had been in Bangladesh for several months earlier in the year, staying in a village where there were cows. Her husband was 'in his element' there and found it hard to come back.

Nasima did not think that Sami was particularly close to his father who was 'not much use' in putting his foot down. She acknowledged that Sami could be confused about whether he was supposed to be like his mother's 'little husband', and thought it was his responsibility to look after her. She agreed that he may have received mixed messages and was amused and fatalistic about this.

Subsequent appointments were held in a clinical room in the Children's Centre used by the Under-Fives service. Sami particularly enjoyed playing with a toy that made a sound like a cow when squeezed. He was interested in what might be inside. I raised the question with Nasima: What did Sami think would happen if he let his mother go? Using a rather fierce-looking lion with two lion cubs, Sami's play indicated his preoccupation; Would there be more babies? Nasima herself was more relaxed and enjoying greater freedom. Although Sami was not spending time with his father, he was doing things with his uncle (his father's brother) such as cleaning his car and going about with him. It appears that, in Bangladeshi families in the East End of London, uncles as well as fathers may play a role in placing a wedge between mother and son.

After three appointments Sami became settled in the playgroup, and prepared to let his mother go. Nasima felt less worried about him and thought that our work was finished. However, she was less certain about her own future and what she would do next. Before she married, Nasima did shop work, which she enjoyed. Her husband did not want her to do this kind of work now because it meant being in men's company, which was considered inappropriate on religious grounds. Her plan was to do a childcare course and voluntary work for Sure Start which would involve work with mothers and children.

Two months later, Sami was re-referred for aggressive behaviour at home and in the nursery. He had punched another child, hit his grandmother, taken a knife from the kitchen drawer and threatened to kill everyone. Three weeks later, Nasima told me that she was two months pregnant. She stressed that this was a planned pregnancy. She and her husband discussed it. If she had another baby now, she could do a course or work later on. She was optimistic about the future but acknowledged that Sami would find the new baby difficult and would need help to prepare for it.

Nasima attended appointments roughly fortnightly, throughout her pregnancy. She recognised that Sami had some awareness of the pregnancy and feelings of being displaced. Sami's play continued to be very expressive. Talking about his feelings reduced the violence considerably. Nasima also acknowledged that Sami was talking more about his father in our sessions, and was closer to him. She involved him in coming to pick them up afterwards. Though Hussein never attended the appointments, there was a sense of a stronger family unit.

However, towards the end of the pregnancy Nasima became increasingly unwell. She complained of headaches, nausea and back pains, and the burden of household tasks imposed by her mother-in-law. What she took to be her mother-in-law's hostility exacerbated her anxiety about the new baby and how she would cope. Staff in the Children's Centre became concerned about her state of mind. She was unable to attend her final appointments before the baby was born because she was unwell. I alerted the GP and health visitor about my concerns about her mental state and the likelihood of postnatal depression; the GP was in touch with community psychiatry.

The birth itself was uneventful, Nasima told me four weeks after it. She found it physically much less painful than the birth of Sami. In our sessions Sami was able to say that there was a 'new baby'. Putting some of his ambivalence into words appeared to help with an upsurge of so-called 'wild behaviour' and newly emerging difficulties in getting him to sleep. Sami also had to contend with starting nursery school at the same time. Nasima herself was overflowing with distress. She complained particularly that her mother-in-law spied on her, had made a slave of her, and that she could do nothing right. At the same time Nasima was imposing very strict demands on herself, reducing her food intake drastically and prolonging the hours spent doing housework.

Nasima was worryingly depressed. She said that she felt completely trapped, and that she had done nothing with her life. It was all over and she was only 25 years old. She was very frightened of talking about her situation because she was afraid that it would get back to the paternal grandmother and that she would be punished. Her descriptions suggested paranoid ideas. The situation was made worse when her own mother told her that it was her duty to stay where she was in her in-laws' home while the baby was still so young. Nasima was placed on medication but the paranoid ideas continued.

The situation was discussed at a professionals' meeting with the GP, the health visitor, who also expressed her concerns to the baby's father, and the staff at Sami's school. The possibility of admitting Nasima to hospital was considered. It was decided to avoid admission if possible. It would have introduced an extra source of stigma, further alienating Nasima from her family. The situation required Nasima to be helped to discover the resources that might be available to her in her extended families: her own and on her husband's side. It was also important to try to avoid destabilising Sami further.

Staff at the nursery school were fully aware of the situation and tolerant of a new habit Sami developed, namely of taking things home with him from school – a rubber, crayon or pencil – and from home into school in the mornings, particularly toy cars. He needed to adjust to the fact that he had a new little brother and that his mother was not quite herself. He was helped by the school's tolerance, an easygoing dialogue between the teacher and Hussein, who now picked him up at the end of the day, and by the fact that the other children in his playgroup were starting school at the same time.

Nasima received regular visits at home from the health visitor and from a Sure Start parent support worker. I saw Nasima every week over the next few months, to provide a place for her very powerful feelings. These included her anger with her own mother for her firm line now but also for the numerous displacements she had experienced with each of her mother's new babies who came after her. It also gradually emerged that circumstances precipitating the depression included Nasima feeling displaced in her own right within her husband's household, as well as, being a first-born child, through her identification with Sami. During the last months of her second pregnancy, her husband's younger brother married a younger girl who joined the household. Unlike Nasima, who had married the eldest son, this young woman was under less pressure to take on household responsibilities and was allowed to continue at college. Nasima was expected to cook for her, ready for when she came home. Nasima expressed her distress and jealousy about how, in addition, this new marriage had eclipsed the birth of her baby and Sami's start at 'proper' school.

Nasima considered making a housing application on mental health grounds so that she and her husband and children could move out of the family home. However, she did not go through with this. One factor was that Nasima persuaded her husband to support the idea; he began to acknowledge Nasima's experience of victimisation and loneliness. A small thing, like their going on shopping trips together, and his suggesting that they stop off for a burger or pizza, mattered a great deal to her. In fact, she liked her young sister-in-law and acknowledged that it was good to have young female company. She was eventually able to broach with her the subject of the uneven burden of household tasks, and to enjoy her position of greater responsibility and experience. She began to appreciate aspects of communal living and that moving out with two small children might not be realistic.

By the time the baby was a year old, Sami had stopped needing to have his pockets searched and was more integrated at school. The 'old woman' was all right really and Nasima had started again on a childcare course. She planned to work as a childcare assistant when the baby moved to nursery school. This plan was solid and realistic.

Given this relatively satisfactory outcome, it is perhaps surprising that admitting Nasima to hospital had been seriously considered. It was successfully avoided through making extra resources available and utilising community services. This network functioned somewhat like an extended family around the mother, baby, young child and father at a time when Nasima's own family was not functioning well for her. Through being able to make use of these resources, Nasima felt attended to and cared for by her community. This further helped her integration into the neighbourhood.

Miah and Vijay

Miah is a Hindu, the second youngest child in a large South Indian family. She is thus part of a minority Asian group living in a largely Bangladeshi community. Nevertheless, the family is well settled in the area. Miah came to the UK when she was 10 years old. Before she became pregnant, in her early twenties, Miah was admitted to hospital for two weeks for what was described as a psychotic depression. In her mid-twenties, Miah became involved with a young Muslim man from Pakistan. He was using drugs. Her family strongly disapproved of the relationship. Miah became pregnant and decided to keep the baby. Her parents and most of her siblings disowned her. The relationship between Miah and the father of her baby broke down during the pregnancy. Unfortunately, Miah's mother became seriously ill and tragically died before Miah's baby was born and before Miah and her mother could be reconciled. Miah's father refused to allow Miah to attend the funeral.

Under such circumstances, the risk of postnatal depression is high. Miah gave birth to a healthy baby boy, Vijay, at term, but the labour was protracted and eventually required emergency intervention and a forceps delivery. Miah suffered a puerperal psychosis a few days later. She was admitted to a mother and baby unit in preference to a psychiatric ward, so that the baby could remain with her. There was no other immediate family to take care of him.

Miah and Vijay were referred to CAMHS by a health visitor when Vijay was 16 months old. The health visitor had arranged for a nursery place for Vijay, as a support for Miah, but Vijay would not be separated from her. Miah ostensibly wanted help with enabling him to do this and to manage his behaviour.

At the first appointment it became apparent that Vijay was not ready to separate because Miah herself was not able to do without his company and his need for her; she felt she would feel terrible without him. Our work focused on taking smaller steps. Aiming to meet fortnightly, these included helping Vijay to understand that people and things continued to exist even when he could not see them, practising sharing with his mother and moving towards sleeping in his own bed.

At the second appointment Vijay was plainly pleased to see me but Miah was extremely distressed. She had tried to play 'hide-and-seek' with Vijay, following what I had said. She had hid from Vijay but he did not come to find her. Miah had screamed at him in anger, 'You stupid boy!' Vijay had been frightened and upset. Miah felt guilty. The health visitor had said she expected too much from him. Miah was afraid that Vijay was mentally backward or did not care enough about her to look for her. Vijay looked very worried as Miah recounted this.

To reassure Miah I hid a small toy, a baby Russian doll, inside a larger one, and encouraged Vijay to find this, which he did with evident pleasure, Miah joining in with the game. I suggested that, rather than not caring about her, Vijay might have missed her and worried where she was. Miah was intrigued by this possibility. She noticed he had become more clinging lately and was interested in the idea that this meant she was important to him.

This belief in her value to Vijay contributed to her becoming more confident in taking him out and meeting new people. She renewed relations with one of her brothers and a sister, though she remained perpetually fraught about the lack of reconciliation with her father. Miah and Vijay also joined a playgroup. Miah was pleased that Vijay was a gregarious child. However, she thought he looked like a baby beside the other children, as if he would never catch up. In her family she had always felt that she had been the unsuccessful 'baby', as if she would never be an adult.

As we approached the summer holidays, when there would be a break of five weeks in our work, Miah voiced her worry that Vijay would 'go off with anyone'. She thought the other mothers at the playgroup 'looked down on' her. An elderly aunt to whom she was close died. This brought back memories of her mother's death, which had occurred in August. Miah was very depressed. She was taking antidepressants erratically; she complained that they did no good and that everyone let her down.

The health visitor and I were concerned about Miah's mental state and that she might need a hospital admission. It seemed imperative that Miah should find another way of coping, for her own sake and for Vijay, who would have needed a foster placement. I contacted the Coordinator for Children in Families with Mental Illness. The case was flagged as one in which the mother's needs and the child's needs required consideration within the same framework. Thus, from Child Mental Health, I communicated directly with the GP, health visitor, social services and also with adult psychiatry. The psychiatrist changed Miah's medication, arranged for more frequent follow-up and referred her to adult psychology for an assessment to consider work for Miah in her own right, alongside the parenting support provided by CAMHS. In this way the services communicated with each other and were embedded in a wider care structure.

It took time for Miah to recognise and use the relations between the different services in a positive way. At our first session back after the holiday, Miah complained about the very long break. She was tearful about the anniversary of her mother's death, about not being well, and about having to go to the hospital for blood tests. She was angry with her social worker, who had turned up on her doorstep, she felt, without warning. She did not go to the playgroup, she had not seen her psychiatrist, she did not go to the health visitor because *her* health visitor was on holiday and, although she had been given the name of another one, she was not going to see someone she did not know! I commented that this was a very bad time for me to have gone away. Miah heartily agreed! Vijay brought his mother a tissue and wiped her eyes.

Miah's ability to express her rage at what she experienced as abandonment was possibly conditional on the fact that actually there was more help around, even though her complex feelings meant that she was not able to access it. This situation illustrated what I came to understand as a pattern whereby in her anger Miah would cut herself off from the resources she needed, mirroring what she experienced as resources being withdrawn from her. This route ultimately left Miah more isolated, self-blaming and depressed. Understanding was achieved through trying to make sense of Vijay's behaviour and developmental struggles.

Vijay himself appeared to have managed well during the holiday. Pleased that I remembered the Hindi word for 'car' (and therefore remembered something about him), he initiated a game of 'hide-and-seek' through making the toy car disappear down the stairs of the doll's house, Vijay getting great pleasure in bringing back the lost toy. Vijay was also being more adventurous. His mother was allowing him to play with the children who lived opposite and he knew their names. Miah said that he was showing more jealousy if she talked to other children.

This expression of jealousy may have indicated that Vijay had a greater sense of what was his and what he could lay claim to. It was possible to show Miah how Vijay's behaviour suggested greater internal reliability. When the family arrived at the clinic, he would ring the bell with great enthusiasm; Vijay was in no doubt, even though he could not see me, that I would be there. I commented on Vijay being more grown up. Miah said that a few days earlier, Vijay had been looking at old photographs, fascinated by himself as a baby and calling himself 'baby' as if he now knew he had moved on. Miah repeated again that she was afraid Vijay would leave her.

However, a month later something had shifted. Miah was clear that Vijay was ready for nursery. Vijay's play in the sessions was increasingly exploratory. He would search for things that had been hidden in unexpected places; and if they were not where he anticipated, he would not give up but look somewhere else. His mother pointed out that he was now sleeping in his own bed and she did not need to leave the door open to her room next door. Vijay started nursery two months later when he was 2 years 9 months old, part-time initially. The nursery was attached to the school that Vijay would eventually be attending; he would join the nursery class of the school at age 3 years 3 months.

Asked how she would spend her time when Vijay was in the nursery Miah said that she needed to sort out her old photographs, and find a home for all Vijay's old baby clothes and toys. Vijay said very firmly, 'No!' In addition to a literal need to make space, Miah's sorting could be taken to describe metaphorically the kind of internal sifting through that she needed to do, repositioning herself in relation to her internal family, like the different Russian dolls that so intrigued Vijay. In recent months I had heard a little more about Miah's family. Miah was plainly in touch with what they were all doing, even though she was in direct contact with very few of them. At the first session after Vijay had started nursery he asked to 'play that game again', hiding the Russian dolls. Miah volunteered that her father was in India, visiting the family village. Apparently he believed he needed to go there before he died, and maybe he would die there. Miah became upset.

Meanwhile, Vijay had started to play with the toy fire-engine that had fallen under the couch. 'It's stuck! It's stuck!' he wailed urgently. 'It's lost! It's gone, lost', in a desperate tone, even though we all knew that Vijay was now very capable of recovering objects that were out of sight. Miah cried more piteously. She said that she had become aware suddenly that her father was getting old. Her concern for him provided the opportunity for Miah to talk through for the first time the history of her rift with her father, and her regrets.

As Vijay was about to start proper school, Miah's family called upon her for help in a way that demonstrated greater tolerance and that they recognised her increased competence and adult status. Ironically this revived the difficult memories surrounding Vijay's birth. At his request, Miah agreed to stay with her brother and his wife to help out while her sister-in-law had her first child. Vijay would stay with Miah's sister and her family. In the event the new baby's birth was complex, involving a protracted labour and an emergency caesarean. The new mother needed a lot of care at home. In the session afterwards, Miah was upset and angry at having to go through this alarming experience. It had brought back the horror of her experience of Vijay's birth. Miah went on to describe the feeling of being totally on her own with the terror and pain of Vijay's birth and most particularly the shame: being strung up, her legs in stirrups, not knowing what was happening. I commented that it was as if she experienced herself as under sentence as a criminal; she agreed.

Miah felt depressed and confused again around this time, even though in reality she had been helpful to her family who were appreciative. Her confusion was probably compounded by the fact that Vijay had coped well without her and was now settling into full-time nursery. Miah felt she could not talk to the school staff, that they did not tell her what he had been doing and that they looked down on her. Miah told her health visitor that she was not coping and the question of an admission was again raised. By this time some elements of a repeating pattern were becoming clearer. A drop in self-esteem followed significant separations, and with this an increase in paranoid anxiety about being at the butt end of others' negative criticisms, in the way in which she perhaps always felt scapegoated within the family. The degree to which Miah became isolated during this time was alarming. This time the care plan involved the Family Welfare Association (FWA, now Family Action) which visited twice a week to support Miah and to provide some direct intervention into how she might play with Vijay at home.

However, there was another factor contributing to Miah's disturbance; she was two months pregnant following a reunion with Vijay's father at the time of Vijay's birthday. Miah was confused and shocked. She knew that the young man would not stay around. She was again certain that she would keep the baby who, it turned out, would be a girl.

Like Sami, Vijay showed a period of disturbed behaviour in the early days of his mother's pregnancy. Miah was enormously supported by the FWA, whose staff remained consistent and who she experienced as non-judgemental. In our work, telling me her news provided an experience of facing up to what I might think and whether I would blame her, and of revisiting telling her family about her first pregnancy. It was important that I did not disguise my surprise and allowed her to explore what she wanted and what was realistic. She no longer felt that a second pregnancy would be disloyal to Vijay. She clearly thought a little girl would complete her family and that Vijay would in time benefit from a younger sister (as she now believed her elder brother had done from her arrival). She also felt that she had learned something about herself and looking after babies.

We had several months for Vijay and Miah to get used to this event and for Vijay to talk about the new baby coming. But for Miah the risk of a second puerperal psychosis was high. It was arranged that Vijay would stay with her brother and his family, with their new baby who Vijay had got to know. Miah's sister would be with Miah at the new baby's birth and would stay with her for a week after she came home. The adult mental health team monitored Miah's state regularly in the last weeks, visiting her at home.

Miah's daughter Sara was born two weeks early. There was some tearing but otherwise the delivery was normal. Miah chose to stay in hospital for a few days after the birth so that she could feel looked after and to increase her confidence before going home. She enjoyed the company of the other mothers. Breast-feeding was established relatively easily. Miah missed Vijay and felt weepy on the second day but showed no psychotic symptoms. Her only complaint was that a nurse had been sharp with her, telling her that she needed no instruction in bathing the baby as she had had a baby already! Miah would have liked more nurturing. Otherwise, she had not been taken by surprise by the birth experience; it was strikingly ordinary. Miah felt that she was a mother just like other mothers.

Miah and Sara attended regularly over the next six months, often accompanied by Vijay. Miah enjoyed helping him with his feelings and the increasing playfulness between the children. Miah remained prone to depression, but her greater capacity for self-observation contributed to increased resilience over the years ahead.

Conclusions

There are several 'babies' intended in my subtitle, 'Who cares for the babies?' Most obviously, I have underlined the emotional and psychological needs of babies anticipated by women whose mental health may become compromised by their arrival. I have also drawn attention to the 'baby' aspects of the first-born children whose needs for mothering are not reduced by a sibling's birth and the importance of including them in planning. Third, I have illustrated the needs of mothers themselves for support and care at a time when their capacities for caring for others and keeping a balanced perspective may be swamped by primitive emotions, unusual ideas and extremes of feeling.

In the two cases described I have illustrated how the baby's first two years are times of developmental opportunity for parents as well as children. The thrust of development is largely organised by changes in the infant: for example, through establishing basic rhythms, the growth of attachment and the need for separation, for relationships with fathers, other children and other relatives, and for opportunities for learning and exploration. The Under-Fives counselling described here depended on alerting the mothers to their infants' developmental dilemmas, enabling them to identify these areas in themselves. What had things been like for them, for example, when they had to give way to younger siblings? I also underlined the degree of change in parents' sense of themselves that came with parenting achievements.

With respect to the second babies' births, the work was different in the two cases, because of different psychopathologies and because the women were in different places psychologically. Miah's second delivery and post-partum period were remarkably ordinary and confirmatory of her competence. By contrast Nasima's second pregnancy appeared to have unleashed the mental-emotional disturbance.

On the other hand, this difference may be more apparent than real. For Miah, experiences and challenges prompted by Vijay's development brought her up against painful memories and emotions that she used the psychotherapeutic context to talk about and to some extent work through. These included the traumatic loss of her mother, her family's censure, reinforcing her belief in herself as the least wanted child in the family, and her sense of isolation and humiliation at Vijay's birth. With the second baby's birth, she was more able to feel, observe and think about her emotional states rather than expressing them in psychotic sympto-matology. Furthermore, the support from statutory and voluntary sectors allowed her to be more communicative with her own family. Her responses to their needs brought home the fact that she did, after all, have a family, within which she could regard herself with some degree of respect.

In Nasima's case, her responses to both of her pregnancies indicated the degree to which achieving greater separation from her own mother was a process set in motion by the pregnancies and childbirth. She also needed to address the losses and disruption to her life produced by her arranged marriage, which she eventually accepted with some appreciation and equanimity.

The depression and degree of risk in each case needed firm psychiatric manage-ment. This provided the umbrella of safety that allowed the psychotherapeutic work to continue. Avoiding hospitalisation minimised effects of separation and discon-tinuity for each family and enabled each parent to find meaning in her experience. In addition to CAMHS and adult mental health services, the voluntary sector played a key role in each of these cases. The relative informality but reliability demonstrated by this sector contributed to the mothers' greater sense of being known and kept in mind. To some extent it provided functions of the extended family, which is generally more implicated in supporting parenthood, even in white Western cultures, than is often assumed (Kagitcibasi 2005). These services allowed the mothers to feel part of their communities and connected to support systems around them including the company of other parents. Both Nasima and Miah are now better placed to get help for themselves if necessary in the future.

References

Bennett, P., Midde, F., Green, E., Heron, J., Seguirado, R. and Lambert, D. (2007) Bipolar affective puerperal psychosis: Genome-wide significant evidence for linkage to chromosome IG. *American Journal of Psychiatry* 164: 1–6.

Brockington, F. (1996) *Menstrual Psychosis and the Catamenial Process.* Bredenbury: Egry Press.

Friedman, T. (2010) Psychiatric mother and baby units. In D. Kohen (ed.) *Oxford Textbook of Women's Mental Health.* Oxford: Oxford University Press, ch. 21.

Harris, M. (1987) Depressive, paranoid and narcissistic features in the analysis of a woman following the birth of her first child and the death of her own mother. In M. Harris-Williams (ed.) *Collected Papers of Martha Harris and Esther Bick.* Perthshire: Clunie Press.

Kagitcibasi, C. (2005) Autonomy and relatedness in cultural context: Implications for self and family. *Journal of Crosscultural Psychology* 36: 403.

Leigh, B. and Milgram, J. (2008) Risk factors for antenatal depression, postnatal depression and parenting stress. *BMC Psychiatry* 8: 24 (accessed April 2012): www.biomedcentral.com/bmcpsychiatry/.

National Institute of Clinical Excellence (NICE) (2007) Antenatal and post natal mental health; Clinical management and service guidance (CG45) (accessed March 2012): www.nice.org.uk.

Ramanunjam, R.K. (1992) Towards maturity: Problems of identity seen in the Indian clinical setting. In. S. Kakar (ed.) *Identity and Adulthood.* Delhi: Oxford University Press.

Robertson, M.M.A., Jones, I., Haque, S. and Craddock, N. (1995) Risk of puerperal and non-puerperal recurrence of illness following affective puerperal (post-partum) psychosis. *British Journal of Psychiatry* 186: 258–259.

Thomson, R. and Kehily, M-J. (2011) *Making Modern Mothers*. Cambridge: Polity Press.

Urwin, C. (2005) A Sure Start rapid response service for their parents and their Under Fours. In J. Lauder, S. Blake and D. Daws (eds) *Reflecting on Reality: Psychotherapists at Work in Primary Care*. London: Karnac.

Urwin, C. (2007) Doing infant observation differently: Researching the formation of mothering identities in an inner London borough. *Infant Observation: The International Journal of Infant Observation* 10(3): 239–253.

Urwin, C. (2009) Separation and changing identity in becoming a mother. In S. Day Sclater, D.W. Jones, H. Price and C. Yates (eds) *Emotion: New Psychological Perspectives*. London: Palgrave Macmillan.

14 Reflections
What does the future hold for the Children and Adult Mental Health Project?

In Part I we identified an unending and relentless process of loss and change to which both staff in organisations, and no less the families with whom they worked, were subject. The project has, inevitably in times of economic and political upheaval, also suffered loss and change, as well as several unrealised aspects; these included an attached health visitor with her special knowledge of infants and under-fives; a dedicated youth worker to provide more activities and group work with children; more learning opportunities for school staff about the impact on children of parental mental illness, and a parenting programme specifically designed for this group of parents. A parent who had attended such a programme commented that it had made her feel like any other parent with ordinary parenting difficulties. That these developments did not materialise was attributable not only to the intense competition for limited funding, but also to continuing uncertainty about the ability of the agency structures at senior level to establish a joint commitment to the project which could adequately contain and sustain staff members' energy and morale.

Economic problems have brought about cuts in services. The untimely and unplanned early retirement of the coordinator left the newly formed team lacking leadership at a time when posts and whole teams were vulnerable. The result was indeed that her post was subsequently cut from the budget and the children's specialists expected to take on additional responsibilities. The cross-agency arrangement for management and supervision which is important in containing anxiety and modelling joint working was lost and team management eventually moved into Children's Social Care.

It is a reflection both of team members' strengths and of the commitment of the new manager and the borough to the work of CHAMP that, despite these changes and ongoing uncertainty about the team's future, the project continues, while seeking longer-term funding.

A small number of other projects also building close working links between adult mental health and children's services were generous in sharing knowledge, time and information, and our contact with them was both inspirational and enabled us to learn a great deal. These included in particular the Parental Mental Health Service at Parkside Clinic (BKCW),[1] the Hackney Parental Mental Health

Team, and the Cape Project. The latter project was, like this one, largely focused on relations between local authority children's social care and adult mental health. Some of these initiatives have not been sustained in their original form as a result of failure to attract mainstream funding, while some newly established services have fallen victim to current cuts in public sector spending.

However, in the decade since the Child and Adult Mental Health Project started, there has been a rapid growth in the area of parental mental health and child welfare, with a number of developments both led by government agencies such as SCIE, and taken up by the voluntary sector, such as Barnardo's, Family Action and Rethink Mental Health. Much of the knowledge gained from these agencies has become embedded in practice, and incorporated into professional training. For example, the Royal College of Psychiatrists has made clear what is expected of psychiatrists in supporting parents as patients. Individual professionals, finding their specialist teams axed, have moved elsewhere, maintaining their interest in parental mental health, and teaching or consulting to others. There remains a strong voice from children and parents demanding change.

Local authorities have met the demand in a variety of ways, through protocols, joint senior management initiatives and by appointing 'cross-over' posts such as the coordinator. However, we would argue that experienced children's social workers placed *full-time within adult mental health teams* can make a real difference to the culture and practice of those teams. Since the 1989 Children Act which specifically required working in partnership, they have developed considerable skills in working in partnership, first with parents, and also with a range of other agencies. For those who also have an interest in and an aptitude for work with mental illness, the new role of children's specialist in adult mental health offers a valuable and growing specialism. Experience in this project suggests that this is a highly skilled and specialist area of work which merits specialist training. Modules on parental mental health and child welfare should form a part of all post-qualifying courses for social workers, while all the disciplines will find value in courses focusing on inter-professional working in mental health, or on organisational and consultation skills.[2] In such courses difficult areas, for example, the differences in the understanding of confidentiality, can be examined, explored and worked through.

Children's social care is often concerned primarily with child protection; in contrast these posts are focused on preventing crises and on early interventions with children, their families and the professionals working with them to ensure that vulnerable children do not remain hidden.

Early intervention can mean very early help provided to mothers and infants or under-fives. This focuses on a mother's sensitivity to her infant, and her capacity to see him or her as a person in their own right, free of parental preoccupations. Awareness of the importance of early infant relationships to later abilities to cope with life's struggles has increased, and such early intervention now has the support of the three major political parties, not least because of its cost-saving implications (Allen 2011).

Allen points to other interventions as also being considered early:

- Identifying and targeting vulnerable children for help at an early stage in their school life can prevent problems leading to social isolation, underachievement or possible exclusion.
- Targeting vulnerable children and supporting them and their parents before a crisis develops is likely to reduce the risk of separation through hospitalisation or being accommodated long term by the local authority.
- Systemic interventions with teams can make a significant difference to partnership working across agencies with different and sometimes competing priorities and can prevent conflict from developing.
- The core work of the children's specialists in adult mental health, of building relationships to ensure communication between agencies when they are involved with families with mental illness, can ensure early planning, co-ordination of visits, and a better service to the family.

Reflections

As well as developments in services there has also been a blossoming of research about what children think and want, and increasing understanding of how to talk to children with their parents about the illness with which both live, and its effect on their lives. Freud's theory that memories and trauma, perhaps arising from early childhood experience, which remain buried, then cannot be processed or under-stood, is relevant and important. When such experiences cannot be brought into the light of day for re-examination and evaluation, they remain unavailable for thinking, and they are likely to persist, being re-enacted in current relationships, distorting perceptions, and disturbing the sense of self.

For children who have witnessed bizarre or frightening events, the construction they place upon them and the stories they weave around them are likely to be much more frightening than the reality. Talking to children and giving them truthful but age-appropriate explanations of what they are seeing around them has been a central theme, and we now see that children are 'becoming visible' and their views are being heard.

Talking with a child or with a family about a parent's illness can mean experiencing their pain and suffering, witnessing their loss of the parent that they knew, their anger and confusion. This can leave us feeling powerless and sometimes reminds us of our own buried feelings, so that we do not wish to hear, and defend ourselves against such pain. Parental mental health teams where they have been established have usually been in CAMHS settings (notably Parkside Parental Mental Health Service). Some children and some families will value and benefit from the safety of regular sessions with experienced staff members who bring a range of skills to the understanding of the dynamics of family and individual relationships. These may include family therapy, or longer-term work with a child psychotherapist.

For many others, resources within community services and the voluntary sector can meet many of their needs. However, it is those professionals in closest contact with families and their children, that is, community mental health team staff, who can answer questions and demonstrate their interest, adopting a holistic approach to their work and one that is determined by ordinary human interest, rather than by 'performance targets'. This may be unfamiliar work, and staff members have asked for training in 'talking to children' which is now more readily available from CAMHS. Nevertheless it may remain a formidable task for staff whose dominant anxiety and first priority must be the ill adult who may be acutely disturbed, suicidal, or even homicidal.

Listening and talking to children and providing answers to their questions enables them to hold a coherent narrative of their lives and experiences which brings understanding and strengthens their ability to manage future disruptions. What is crucial in talking to children and their families is that ideas of blame are inappropriate. Children too easily blame themselves for their parent's illness, while parents are exposed to society's doubt about whether they can be effective parents, to their own harsh self-critical attitude, as well as perhaps to internal negative and punitive voices.

Our blaming culture is pervasive. It too easily dominates our childcare agencies and mental health trusts, reflecting media preoccupations. There are many barriers to inter-agency joint working, including theoretical differences, professional rivalries, pressures of time and workload, lack of clarity about roles, and organisational constraints upon communication. These can be overcome with determination and by making space for non-judgemental talking. Such talking can help increase understanding of the other, build relationships and trust, and counter the 'blame culture' which is often such a feature of inter-agency work.

Taking time for 'getting to know you' and building relationships with colleagues in other teams or professions can create a non-blaming environment facilitating early interventions, joint planning and future consultations.

What is so important to this process is the recognition and understanding of the impact of mental disturbance and suffering on those who are working with it 'day in, day out'. The ill adult seeks to rid him- or herself of unbearable feelings of loss and pain. He or she gets rid of such feelings by projecting them onto others who can become easily overwhelmed. There is frequently a fragmented state of mind which can produce a paralysed state in the recipient, whether staff members of the team, family member, or child, where thinking is rendered almost impossible. The resulting anxiety about what might happen then comes to dominate, and thinking becomes impossible. Louise Gallagher bears witness to the frustrations of the work as she encounters what appear to be resistance and inertia in mental health staff, but finds that over time, her persistence, patience and a non-blaming stance can break through.

It is important that all the authors contributing to this book either have worked in or are currently working in or closely linked with the same large mental health trust. Despite working in separate localities, boroughs or services they have over the years come together in various ways and in different forums to share knowledge and understanding of the work, as well as frustrations, losses and difficulties. Awareness of such a network of colleagues around one can become an internal resource and source of strength for otherwise relatively isolated project staff.

To work against these powerful unconscious forces is complex and disturbing, provoking intense anxiety. It requires stamina, understanding and a containing organisational base. It is life-supporting, life-affirming work.

Notes

1 Parental Mental Health Service, Parkside Clinic (Brent, Kensington and Chelsea, Westminster).
2 City University: M.Sc. or Postgraduate Diploma in Inter-professional Practice (Child and Adolescent Mental Health); Tavistock and Portman NHS Foundation Trust: Consultation and the Organisation; psychoanalytic approaches (Ref D10).

Reference

Allen, G. (2011) *Early Intervention: The Next Steps: An Independent Report to H.M. Government.* Early Intervention Review Team. Her Majesty's Government.

Appendix
Origins of CHAMP

In 2002, shortly after being appointed as coordinator, RL was given an opportunity to apply for a millennium grant administered by the King's Fund. Applications were invited from mental health service users and professionals for a grant of £2,000 to set up and run a new mental health project lasting for two years. In addition to the grant successful applicants were to attend a King's Fund leadership and project management course lasting for ten days. RL put in a proposal to run a group for children, offering a programme of activities, trips and visits for the children of mental health service users in the borough. In addition to providing social activities, the aim was to offer peer group support and an opportunity to increase children's understanding of mental illness and to have access to relevant information. This group was given the name CHAMP, standing for Children and Adult Mental Health Project, but the children who formed the group interpreted it as their name, that they were champions, a much better idea! However, it is one that can all too easily be distorted if people talk about children known to the project as CHAMP children, when it becomes yet another stigmatising label.

Outings

Over the two-year period thirty-two children of all ethnic groups in the borough attended twelve outings or activity sessions arranged during each half-term and school holiday. Twelve children attended regularly, forming a core group. A profile of these children is given below. Trips included visits to the London Eye, the Natural History Museum, the Lord of the Rings exhibition, two seaside resorts, an outdoor activity centre, and a theatre trip as well as art and drama workshops held locally. Later we were able to offer an overnight camping trip assisted by scouting volunteers.

We sought to involve children in deciding on places to visit, but they invariably suggested bowling, arcades, the zoo or an amusement park, all of which they had visited several times on school trips or with family. Their experience of places to visit was extremely limited and we wanted to extend their horizons while still introducing places they might be able to visit with their family or, when older, with friends. They particularly enjoyed the outdoor centre where they could try out new activities, such as rock climbing, go-karting and canoeing, so gaining self-confidence. One child had admitted anxiously that he did not know what a canoe was, but after having a go, said proudly, 'I have done something I've never done before'.

All the children were impressive in their readiness to join in, to have a go and to have some fun, even on cold, wet days. At first we asked children to bring a packed lunch, but rejected this in favour of pizza or barbecue lunches which they enjoyed and helped organise, thus increasing group cohesion and a sense of belonging.

Profile of the children

The criterion for children coming on the trips was that they have a parent or some-times older sibling who was in regular contact with one of the community mental health teams. While there are many organised clubs and children's activities available in the borough, experience indicated that the children of mentally ill parents did not access these activities, and remained socially isolated. In addition, the knowledge that these outings could only be accessed through their mental health professional gave parents confidence that their children would be looked after, and that their CMHT was interested in their needs as a family. We also required parents or partners to be sufficiently organised to bring children on time to a meeting point and to collect them afterwards. It was not practical to collect children from widely scattered homes and experience taught us that when parents or other family members could not bring them, there could be a level of neglect which was not being attended to by the professional network. In this case the children need basic care, not day trips. Two children under 10 years of age were collected from home and brought on one trip by their care coordinator. Their mother was still in bed, the children not ready or fed, and the group was delayed waiting for them. They did not have a packed lunch as arranged and felt stigma-tised when this had to be provided for them. Worryingly, other children in the group commented on how small these two children were and were troubled by this. These 10-year-olds could recognise neglect when they saw it. The purpose of the group was not to 'rescue' children, but to support those children and their parents who try to do their best in difficult circumstances. A youth worker who assisted us commented that the group did not present the challenging behaviour that he was used to dealing with. This reflects the way in which these children have learnt to keep a low profile, not to make their own needs felt because the needs of their parents are so overwhelming and they do not want to risk 'rocking the boat'. Yet among this group were seven children who had been referred to CAMHS, three who had in the past been subject to child protection procedures, and one who had a heart problem.

The families

Two children came from families in which both parents had a mental illness, and two others from families in which one parent suffered from a personality disorder with depression and repeated self-harming, while the second parent had an alcohol problem. Many parents also had physical illnesses, including diabetes, and physical disability. Two children lived with a single parent.

The group

It was some time before the children remembered each other's names or engaged directly with each other rather than through the adults. The regularity of the trips and the provision of art and drama sessions helped increase a sense of group identity. A quiet time for the group to be together was provided by the art therapist, enabling the children to be more relaxed in each other's company and to interact more.

Feedback

On the last of the funded trips we asked the children to write down or draw what they thought about the outings. They all joined in this task with enthusiasm, organising themselves into small groups, keen to give their feedback. Their comments included the following:

- 'Adults and children can have fun together'
- 'CHAMP is good because it takes kids out so they don't get up to bad stuff'
- 'I think it's good and fun that we do different things'
- 'I like having fun and going on trips because it's better than being alone and watching TV'
- 'Going out without your parents is good because they don't worry about you all the time'
- 'Can you send the letters to us, not to our parents?'
- 'Where are we going next time?'

Unexpected outcomes

The outings stimulated much interest for mental health staff members, who began to approach the coordinator to ask if a child of one of their clients could come on the trips and even if they could come themselves. Seven staff volunteered to come along to help and commented that this had helped them appreciate family strengths and to be more aware of children's needs.

We found immense satisfaction in seeing the children's obvious enjoyment and were moved by their pleasure in the simple, ordinary activities and their gratitude.

Index

academic achievement 110–11
accessibility 10, 34, 110, 111, 117, 164, 170
adaptive coping 21–3, 28, 42
Ali, Rushanara 65
Allen, G. 193–4
Andersen, T. 120
anger 18, 40, 41, 49, 54, 101, 102, 164, 183, 185, 186, 194
anxiety 50–1, 54–6, 57, 83–6, 101
assessment: CHAMP in education 133; and CMHTs 109; perinatal work 97–8, 99–100
Assistant Director for Safeguarding Children 8
attachment relationships 34–5
attachment theory 11, 14, 34

Bailey, D. 84
Barnardos 74, 167, 193
Bartlett, P. and Sandland, R. 67
Bedingfield, D. 70
Behaviour Support Team (BST) 130, 132, 133, 134, 135
bereavement, and perinatal work 96
Bion, W.R. 49, 52, 53, 57
bipolar disorder, and post-partum depression 168, 178
blame/blaming: children 18, 79, 84, 167, 195; patients 18, 24, 42, 167, 186, 188, 195; professionals xii, 11, 50, 56, 57, 59, 67, 72, 79, 84, 85, 86, 87, 107, 119, 124, 142, 195
borough: children's services 71; health and social care 66–7; health: physical and mental 65–6; immigration 64–5; mental health services 67–9; poverty and deprivation 65; racial violence 64–5; social context 63

boundary setting 21, 37
Bowlby, John 32; *see also* attachment theory
Britton, R. 46–7, 50, 52, 54
Bromley, C. 16
Buchanan, J. and Corby, B. 118–19
bullying 40, 52, 133, 139
Butler-Sloss, E. 70–1

CAMHS (Children and Adolescent Health Services) 10, 59, 81, 86, 131, 180, 194, 195, 198; avoided by families 82; and children's specialists 108; multidisciplinary clinic team 146–7; post-partum depression 185–9, 190; *see also* systemic practice; Under-Fives project
Campaign to End Child Poverty 155
Cape Project 193
Cardwell, A. and Britten, C. 81
care coordinator 87–8, 89, 90, 92 n2, 112, 137–8, 198
Care Programme Approach 59, 68, 113, 150, 169, 170, 171–2
Carers Connect Project 152–3, 159
carers, children as 3, 140
caring as balanced 28
caring as reciprocal 21–3, 28
Centre for Excellence in Outcomes: *Grasping the Nettle: Early Intervention for Children, Families and Communities* 151
CHAMP (Children and Adult Mental Health project) 1, 10, 59, 68–9, 77–9, 112, 114, 145, 192; and children's specialists 114–15; establishment of 117, 197; and Family Action: Building Bridges 154; funding 132; *see also* CHAMP children's activities group;

CHAMP in education; CHAMP specialist teacher; systemic practice
CHAMP children's activities group 125, 197–9
CHAMP in education 129–30; assessment 133; early intervention 131–2, 140–1; education background 130–1; establishing trust 134; evidence-based approaches 130–1; inter-agency partnerships 134, 142; multi-agency working 131–2; and partnership approach 130–1; scientific practice 131; supervision 134; values and culture of 134
CHAMP specialist teacher 111, 132, 134; advisory role 135–6; aims and objectives of 133–4; and awareness 141–2; and children 138–41; and child's school experience 134–5; and CMHTs 137–8, 141, 142, 198; and parents 138; the school and its staff 135; skills of 141
change: children's experiences 18–19; impact on professionals 71–4; resistance to 55, 56
Charity Organisation Society (COS) 149
child protection 5, 7–8, 9, 10, 59, 70, 95, 113, 117, 124, 132, 145, 193; and the coordinator 82, 87, 92; Munro on 146; parental mental illness 167, 168; regulations and policies 172–4; under-age children 169
childhood conflict, reworking in adulthood 96, 102–3
children 166–7; affected by parental mental illness 3, 4; awareness of 3–4, 43, 141–2, 194; blame/blaming 18, 79, 84, 167, 195; death of a child 3, 5, 6, 7, 8, 9, 45, 77; dangers facing 4; developmental stages 50; fear of 84; hidden 3, 4; impact of parental mental health difficulties on 33–42; parental roles 41; removal of 3, 33, 41, 164; of single mothers 3, 112; social isolation 3, 15, 22–3, 41, 132, 135, 139, 194, 198; wants 167; working with CHAMP specialist teachers 138–41; as young carers 3, 140
Children Act (1948) 69, 149
Children Act (1989) 70–1, 171, 193
Children Act (2004) 9, 12 n1, 71, 91, 171
Children's and Adults Social Services 153
Children's Centres 110, 180
Children (Scotland) Act (1995) 174
Children's Departments 149
children's experience: in their own words: adaptive coping 21–3, 28, 42; caring as balanced 28; caring as reciprocal 21–3, 28; caring for parents 19–21; developing awareness 16; help-giving 27–8; lack of continuity 26; living with change 18–19; parent–child relationship 19–23; positive relationships 28; self-sufficiency 26; shared experience 25–6; uncertainty 18–19; understanding mental health 16–18; use of resources 23–6; views of help 26
Children's Services 69–71, 106, 133
Children's Social Care 71, 72–3, 100, 103, 113, 122, 154, 192
children's specialists 193, 194; and CAMHS 108; and CHAMP 114–15; and children of single mothers 112; and children's academic achievement 110–11; and CMHTs 107–8; and community resources 109–10; continuity of relationships 115; and coordinator for children in families with mental illness 106, 107; and early intervention 113; effectiveness 114; management, supervision and support 107–8; prevention work 113; setting up post 106–7; social isolation, reducing 106, 111–12; working across agency boundaries 113–14
Children's Trust 71, 131
Children's Workforce Development Council (CWDC) 106
Chin, J. 59–60; *see also* Daniel, G. and Chin, J.
Cleveland Inquiry 70–1
Climbié, Victoria 8, 12 n1, 71, 72, 171
Clunis, Christopher 68
CMHTs (Community Mental Health Teams) 15, 68–9, 78, 81, 92 n2, 170, 194–5; and assessment 109; and children's specialists 107–8; early intervention 109; and Family Action 151, 159; and CHAMP specialist teachers 137–8, 141, 142, 198; *see also* systemic practice
Common Assessment Framework (CAF) 124, 133
Community Care 2, 163, 169

Community Care Act (1990) 67, 68
Community Mental Health Nurse 160
Community Treatment Orders 68
consistency 28
containing structures xii, 40, 47, 55, 57, 60, 68, 73, 86, 88, 90, 97, 98, 100, 102, 103, 104, 107, 192
Cooper, A. and Dartington, T. 57–5, 71–7, 74, 147
Cooper, A. and Lousada, J. 66
coordinator for children in families with mental illness 8, 77, 92 n2, 145, 192, 193; appointment of 81–2; and child protection 82, 87, 92; and children's specialists 106, 107; crossing boundaries 83–4; and Family Action: Building Bridges 151–2; first four years 86–8; joint working meetings 88–90; and Multi-agency Behaviour and Social Inclusion Network (MABSIN) 131–2; post-partum depression 186; and resources 83; service development 91–2; setting up role 82–3; team responses to 83–6
Copenhagen High-risk Study 166
creative collaboration 56–8
Crisis Intervention Service (CIS) 94, 95–6, 97, 103, 104
Crossing Bridges (Mayes *et al*; DoH) 73
cultural awareness 7, 14, 32, 57, 59, 69, 72, 113, 155–6, 174, 180–1, 190
custody, loss of 33, 41, 164

Daniel, G. and Chin, J. 59–60, 116–17, 119
Daniel, K. 60, 118
Davis, L. 70
Denborough, D. 117
Department for Children, Schools and Families 172
Department of Health 8, 172
Department of Social Services 71
depression 50, 51, 54, 66; paternal 165; *see also* post-partum depression
depressive position 49–50
despair 52–4, 55
discipline 37, 40
distraction 24
domestic violence 113, 134; and perinatal work 97, 101, 103
Drug Dependency Unit 119
duty of care 83

early intervention 193–4; CHAMP in education 131–2, 140–1; children's specialists 113; CMHTs 109; Family Action: Building Bridges project 151; perinatal work 94–5, 104
Education Social Work Service 132
emotional withdrawal 34, 37, 38
Every Child Matters (DfES) 71, 91, 133
evidence-based approaches 130–1, 147

Family Action 81, 145, 149–50, 153–4, 188, 193; and CMHTs 151, 159; partnership approach 152–3, 156–7, 161
Family Action: Building Bridges project 81, 145, 150–2; and the Carers Connect Project 152–3, 159; case examples 157–61; and CHAMP 154; and the Community Mental Health Nurse 160; and coordinator for children in families with mental illness 151–2; early intervention 151; and the Family Visiting Project 153–4; long term support 157; staff support 155–6; working in culturally diverse borough 155–6; and the Young Carers' Project 161
Family Action Training and Development Department 156
family support workers 151–2, 155
family, the: break-down of 41; hard to reach 140–1; and housing policy 63; sanctity of 70
family therapy clinic 122–3, 125
Family Therapy Conference (1975) 149
Family Visiting Project 153–4
Family Welfare Association 81, 145, 149, 188
Fatherhood Institute: 'Think Fathers' 165
fathers: depression 165; role of 112
fear: of children 84; displacement of 84; perpetual 40; removal of children 3, 33, 41, 164
Fredman, G. and Fuggle, P. 118
Freud, Sigmund 11, 49, 53, 194; *Mourning and Melancholia* 50; and psychotic processes 51, and repeating 48
funding 78, 92, 106, 192; budget cycles 77; CHAMP 132; voluntary sector 156–7

Gittins, D 4
Gosling, P. 79

grief 49, 50, 64, 164
guilt 40, 41–2, 50

Hackney Parental Mental Health Team
    192–3
Hall, A. 117
Halton, W. 58, 87
happiness, worry about showing 40–1
Harris, M. 179
Head of Behaviour Support 131
help-giving 27–8; context 28–9
Hill, Octavia 149
Hinshelwood, R.D. 45, 52–3, 55, 72–3, 84,
    86
Hinshelwood, R.D. and Skogstad, W. 3,
    85
Hoffman, E. 119–20
hospitalization 3, 4, 10, 19, 35, 38–9, 41,
    42, 67, 68, 109, 139, 146, 153–4, 161,
    164, 166, 169, 174, 180, 183, 184, 186,
    188, 190, 194
housing policy 63, 66
Howe, D. 45–6
Hoyle, L. 56
Hughes, Beverly 165
humanism 11
human rights 73, 83

identification 52, 55, 56, 77, 107, 183
identity 39; mothers 97, 179, 183–4
illness, use of term 31
immigration 64–5, 129, 181
independence 39
inertia 55
information 113–14
insight, lack of 53–4
inter-agency work 4–6, 56–8, 194;
    capacity to relate 60; and CHAMP in
    education 134, 142; and children's
    specialists 113–14; difficulties of 7–10;
    and human organisation 58; and
    physical presence 59–60; and reflective
    space 58–9; systemic approach to
    meetings 59
Interface development coordinator 8, 77
Interpretative Phenomenological Analysis
    (IPA) 15
invulnerability, feelings of, in children 40
isolation *see* social isolation
Jarman Underprivileged Area Score 65
joint working 6, 9, 49, 81, 107, 108, 110,
    118, 156, 170, 192, 195; meetings 59,
    88–90; *see also* inter-agency work

Kidstime 28
King's Fund 92, 197
Klein, Melanie 49, 50, 51, 57

Laming, Lord 12 n1, 72
Lancaster, S. 31
Lane, D.A. 130
Lane, D.A. and Corrie, S. 131
language 7, 31, 59, 69, 81, 118, 129, 137,
    138, 155
Lead Officer for Social Inclusion 131
Lessing, Doris 49
loneliness 22–3, 164, 181, 184; existential
    loneliness 179
Looked After Children 118
Loshak, R. 83, 85
loss 49–50, 54, 72; impact on professionals
    73; perinatal work 96; recovery from
    49
Lucas, Richard 48, 49, 53–4

MacLeod, Mary 151
making meaning 34–6
McLean, D. *et al* 73
meaninglessness 52–4, 55
memory project 117
Mental Capacity Act (2007) 68, 174
Mental Health Act (1959) 67
Mental Health Act (1983) 167, 169–70,
    174; Code of Practice 68, 166–7
Mental Health Trust 146, 154
Menzies-Lyth, Isobel 56
Miller, A. 131
Minuchin, S. and Fishman, H.C. 117
mirroring processes 52
mothers: and identity 97, 179, 183–4;
    relatedness with own mother 179–80,
    183, 184–5
Multi-agency Behaviour and Social
    Inclusion Network (MABSIN) 131–2
multi-agency working: CHAMP in
    education 131–2; and responsibility
    113–14
multidisciplinary approach 47–8, 73, 95,
    146–7; perinatal work 100
Munro, Eileen 46, 56, 115

National Children's Bureau 74, 91
National Patient Safety Agency: Rapid
    Response Report 172–3
National Service Framework (1999) 68
Navarro,T. 47
New Types of Worker (NToW) 106

NHS and Community Care Act (1990) 67, 68

NICE 48–9, 171

NICE guidelines: pregnancy and perinatal period 168; schizophrenia 48–9

normality, construction of 16

otherness 54, 112

paranoid-schizoid position 50–1, 58

Parental Mental Health Forum 133

parental mental health: impact on children: and attachment 34–5; and coherent narratives 35–6; and development 38–40; and health 36–8; and making meaning 34–6; and mental health 39–40; physical neglect 36; and relationships 40–2; and safety 36–8; and socializing 40–2; and well being 39–40

Parental Mental Health Interest Group 132

parental mental health workers, effectiveness 114

parental mental illness: and child protection 167, 168; children affected by 3, 4; and the psychiatrist 167

parent–child relationship: children's experience 19–23; perinatal work 101–3; reversal of 40–1, 140

parents: concerns of 163–5; impact of mental health difficulties on 32–3; independence of 23–4; protectiveness towards 40; and school 41; shared experience 25–6; as unavailable 22–3, 102; wants of 165–6; working with CHAMP specialist teachers 138

Parents as Patients: Supporting the Needs of Patients who are Parents and their Children (RCP) 167, 174

parents' care plan approach (CPA) 137

Parkside Parental Mental Health Service 81, 82, 192, 194

Part 8 Review 6–7, 9, 68, 77, 81

partnership approach 193; and CHAMP in education 130–1; Family Action 152–3, 156–7, 161

Patients as Parents: Addressing the Needs, Including the Safety, of Children whose Parents have Mental Illness (RCP) 74

perinatal mental health worker 77

perinatal work: anxiety 101; assessment 97–8, 99–100; and breakdown of relationships 97; case studies: Miah and Vijay 184–9; case studies: Nasima and Sami 180–4, 190; consultation 97; and domestic violence 97, 101, 103; early intervention 94–5, 104; loss and bereavement 96; and mothers' identity 97, 179, 183–4; NICE guidelines 168; parent–child relationship 101–3; reworking childhood conflict 96, 102–3; suicide 98, 100, 101; stress in infants 100

Poor Law 67, 69

post-partum depression 146; and arranged marriage 180–1, 190; biological factors 178–9; and bipolar disorder 168, 178; and CAMHS 185–9, 190; case studies: Miah and Vijay 184–9; case studies: Nasima and Sami 180–4, 190; and coordinator for children in families with mental illness 186; psychiatrists 186, 190; second or later-born babies 178, 182–4, 188–90; traumatic births 185, 187–8; voluntary sector 190

Powell, Enoch 67

Primary Care Trust (PCT) 106, 154, 155, 157, 170

Princess Royal Trust for Carers 74, 158

professionals: absence of concern 84; anxiety 54–6, 57, 83–6; blame/blaming xii, 11, 50, 56, 57, 59, 67, 72, 79, 84, 85, 86, 87, 107, 119, 124, 142, 195; change and instability 71–4; defences 55–6, 57, 84; and distancing 86; impact of loss on 73; impact of working with mental illness on 5–6, 54–6; inertia 55; lead professionals 133, 136; recruitment from ethnic minorities 69, 72; referral forms 87–8; self-reflectiveness 85–6; support for 155–6

projective identification 52

psychiatrists 146, 193; and parental mental illness 167; and parenting under-age children 169–70; and post-partum depression 186, 190; and pre-conception period 168; and pregnancy and perinatal period 168–9; safeguarding children: regulations, policies and procedures 171–4

psychoanalysis 48–9; depressive position 49–50; guilt 50; meaninglessness and despair 52–4, 55; paranoid-schizoid position 50–1, 58; psychotic processes 51–2; separateness of being 54, 180

psychosis 45

psychotic processes 51–2
public awareness 28–9

racial violence 64–5
Ramanunjam, R.K. 181
recovery from loss 49
Reder, P. and Duncan, S. 9
Reder, P. *et al* 7, 8, 71, 114, 116
resentment 40
resilience 11, 14, 21, 35, 42, 137, 139, 140, 141
responsibility: children 40; and multi-agency involvement 113–14
responsiveness 34, 121–2, 150; role responsiveness 52
Rethink Mental Health 193
Rey, Henri 86
rights of the child 73, 83, 171
Royal College of Psychiatrists 4, 74, 166, 173–4, 193
Rutter, M. and Quinton, D. 39, 117

Safeguarding Children's Board 91
schizophrenia 48–9, 164, 166, 168
Schizophrenia Clinical Guidelines (NICE) 48–9
school 25–6, 78; parent's interaction with 41; secondary transition 140; *see also* CHAMP in education; CHAMP specialist teacher
Schore, A. 100, 102
SCIE 74, 171, 193; Guide 30. Mental Health and Child Welfare: A Guide for Adult and Children's health and Social Care Services 151
self, sense of 51
self harm 98, 99, 178; children 39
self-sufficiency 26
separateness of being 54, 180
separation 4, 9, 19, 33, 39, 41, 82, 84–5, 90, 164–5, 166, 175, 180–1, 185–6, 190, 194
Sexton, Anne 3
Shah, S. and Goodbody, L. 40
shame, sense of 41
social entrepreneurs 92
Social Exclusion Unit 74
Social Inclusion Panel (SIP) 131
social interaction 25–6, 28
social isolation 7, 10, 17, 26, 33, children 3, 15, 22–3, 41, 132, 135, 139, 194, 198; reducing 106, 111–12
Social Services Department 145

Sohn, Leslie 51–2
Solarin, N. 110
splitting xi, 50, 52, 53, 57, 84
staff turnover 9, 55, 72, 115, 156
Stevenson, O. 45, 46
stigma/stigmatisation 3, 4, 16, 29, 33, 35, 36, 41, 118, 197, 198
suicide 38, 55, 66, 95, 98, 100, 101, 178
Summerscale, Kate: *The Suspicions of Mr Whicher* 70
Summer University 112
Sure Start Children's Centre 146, 180, 181–2
systemic approaches 14–15
systemic practice 194; barriers to collaborative work 116–17; 'both/and' approach 119–20; externalising 124–5; family therapy clinic 122–3, 125; good inter-professional relationships 123–4; joining 117–19; multi-systemic approach 120–2; utilising resources to effect change 125–6

talking 24–5, 27–8, 35–6, 42–3, 84, 95, 194
Target, M. and Fonagy, P. 112
Tate, S. *et al* 120, 124
Tavistock Institute of Marital Studies 56
Team Around the Child (TAC) 110, 124, 136, 142
Team Around the Family 124, 142
theory: managing difference 47–8; need for 45–7
Think Child, Think Parents, Think Family (SCIE) 74
Think Family 71
Topping, K. 130
training 193, 196 n2; family support workers 155–6
trauma 49–50, 51, 72
Tree of Life 125

Under-Fives project 180, 189
United Nations Convention on the Rights of the Child 166
Urwin, C. 86

voluntary sector 28, 72, 78, 106, 111, 194; funding 156–7; post-partum depression 190; *see also* individual projects

White, C. and Edgar, G 66
White, M. 124–5

Widgery, David 64
Williams, Paul 49, 52
Winnicott, D.W. 94, 95, 97, 145
Woodhouse, D. and Pengelly, P. 10, 56–7,
    58–9, 73
Working Together (DoH) 9, 71, 171

Yelloly, M. A. 11
Young Carers project 26, 28, 161
Young, Michael 63

Zito, Jonathan 67–8